Advance Praise for *Digital M
Learner Identity*

"This book reflects two of the many strengths of John Potter's work in the field of media education. The research is rooted in his experience as an educator of children, young people, and teachers, and has an authority in practice. It also challenges us to think differently about our understandings of identity, digital media, and curatorship, and encourages us to engage actively with new concepts of literacy in a digital age."

—Avril Loveless, School of Education,
University of Brighton, UK

"Potter's clarity of thought and innovative use of the metaphor of curatorship produces valuable insights into the ways in which children use digital media to negotiate culture, identity, and social roles. Rooted in long experience of classrooms and in detailed empirical research, it is an essential read for researchers, students, and practitioners in the fields of literacy, new media, and childhood studies."

—Andrew Burn, DARE (Digital/Arts/Research/Education),
Institute of Education, University of London

"This book makes an original and important contribution to scholarship in new media. Based on a study of children's autobiographical filmmaking, John Potter vividly illustrates the explanatory power of the metaphor of curatorship. This is essential reading for those interested in new literacies and media studies."

—Guy Merchant, Sheffield
Hallam University, UK

Palgrave Macmillan's Digital Education and Learning

Much has been written during the first decade of the new millennium about the potential of digital technologies to produce a transformation of education. Digital technologies are portrayed as tools that will enhance learner collaboration and motivation and develop new multimodal literacy skills. Accompanying this has been the move from understanding literacy on the cognitive level to an appreciation of the sociocultural forces shaping learner development. Responding to these claims, the Digital Education and Learning Series explores the pedagogical potential and realities of digital technologies in a wide range of disciplinary contexts across the educational spectrum both in and outside of class. Focusing on local and global perspectives, the series responds to the shifting landscape of education, the way digital technologies are being used in different educational and cultural contexts, and examines the differences that lie behind the generalizations of the digital age. Incorporating cutting-edge volumes with theoretical perspectives and case studies (single authored and edited collections), the series provides an accessible and valuable resource for academic researchers, teacher trainers, administrators, and students interested in interdisciplinary studies of education and new and emerging technologies.

Series Editors:

Michael Thomas is a senior lecturer at the University of Central Lancashire and editor in chief of the *International Journal of Virtual and Personal Learning Environments* (IJVPLE).

James Paul Gee is a Mary Lou Fulton Presidential Professor at Arizona State University. His most recent book is *Policy Brief: Getting Over the Slump: Innovation Strategies to Promote Children's Learning* (2008).

John Palfrey is the head of school at Phillips Academy, Andover, and a senior research fellow at the Berkman Center for Internet & Society at Harvard. He is coauthor of *Born Digital: Understanding the First Generation of Digital Natives* (2008).

Digital Education
Edited by Michael Thomas

Digital Media and Learner Identity: The New Curatorship
By John Potter

Digital Media and Learner Identity
The New Curatorship

John Potter

DIGITAL MEDIA AND LEARNER IDENTITY

First published in 2012 by
PALGRAVE MACMILLAN®
in the United States—a division of St. Martin's Press LLC,
175 Fifth Avenue, New York, NY 10010.

Where this book is distributed in the UK, Europe and the rest of the world,
this is by Palgrave Macmillan, a division of Macmillan Publishers Limited,
registered in England, company number 785998, of Houndmills,
Basingstoke, Hampshire RG21 6XS.

Palgrave Macmillan is the global academic imprint of the above companies
and has companies and representatives throughout the world.

Palgrave® and Macmillan® are registered trademarks in the United States,
the United Kingdom, Europe and other countries.

ISBN 978-1-349-43455-8   ISBN 978-1-137-00486-4 (eBook)

DOI 10.1057/9781137004864

Library of Congress Cataloging-in-Publication Data

Potter, John, 1938–
    Digital media and learner identity : the new curatorship / John Potter.
        p. cm.—(Digital education and learning)

        1. Media programs (Education)—United States. 2. Mass media and
    youth—United States. 3. Digital media—Social aspects—United States.
    4. Technology and youth—United States. I. Title.

LB1028.4.P62 2012
371.33—dc23   2012024715

A catalogue record of the book is available from the British Library.

Design by Newgen Imaging Systems (P) Ltd., Chennai, India.

First edition: December 2012

10 9 8 7 6 5 4 3 2 1

Transferred to Digital Printing in 2013

*For Janet, Alice, and Jack with
love and thanks*

Contents

Illustrations

Figures

Series Foreword

Much has been written during the first decade of the new millennium about the potential of digital technologies to radically transform education and learning. Typically, such calls for change spring from the argument that traditional education no longer engages learners or teaches them the skills required for the twenty-first century. Digital technologies are often described as tools that will enhance collaboration and motivate learners to reengage with education and enable them to develop the new multimodal literacy skills required for today's knowledge economy. Using digital technologies is a creative experience in which learners actively engage with solving problems in authentic environments that underline their productive skills rather than merely passively consuming knowledge. Accompanying this argument has been the move from understanding literacy on the cognitive level to an appreciation of the sociocultural forces shaping learner development and the role communities play in supporting the acquisition of knowledge.

Emerging from this context the Digital Education and Learning series was founded to explore the pedagogical potential and realities of digital technologies in a wide range of disciplinary contexts across the educational spectrum around the world. Focusing on local and global perspectives, the series responds to the shifting demands and expectations of educational stakeholders, the ways new technologies are actually being used in different educational and cultural contexts, and examines the opportunities and challenges that lie behind the myths and rhetoric of digital age education. The series encourages the development of evidence-based research that is rooted in an understanding of the history of technology, as well as open to the potential of new innovation, and adopts critical perspectives on technological determinism as well as techno-skepticism.

While the potential for changing the way we learn in the digital age is significant, and new sources of information and forms of interaction have developed, many educational institutions and learning environments have changed little from those that existed over one hundred years ago. Whether in the form of smartphones, laptops, or tablets, digital technologies may be increasingly ubiquitous in a person's social life but marginal in their daily educational experience once they enter a classroom. Although many people increasingly invest more and more time on their favorite social media site, integrating these technologies into curricula or formal learning environments remains a significant challenge, if indeed it is a worthwhile aim in the first place. History tells us that change in educational contexts, if it happens at all in ways that were intended, is typically more "incremental" and rarely "revolutionary." Understanding the development of learning technologies in the context of a historically informed approach therefore is one of the core aspects of the series, as is the need to understand the increasing internationalization of education and the way learning technologies are culturally mediated. While the digital world appears to be increasingly "flat," significant challenges continue to exist, and the series will problematize terms that have sought to erase cultural, pedagogical, and theoretical differences rather than understand them. "Digital natives," "digital literacy," "digital divide," and "digital media"—these and such mantras as "twenty-first century learning"—are phrases that continue to be used in ways that require further clarification and critical engagement rather than unquestioning and uncritical acceptance.

The series aims to examine the complex discourse of digital technologies and to understand the implications for teaching, learning, and professional development. By mixing volumes with theoretical perspectives with case studies detailing actual teaching approaches, whether on or off campus, in face-to-face, fully online, or blended learning contexts, the series will examine the emergence of digital technologies from a range of new international and interdisciplinary perspectives. Incorporating original and innovative volumes with theoretical perspectives and case studies (single authored and edited collections), the series aims to provide an accessible and valuable resource for academic researchers, teacher trainers, administrators, policymakers, and learners interested in cutting-edge research on new and emerging technologies in education.

With these aims in mind, we welcome this new book to the series by John Potter from the Institute of Education, University of London. This original and fascinating work presents a strong evidence-based engagement with the themes of curatorship and the "learner-as-producer" and creator of digital content. In his groundbreaking discussion of children's use of video in UK primary schools, Potter demonstrates how digital media can be a powerful tool with which young children can create, disseminate, and learn to understand their multicultural identity in new and compelling ways. Indeed, the autobiographical videos provide numerous insights into the multilayered process of making and unmaking digital identities from both technological and cultural perspectives. The concept of the "new curatorship" is both timely and provocative and should prove valuable given the increasing focus on digital media literacy in the school sector worldwide. Potter's book is a welcome contribution to the Digital Education and Learning series and represents a significant step forward in researching the digital media practices of young children.

Series Editors
MICHAEL THOMAS
JAMES P. GEE
JOHN G. PALFREY

Foreword: Thinking about the New Curatorship

What do a map of the Windward islands made from cane and shell, a teddy bear called Alan Measles, and a pot thrown and presented with applique featuring the panoply of London life have in common? The answer lies in the physical gathering of collected objects from a museum, a personal collection, and a piece of commissioned work for "The Tomb of the Unknown Craftsman," an exhibition at the British Museum in 2011–2012 by the artist Grayson Perry. In this show, Perry pulled reference points from his own life and work into alignment with objects chosen from the museum collection. As he wrote in the exhibition catalog,

> The British Museum holds eight million objects from every corner of the globe. Why not, I thought, make the works I am inspired to create and find objects in this vast collection that respond to them? Somewhere in its endless storerooms there must be objects that echo my concerns and styles. (Perry 2011, p. 11)

This is an active version of making new meanings from found physical objects and texts by placing them alongside things that you make yourself in order to "echo concerns and styles," find some markers of identity, and communicate them. If we map this practice with real physical objects onto the virtual, we can think about how meanings are made in digital media using, sounds, text, images, and clips. This active *curatorship* becomes, perhaps, a useful metaphor to describe an emergent literacy practice in new media production.

In fact, there is frequent and growing use of the word "curated" to describe what the authors of blogs and other online spaces actually do.

Whereas in earlier times, the apposite verbs used to credit an author would have been simply "written," "edited," or even "created," it is quite clear that they don't capture all the self-representational activities or *practices* in digital culture that the verb "curated" does. This is because *curating* a space is not only about writing or creating within it but also collecting, distributing, assembling, disassembling, and moving it across different stages. In other words, it is an active practice that is larger in its reach, scope, and nature than the others but which contains and subsumes them. The meaning in the eventual exhibited form of video, visual art, music, or other text, is made from the previously selected resources by knowing how the resources and forms work together across the many available modes of communication. In digital culture, curating is, in its most sophisticated form, about organizing how these different resources work *intertextually* to make meaning and this is a new process, resulting from human agency in the changed social arrangements, practices, and artifacts of new media (cf. Lievrouw and Livingstone, 2006, p. 2).

Of course, appropriations, quotations, and borrowings are, and always have been, a commonplace in music, visual arts, literature, and filmmaking and in every form of cultural expression from the first stories onward. What has changed is the way in which those who have access to the digital artifacts at their fingertips have the means to take and remix content, to publish things that they have made alongside things they have created and establish new relationships between the elements to make new meanings. This is not to suggest for a minute that this activity is open to all and that we have arrived at some form of techno-utopia in which full participation in this practice is a given and everyone is making and exhibiting in new media. There are still deep economic divides within societies in the developed world and in the developing world, and there are also those with the ability and the access who choose not to engage in this way with social media. Nevertheless, it is important to acknowledge that, at different levels, something like this is going on in very large numbers of social media spaces and that distribution and publication of these media are switched on and off regularly, managed and shown, to some, to all, or, possibly, not at all.

It seems to me that this is more complex than authorship; curatorship is a form of metaauthorship, understanding the relationships between texts of all kinds: moving image, still image, print, and more. The performance of this act of curatorship has become important in what Giddens (1991) has described as the self-reflexive project of identity in late modernity, useful as a means of creating what he refers to as ontological security. Travelling, working, on holiday, with family, without family, at an event, seeing a band, a film, a play, or doing nothing are all open to record and storage, alongside what passes for the personal moment of insight or reflection, carefully crafted for a status update or blurted out and retracted later. These can be added to the collection and published or not, added to something that was found, posted in a response in a network. It can also be added to a specific kind of text for a specific sort of an audience, including getting a job; what is a CV or resume if not a kind of slow blog of a person's achievements and dispositions? And where would we be if we could not dismantle, rearrange, and alter the things we uploaded that were no longer appropriate to the current meanings we want to make? It is, of course, due in part of the mutable and provisional nature of digital media that it becomes possible for some of us to exert this kind of human agency.

This book is about looking for the roots of this process of curatorship in some of the tools and practices of new media authoring, specifically digital video production, and to try to provide some justification for claiming it as a new literacy practice, albeit one that subsumes other forms and modes. Specifically, the book looks at the assembly of short video productions into a whole, in which the authors have assembled songs, clips, self-authored or not, shared or individual to make intertextual meaning under very specific conditions. The authors of the short films in this book are not adult. They are children in the first decade of the twenty-first century. Without wishing to saddle them with a generational name or set of characteristics for all of them to live up to, it appears that the way in which they work with the tools of planning, shooting, and editing, in order to assemble their curated productions, represents a way of being active in media literacy that is predicated on being able to take advantage of onscreen shaping of meaning through editing. I am thinking here about the ways in which a whole series of craft skills have been subsumed into those editing spaces onscreen and how the distance between getting the visual material to those screens has been shortened by the uses of small but powerful handheld cameras, either on phones or not. I am thinking also about how the distance from edited form to exhibited form has been shortened further still in the networked world.

To account for this new practice, we have to look at a range of different but intersecting fields of theory and analysis. For the ways in which the different modes within and between texts operate and make meaning, some version of multimodal theory will be essential in the analysis. However, in order to account for and understand whatever that analysis reveals, some versions of sociocultural theory, particularly in respect of identity, will also be essential; as Burn (2009) has argued, theories of text and signification essentially need to be partnered with cultural theory for them to represent and offer a critique of the experience of production in lived culture. Alongside all of these will come some form of thinking about what it means to be literate in this century. Certainly, it is no longer tenable to think only of print literacy, while acknowledging this as a vitally important component of lived culture; it simply is not the only or even the dominant mode of communication and hasn't been for many years.

This book arose out of a wish to account for representational practices in new media that is cognizant of the theories and discourses of cultural studies and multimodality and that, hopefully, contributes some thinking about ways of looking at the educational experience for learners and teachers in the digital age.

Acknowledgments

I would like to thank all my family, friends, and colleagues who have talked this through with me at home, at seminars, and at conferences. On the home front, this means the principal supporters: Janet, Alice, and Jack; also my dad, Tony, my sister Frances and her family, Jimmy, David, and Roisin. Lots of friends have put up with me going on about it and still remained supportive throughout; here, I should mention in particular my deadline coach and role model in how to complete things on time: Richard Frost. I would like to thank Andrew Burn and Neil Selwyn for their huge support and encouragement in this and many other projects over the last few years. Others have, at different times, played a big part in shaping the thinking behind it, including David Buckingham, whom I was lucky enough to have as codoctoral supervisor with Andrew a few years ago. There are many other friends and colleagues with whom I have had conversations in different settings about the work in and around this book and I thank you all. I would like to mention in particular, Guy Merchant, Jackie Marsh, Rebekah Willett, Di Mavers and Martin Oliver – all of whom gave great advice and encouragement during my doctoral study, formally and informally, as did fellow researchers, Becky Parry and Oystein Gilje. Thanks are due also to Michael Rosen for providing the vision on so many occasions of an educational system that can and should be responsive to the wider lived experience of learners. Thanks to Annie Keogh for permission to use her photograph for the cover art. Finally, I owe a huge debt of gratitude to all the people who supported this project and, in particular, to the children and schools who became partners in the process.

JOHN POTTER
London, August 2012

CHAPTER 1

Media, Culture, and Education

I had the experience last year of bearing witness to a life lived entirely offline. In clearing my late aunt's possessions and memorabilia from a house in which she had lived for more than 50 years, there was an opportunity to reflect on which aspects of our lived experience are exhibited and shared and how. My aunt was a very private person in an era in which it was perfectly possible to have no sense of obligation to share or display details of one's life for all, or even for some, to see. She never married. She served the local community as a nurse for all her working life and later as a volunteer working with refugee families. Among her possessions, and hidden from view, were her swimming certificates, school photos, and her volunteer red cross membership during which, aged about 14, she tended to the injured in the bombing of London in the second world war. She regularly kept the slenderest of diaries from the 1950s, most entries so short that they were like distant ancestors of the tweet, the current 140-character summary of history and responses, hers dictated not by a social media site but by the amount of space available in the entry spaces in which she wrote with her pen. We learned how she reacted to some of the notable events of the twentieth century ("Terrible news from Dallas today," "Some men walked on the moon," etc.) alongside short notes on outings, family, and friends. Looking through her house for evidence of twenty-first-century devices, one struggled to find more than a set top box for her TV. There was no computer and her mobile phone, largely unused, was not the smart mobile network hub that large numbers of us carry with us 24/7. Hers was a life lived entirely offline and one which is, in the richer parts of the developed world, an increasingly rare thing. She never sent an e-mail, let alone posted a picture of herself online. The images we found were hidden in boxes, cupboards, and drawers, far from view in determinedly old-media formats. We found a slide projector and a crate of transparencies. To access these images now, we will have to track down a particular bulb and, of course, we will be dependent on the panoply of contemporary tools for such purposes: search engines and online shops, all essential to find the means with which to open a window to the past.

I do not subscribe entirely to the generational arguments about learners, although I believe that they have been worth having and continue to produce interesting debates in respect of education particularly (see, e.g., Thomas 2011). However, the more extreme examples of lives lived offline rather than online, such as my aunt's, do genuinely illuminate the differences between full participation in the dominant modes of human communication and decisive nonparticipation, making decisions about how you live your life that take you out of that present moment. Nowadays, the personal diary is public, if we want it to be, and our reactions to world events, and those closer to home, can be instantly shared at 140-character speed, in a longer status update, on a blog, or in a media production. It's a choice, in the richer parts of the world, that many are exercising, and have been doing so for many years, to publish online, broadcast, and exhibit from the raw material of their lives. While most of the commentary focuses on the enabling features of the various technologies, sometimes to the point of determinism, others prefer to place the digital in the mix somewhere alongside the rest of lived experience and to view this with cultural studies or even within an anthropological frame. This approach to the technology is the one I favor. I am more interested in lived culture as it is experienced in the present, using the current modes and media of expression, in which human agents determine their day-to-day experience, under the very specific conditions of ownership of media devices and spaces.

Of course, as many have pointed out, the apparent freedom to be in control of these spaces and publishing opportunities is still shaped by corporate endeavor, albeit of a somewhat different nature to the media industries of the past; our utterances, pictures, and media collections are happy hunting grounds for advertisers and serve a giant, global marketplace. Notwithstanding the wider picture, at the individual level, if there is an overarching new cultural and literacy practice in the production and sharing of new media of all kinds, it is this metaphorical, metacombination of literacies into what I've called a new "curatorship of the self," an expression of the anchored aspects of our identity and our transient affiliations and choices (Merchant 2006). These are exhibitions assembled, presented, dismantled, and reassembled for different audiences: family, friends, coworkers, employers, fellow campaigners, and so on. In each of these cases, some kind of textual design is employed, either in the components of the individual text, a video clip of some sort, or in their assembly from a range of different material and modes of production into a new whole (a page containing, e.g., favorite videos, status updates, personal productions, profile pictures, tagging on others' online spaces, etc.). In these cases, the decisions and intentions of the designers of these texts is important intertextually; that is, these texts of all kinds, markers, and modes of expression that work together to make meaning on the screen in representing the self and, at the moment they get made, the aspects of the author's own cultural capital are important.

Writing about literacy practices and cultural practices is never far from writing about educational practices, and this book seeks to take a closer look at these cultural phenomena in the context of education. Of course, literacy and education are connected in ways that can be traced right back to the earliest definitions of the word "literacy." Becoming "literate" means, in those ancient, operational definitions of the word, becoming an educated and economically productive member of society. In what Street (2003) describes as the "autonomous" version of literacy, the act of becoming literate confers status and success in and of itself. This version reinforces beliefs and values about the type of literacy students and young people should have access to, through curriculum design and the enactment of policy and practice inside school and outside in the home. There is an emphasis on print literacy in this model since reading and writing are represented as the keys to a communicative mode that can confer success. Reading and writing, print and screen are viewed as essential to growth, to employment, and to personal fulfillment of various kinds. Of course, the major disadvantage of this model is the absence of a way of admitting to the curriculum the changing forms of production in digital culture. There are, however, serious attempts being made in several education systems and by several cultural organizations therein to have literacy reframed to account for the moving image and/or for the digital age. Thus, we have the "new literacies" and various forms and examples of much-contested relatives and descendants from them; two of which are media literacy and digital literacy, of which more will be discussed later.

This book arises from a concern for, and a belief about, the ideological nature of literacy, its roots in lived culture, and in what people actually do and say as part of their daily existence and which has unrecognized value and worth in narrower systems of education. It has, as its central belief, after Street and other cultural anthropologists, a broader view that cultural practices are also literacy practices. These practices have changed in the light of new media, not simply because of technological artifacts but because of how the practices and arrangements around them have changed (Lievrouw and Livingstone 2006). This book takes on board the reframing literacy argument seeking to understand and account for the moving image and other modes in the production of meaning that lead us to be more inclusive of practices in a whole way of life, in other words, not only what people write and read but also what people make and share in media in the other modes available to them: still images, music, speech, moving images, and so on. The argument is not about privileging one mode over another, as it already is in many school systems around the world, but about seeing how all modes taken together operate and produce meanings and markers of identity that might have value in wider educational senses.

This book is being written against the backdrop of concerns over the widening digital divides, between generations and between developed and developing worlds, and between rich and poor within those worlds. Practices, social arrangements, and artifacts are in constant flux and among those practices that are often the slowest to change are education systems. Where these are locked rigidly into narrow and performative measures, true innovation is much harder to introduce. Various writers, academics, and commentators have, in print and on video, suggested loudly that something needs to be done to replace older institutional ways with school systems that are more responsive to changes in cultures, especially the turn toward the digital and the media. The pull is felt inside school culture, like a gravitational effect, but those who seek to make the case for wholesale system change are not always in overall charge of education systems and must depend on speaking directly to professionals and their representatives. Sometimes, the tone they take is wrong, mistaking the slow take up of change to poor teaching rather than the sometimes highly punitive consequences for teachers of stepping outside the system. Governments and politicians in systems under their direct control increasingly take short-term decisions based on political expediency and not on the longer view with the result that school curricula are in a constant state of change but largely pinging between different versions of narrow, traditional forms.

Meanwhile, outside of school, regardless of these debates, changes in the wider culture predicated on the access to powerful, portable media devices are pronounced. Individual access to changed forms of production, the ability to create and to share is often exaggerated and while it is arguable how many people are really making and remixing media content, there is little argument with the fact that, however banal or commonplace it is, in the developed world there is growing personal investment in social media, at home, in the workplace, and on the move. Very large numbers of people have a profile of some sort in social media, a place to collect favorite videos, moments to share, affiliations to underline, relatives and friends to maintain contact with—a cultural space shaped by new media technologies, which, as danah boyd (2011) has written, maintains a "networked public." It is quite natural for those who choose and have the means to do so, to share a mediated and "curated" version of their experience when they make, edit, and present media texts of various kinds from the online CV to the photo gallery, from the blog to the YouTube clip. Whereas in earlier times, apposite words to describe activities around publication may have been "written," "edited," and/or "produced," it is quite clear that they are inadequate to capture *all* the self-representational activities or *practices* in networked, digital culture. The word "curated" does so by subsuming all of those practices and adding others that are possible in social media. This is because curating suggests not just writing or producing but also *collecting, distributing, assembling, disassembling*, and *moving* media artifacts and content across different stages; all of which are potential activities in new media production from posting your status in a social networking site through to making a short clip, sharing an online gallery, or any number of other activities. Curating is about knowing how the different forms you are working with work together to make meaning intertextually and for which purposes and audiences they are successful. To account for it, we have to look at a range of different but intersecting fields of theory and analysis. For the ways in which the different modes within and between text operate and make meaning, some version of multimodal theory is useful. For the issues that lie behind production, particularly of aspects of the self, it will be important to consider aspects of sociocultural and literacy theory, to examine the intersection between media literacy and identity.

The roots of this suggestion that curatorship is an active cultural and literacy practice in new media with its own ways of reading and writing the self, its own lexis and grammar, lie in thinking about how a group of younger learners undertook making some short video pieces about their lives. This is the origin of this book, which addresses the digital production activity of a group of younger learners in order to address the question: What do these changes in lived culture, which are moving us into this curatorial experience of our mediated lives, presuppose for teaching and learning in the twenty-first century?

While a great deal of debate, product promotion, and other endeavor is taken up with trying to define twenty-first-century skills and market solutions for the problem of addressing them in educational settings, there is often a failure to recognize change as primarily institutional and cultural in nature. This is not to dismiss the technological perspective but to ask that it takes its place alongside the cultural and retains an emphasis on human rather than technological determinism. The problem for the developed and developing world is not simply the acquisition of new skills so much as the recognition of new *forms* of skills and dispositions that learners appear to be exhibiting outside formal schooling and how to adapt, incorporate, and value one and the other.

The divide between school and home is not a solid barrier as such but a semipermeable membrane through which things of value travel along with the learners themselves. Some things get left on one side of the divide or the other, or changed in the transition as they are carried though. The suspicion of many educational commentators is that there is simply too much going on outside that is not valued or built upon within school systems. And yet, this is so much more subtle a distinction and sophisticated a process than simply being "down with the kids" and introducing content from what appears to be youth culture; it is about capturing some of the skills, dispositions, and motivations of learners inside and outside the system and valuing a wider range of cultural experiences and communicative modes than some systems presently do.

Around the world, as I have argued above, those of us with the privilege of personal access to the tools of media production, online storage, and social networking, are all now potentially curators of exhibitions of our lives—how we appear, disappear, and realign ourselves to new consumption, to new affiliations, networks, and identities and how, in some cases, we recall older cultural touchstones as part of this process of presenting content to others. The exhibitions we make of this work may take the form of small communications in microblogging, of information we share on social networking sites, of CVs, of blogs, of photosharing, of remixed content we would like others to experience, and of connections we are making. So far, they resemble the usual panoply of new media forms, capable in the right hands of creating compelling representations across a variety of platforms and a variety of spaces. In their forms on both desktop and mobile devices, these sites of exhibition close the distance between happening and distribution, between event and representation. They also blur the distinctions in media forms and coherence, rendering some of the older conceptions of literacy practices *not* redundant, but certainly only partially complete. This book suggests the concept of "the new curatorship" as a new literacy practice in and of itself, something that is aligned with elements of older practices and forms, not as a replacement for them but as a set of skills and dispositions that are inherently new, building on the accrued cultural capital of the consumer and re-presenting itself through production as an ever-changing exhibition of the self and those relationships with others. This book will do more than outline and celebrate this phenomenon in any kind of cheerleading of technology and new media; it will problematize the situation as well as theorize it from a range of perspectives drawn from sociocultural theory and contemporary commentators.

The book will describe the origins of the thinking about the new cura-torship in a study of digital video production by younger learners as well as in projects that sought to elicit something of an agentive voice in research exploring home and school differences in cultural appropriation of media and technology. It will go on to show how this may help reconceptualize educational practice to build on the skills and dispositions of younger learn-ers as curators, *not* as a separate entity but as entrants into the wider society in which their literacy practices and cultural practices are forming in line with the lived experiences and representational practices of the wider world. The book will show that recognizing the curatorial nature of lived experi-ence in the twenty-first century is potentially of huge benefit in educational settings, not to change or diminish that experience by trying to move it inside those settings, but by building on the skills and dispositions of those who are practicing it to enrich the experience of learning in all settings.

Consider the opening of one of the videos in the projects described later in more detail:

> From across the school playground I watch two eleven-year-old boys with a small digital video camera, a tripod, and some props setting up the opening shot in their production. The fair-haired one is holding a small blue toy car at lens height, right in front of the camera and lining up his friend's face in the driver side window, a foreshortening effect that makes it look as though his friend is inside the car. The dark haired boy is crouched down over by the fence looking straight back at him. The dialogue begins:
> "Oh hello Keiron."
> "Oh hello Raymond."
> "That's a lovely Porsche Boxster."
> "Beautiful innit? Beautiful!"
> "Er...how much was it?"
> "About three quid."
> "Where'd you get it from?"
> "Round the sweet shop. It's a fakey."
> "Nooooooooooooo!"

As he speaks, Raymond moves the toy car revealing it as a joke. Since the production was completed I have watched the video many hundreds of times. In the course of the work, my family has also seen this video at home and when someone says, "Where did you get it?," they now inevitably utter it in the strange, high-pitched accent used in the movie. The boys in the produc-tion, created in a primary school in London, have invented a catchphrase, which, in this house, rivals the many pouring out of our screens every day. In media terms, adding part of your production to everyday conversation is something that many production companies employ teams of scriptwriters and editors to do. It was just one measure of the success of this piece in communicating adroitly in media language, and from a position of relatively low experience of production. As a measure of other successful moments of communication, screenings at academic conferences and seminars, where youth media production has been under discussion, have seen participants hailing the sophisticated manipulation of the varied modes of meaning making from the boys' choice of soundtrack, their visual play, their gestures and speech, and their performance of often bizarre sketch material.

This, and nine other videos by classmates, were made during the final weeks of primary school as part of a project that was intended as a celebration of the children's time at the school, a set of recollections in a variety of forms, which would ultimately be placed in a "memory box" alongside physical mementos of growing up and other personally important artifacts, presented in a style inspired by the American artist, Joseph Cornell (1903–1972), who was famous for his collages and memorabilia displayed in cases. They were to be taken home at the start of the summer holidays before of transition from primary to secondary school. These videos are both the starting point and the centerpiece of the arguments about literacy, identity, and new media.

At the time these productions were made, a few years ago, large scale video sharing sites were only just beginning to appear and had not yet exploded in popularity in the wake of new ways of tagging and relating collections of media artifacts to each other. However, one of the boys has subsequently, like many of his age group, gone on to represent aspects of his life as remixed media content created for consumption and communication in, first, MySpace, and more recently in Facebook. Nevertheless, the significance of this book lies in the opportunity not only to see the antecedents of new modes of self publication but also to show an alignment between theories of media production, learner agency, voice, and identity in a new formation around the concepts of curatorship, representation, and exhibition. Those of us living in affluent, developed societies with access to the tools and online spaces of media production are all now potentially curators of our lives—how we appear, disappear, and realign ourselves to new consumption, to new and old affiliations and identities.

Analyzing the videos using a range of media and sociocultural theories enables an understanding of how self-representational forms of new media production can be seen as a process of assembly of aspects of the self into a whole. The children in these videos are not merely producing work that, in a relatively uncomplicated way, as we will see later on, borrows from, quotes from, and appropriates popular media culture that they have consumed. Curatorship emerges as an active practice in itself, one which involves complex, focused, and intentional media reappropriation and remixing. Using the increasingly accessible tools of media production alongside spaces for exhibition and distribution, users, in the form of adult consumers or, in this case, younger learners, are able to take an active, agentive role in new media, as authors of repurposed and remixed media texts. They are simultaneously engaged in activity that allows for different media assets to be arranged and presented as artifacts for different purposes, different audiences. Each time a production is made, users can assemble and recombine material that they have collected, produced, and remixed into a curated work ready for exhibition. In the second decade of the twenty-first century, from their own homes, community centers, and libraries this could conceivably be a display within the "folksonomy" culture of YouTube or similar social media space. In the projects described in the book, created in quasi-formal arrangements within school settings (see later sections for a much fuller description of this environment) the distribution was to peers, teachers, parents, siblings, and carers. In all cases, the purpose is to say something about the self at a specific moment in time, to make something that will stand in place of the producer when the producer is not there. The moment a child realizes that this is what writing in print is all about is a powerful one. Now, in the twenty-first century, producing and making texts with digital media, they rapidly see that this happens with writing in modes other than print as well. Indeed, an aspect that was common across all productions was the way in which the videos themselves helped to make aspects of the children's past lives and current development beyond the curriculum visible where previously in the school they had been invisible. In representing identity at the moment in time in which the production was shot and edited, the learners were also, in addition to responding to the challenge to represent an aspect of their lives at a time of accelerating change, putting down a marker of their changing identity.

One of the contentions of the book is that active, agentive curatorship of media resources in production is a new literacy practice. For the children in the videos under discussion, this practice enabled a presentation of previously invisible versions of the self to be represented in media remixes and reformulations. It is a further contention that there is a degree of accordance with aspects of theories of identity as well as with those of learner or student voice. In addition to observing changes and reflections of the self in relation to the surrounding spaces of school, home, and neighborhood, it was an aim of this project to see if, within some of the productions, it was possible to hear versions of learner or student voice that were not previously audible. The authenticity of these voices may be difficult to prove and highly contested but, allowing for these debates, a key aim was to find a way to analyze carefully the video productions, as well as the associated interview responses, to see if activities and artifacts close to the lived culture of the learners were permitting control and curatorship of media assets. In this, it was important to adopt the view of active assimilation of such assets as derived by those working in the field of new media literacies (Robinson and Turnbull 2005). However, I aimed to investigate this active assimilation in terms of a kind of "curatorship" of media assets, implying collection, assembly, and exhibition. I wanted to position the curatorship of media assets, self-produced (as in the actual shots in the video) or collected from other sources (the music, other images) as an active skill and disposition that bridges *literacy practices* and *identity representation* and is both evident and inherent in children's media production.

While an adapted form of multimodal analysis was used to unlock the modes in the productions, there were further frameworks drawn from media literacy and sociocultural theory that enabled a rich account to be constructed about the purposes, skills, and dispositions of the learners as they represented their identity.

The videos described later in the book were made in the halfway house between formal school settings and more informal social arrangements. Initially, in studying these videos, there was an attempt to answer questions specific to media production. With minimal initial input into the aesthetics and techniques of production, discovering what the makers said and what their videos attempted to say was thought to be potentially useful in describing future pathways into media production with younger learners. What worked and what did not work in these videos, which were made with minimal adult input, could lead to an enhanced understanding of how media production may operate in the future with young learners in projects not only attempting to teach media literacy but also attempting to reveal and hear learner voice. Thus, what I was hoping to discover was something about both the *organizing structures* that were evident in self-authored video production and the *inherent practices of representation* of identity in such production by children in the later years of primary education. I was hoping to answer the following question when I started to think about their short films: What forms and organizing structures are used by young learners when negotiating and representing identity in digital video production?

Personal Contexts for Thinking about the New Curatorship

My interest in self-representation through literacy practice or media production (and the space between them) by learners has been a dominant theme in more than 20 years in education. For the first decade of that time, I worked as a classroom teacher in primary schools in inner London, predominantly in the London Borough of Tower Hamlets and for six of those ten years in a school on the Isle of Dogs. During this time, I held joint responsibility for Literacy and for Information Technology (as it was styled at the time) along with a management role in assessment and record keeping.

The school where I worked was in an ethnically and economically diverse community and the whole area was undergoing enormous change as the social impact of the closure of the docks a few years earlier and the rapid expansion of the building program began to be felt. Roy Porter's social history of London at this time provides a useful context in its penultimate chapter (Porter 1994). The classes I taught in docklands comprised—in more or less equal measure—children from working-class families of former dockworkers, Sylheti-speaking British Bangladeshi children moving east from host communities around Brick Lane, Chinese and Vietnamese speaking children moving down from Limehouse and Poplar, African children, some of whom were refugees from conflict zones, Caribbean children, and small numbers of children from new communities moving into the new accommodation and using the new Docklands Light Railway to commute.

During this time, two major interests influenced my teaching. The first of these was in the range of languages and cultures in the school community and what these could contribute to teaching and learning. This school was an inclusive institution, brilliantly led and staffed with an inspiring group of teachers, that fostered the different languages and cultures as a positive resource. Conversing in more than one code and being able to switch between two, sometimes three, languages was viewed as a positive marker and neither a hindrance to understanding nor to accessing the newly devised National Curriculum in England. In this belief, we were supported by the then Inner London Education Authority (ILEA) in its provision of additional staffing and resources. A number of staff attended in-service training (INSET), which was at the cutting edge of research into bilingualism at that time. Indeed, much of the work in the field that reported positively on bilingualism was carried out in schools like the one in which I worked and continues as a theme in the contemporary analysis of such classrooms (Gregory 1996; Kenner 2005; Sneddon 2000).

At the same time, through reading the work of Jerome Bruner in cultural psychology, on both narrative and culture as key influences in learning, it was possible to see ways of engaging learners through incorporating aspects of their lives, bringing them into writing, and storying with positive outcomes (Bruner 1996). Children's publishing and engagement with audience, alongside performance, was a key feature of the work of the writer Michael Rosen at the time, alongside a well-understood need to develop oracy at a time when writing and reading targets in the form of Standardised Assessment Tasks and Tests (SATS) were beginning to dominate the agenda in schools, through the publication of league tables. Rosen was a regular visitor to the school for workshop activities and I was lucky to take part in a "Languages in Classrooms" working party with him. Rosen's book on children's writing (1989), in which he outlined the concept of "memorable speech" as a key to unlocking children's culture and engagement with literacy, was a huge influence. The line of development from literacy issues and children's culture into an engagement with media culture has been a feature of the work of other writers (Buckingham 2003; Marsh 2004; Pahl and Marsh 2003) and I will say more about this in the subsequent chapters.

The second major influence on my practice and thinking at the time was an engagement with "Information Technology in Education." Increasing numbers of computer resources developed specifically for the education market had just begun to appear in mainstream schools. The late eighties and mid- to late nineties were a time of massive, exponential increases in expenditure on such resources. Funding streams for computers in schools were generated as result of lobbyists who identified the United Kingdom as being at risk of losing economic competitiveness through the relatively poor state of information technology in educational settings (in terms of both equipment and expertise, though the former has always held prominence in "solutions for education" in this country). At the present time, similar debates are being invoked in England over the introduction of a new curriculum based more in the realm of programming and coding, also stated as imperative for the economic competitiveness of the country in the future under pressure from programming enthusiasts and corporations alike (Cuban 2001).

In-service training for teachers back in the 1990s, however, was patchy and software/technology focused with little emphasis on curriculum matters and more on the technology itself. It was unclear how the incoming computers would actually work in schools in a curriculum not designed for them, in buildings that were not suitable for them, and with teachers who were under pressure to deliver results (Selwyn 2002). In fact, a lack of shared understanding of pedagogy has been identified as an early cause of the lack of significant impact of computers in schools over this period of time (Twining 2002b).

The selling of technology has become a theme for some engaged in the study of the field and is a tale well told by Neil Selwyn in the United Kingdom and, earlier, by Larry Cuban from the Californian experience of similar endeavors in the United States (Cuban 2001; Selwyn 2002). David Buckingham brings the situation up-to-date with an account of the present day impact of this drift through the technological determinism of the eighties into the nineties and beyond with a call for media education and not a techno-centric one (Buckingham 2007).

The impact on my own practice of these initiatives in computers in education was significant. In my last few years as a classroom teacher in East London, a Docklands educational Information Technology (IT) initiative was announced that presaged the larger government spend coming along right behind it and that flooded local schools with equipment. Because of my interest in children's writing and in incorporating their world outside school into production and publication, I had high hopes for the cultural and social aspects of the various projects that resulted. I was happy to be part of an early pilot with handheld computers, for example, early versions of the Personal Digital Assistants (PDAs), which have subsequently, years later, turned up in a variety of local and national projects (Kimbell et al. 2005). Children in my class shared the device one between two and were able to take them home. There seemed to be the possibility of employing technology in the service of closer work with the out-of-school cultures of the children along the lines proposed by the academics and writers engaged with bilingual and multilingual classrooms (see above). Certainly, in working without some of the constraints of time or location, children were able to produce drafts for publication of a range of personal stories in the rich vein of curriculum experience suggested by Rosen (1989). It must be stressed strongly that although the project was essentially portrayed in the immediate area as technologically determinist ("look what the PDAs can do"), in our school the focus was on the children as writers and publishers, making meaning from the resources around them. In many ways, these activities presaged later developments with media, of which more will be discussed later.

Over time, however, the projects that were funded became less obviously creative and much more focused on a technologically determinist view. More significant investment and development began to go into providing narrow and atomized experiences with technology that had little or nothing to do with children's culture and everything to do with assessment. It was a stressful time to be a teacher as a series of sweeping and punitive measures centered on inspection by the Office for Standards in Education (OFSTED) were foisted on schools by central government, serving to develop a culture of performance and to narrow the curriculum experience for learners to the easily measured, so-called basics. More and more resource would subsequently be directed toward devices and software that would support the new emphasis on teacher talk and whole-class teaching and away from a more learner-centered engagement with cultures outside the school. Ultimately, this would lead to the widespread implementation of the Interactive Whiteboard in classrooms at all ages, although this is not to deny that there are opportunities to engage in imaginative and collaborative work around this device in the hands of teachers concerned with learner agency and engagement.

Two years of work in East London followed as an advisory teacher for IT in primary and secondary schools. At this time, the funding provided by the government in its National Grid for Learning (NGFL) project began to change the nature of the interaction with technology significantly through the emergence of massively funded, ubiquitous, and safe connections to the Internet. Here again, however, two recurring strands reasserted themselves. The first was the lack of any idea of training for teachers that considered pedagogy to be of, at least, equal importance to technical prowess. Certainly, this was a finding of masters research into training for curriculum uses of the Internet that I subsequently published (Potter and Mellar 2000). Second, the NGFL rushed into areas of expensive "content" production that positioned learners as passive recipients of chunks of information and positioned teachers and schools as consumers of overpriced curriculum material, much of it very poorly designed and of unproven worth in educational settings.

The late children's author Diana Wynne Jones once wrote a book called *Archer's Goon*, in the opening section of which, she defined her titular character as follows, "A Goon is a being who melts into the foreground and sticks there" (Jones 2000). In some ways, this is what has happened with technology in education; it has melted into the foreground of many educational settings and stuck there, uninvited, largely undertheorized as a culturally produced set of artifacts and practices, misunderstood in terms of its impact on pedagogy, and sometimes even unwanted in the classroom. I am suggesting here that one reason is a lack of thinking about these artifacts as cultural objects situated in the lives of learners and teachers alike beyond the school.

After working as an Information and Communication Technology (ICT) advisor, I moved into a lecturing role in initial teacher education hoping to conduct more research and introduce more curriculum and pedagogy-focused courses about the uses of technology in education. Teaching both Literacy and ICT meant that I could work in this way, although it was not really until digital video production became more easily accessible and available that the possibilities to think differently about technology and pedagogy really presented themselves and the way was led by a growing interest in media as a site for cultural experiences and greater connections with learner lives.

Outside work, video production had begun to play a part in my home life. Short videos of my children growing up taken whenever I was able to borrow equipment from work allowed me to record and represent aspects of lived experience. What happened next took me by surprise and changed the way in which I was moving personally and professionally. Early home movie footage shot by my son Jack when he was aged about 4 included a self-authored tour of the house, featuring items that were salient and important to him (cupboards, toilet, etc.)—all at child height. The short clips filmed by my children and friends of theirs on a Sony Mavica camera, a basic low resolution early digital camera, which recorded images to floppy disk, included a range of media references, all repurposed and repackaged into short self-representational video texts. This activity appeared to me to be a nascent new form of literacy production that was worthy of much more detailed investigation. It was enabled by technological advances, such as portable cameras, new file formats, new playback devices, and so on. Yet, it was different from previous technology-enabled activities, occupying a space in the primary years between the subject domains of English and ICT. In secondary schools, as will be seen in the forthcoming chapter, the situation was different, with digital video production introduced within the context of Media Studies where its inherent possibilities as a tool for analysis and production had a ready curriculum space.

In the context of primary education, I began to think of digital video production as an area that represented a new way of relating to technology in education; one which privileged the texts and artifacts produced, and how meaning was made in them, over the technology with which they were made. This interest subsequently extended into other areas, including website production and hypermedia authoring. Digital video production, however, remained a key starting point for moving more into media education and research, pushing the technology into the background and foregrounding media culture. At this point, I began to introduce digital video production in both the courses I was teaching and in my own research. This led me further from the technologically determinist views of much of the ICT in education world and into a much greater negotiation with media education, media literacy, and a wider consideration of cultural texts and artifacts.

The opportunity arose, through an internal scholarship at the university where I was working, for me to gain some professional development and equipment. I joined one of the residential media production courses run by the Apple Teacher Institute, during which I worked alongside people who were also exploring the area between ICT and media; people who were media resource officers, lecturers, teachers, advisors, workers in city learning centers, and so on. The course content, spread over four days, allowed for immersion in the issues around technology use in the production of media, including digital video editing, sound editing, and more. Because of the range of attendees, there were some interesting conversations and debates, ranging from the technical on one side, across to media and cultural theory on the other. I certainly experienced a shift in emphasis from one to the other.

As a result of this shift in emphasis, I began to think of ways in which digital video production could be the site of exploratory research into media literacy in young learners. The projects discussed later on in this book were formulated around a process of self-representation using digital video production. This was not simply in order to engage younger learners with "authentic" or even "relevant" experiences. Authenticity is hard to measure and relevance harder both to prove and to provide (without risking patronizing the end user). It was more about continuing to move away from a "technologically determinist" view toward a "user determining" one, centered within the lived culture, media experiences, and practices of those learners. At the start of this work, on the basis of my teaching experience to date, this meant providing opportunities for self-authoring activities in digital video production and analyzing outcomes using some of the emergent thinking about sociocultural perspectives on education and new media as well as some relevant aspects of cultural studies.

And so, following this introduction, this book is divided into further eight chapters. The second chapter, "Literacy and Production," looks at a range of useful theory in the field, discussing changing conceptions of literacy, particularly as this relates to production, technology, and to the concept of play in learning. The third chapter, "Identity and Storying," considers relevant writing about identity, storying the self, and digital video. The fourth chapter, "Research and Voice," surveys some relevant research into digital video production by learners that has successfully used different models to account for technological factors in video projects, alongside others that have considered the properties of the medium and its relationship to wider filmmaking activity. Those studies that have specifically looked at outputs and relationships to identity and literacy issues related to them are also considered, alongside potential methods for looking at, and thinking about, digital video. The fifth chapter, "Video and Performance," looks in detail at the contexts for video production in the form of a detailed examination of the case study videos. The sixth chapter, "Editing and Coherence," considers editing as the key organizing element of intertextual spaces in the videos, how the many modes in production speak to each other and make meaning. The seventh chapter, "Location and Memory," examines the importance of the locative memory in creating stories of the self as well as how the learner's voice in production and in research around production in a space gets constructed and heard. The eighth chapter, "Theory from Practice," explains in more detail the concept of curatorship as a new literacy practice and how it emerged from close examination of the video texts. The final chapter, "Learning and the New Curatorship," looks at what this concept means for formal education and the "Afterword" presents a manifesto for how this should develop in the future.

CHAPTER 2

Literacy and Production

In recent years, "literacy" has been defined in a number of different ways and claimed by a number of different disciplines within education and related theory. Literacy is prefixed by words that reflect different educational movements, controversies, debates, and, occasionally, attempts to "sell" an educational solution in response to rapid societal and technological change. Thus, it is possible to find examples of any or all of the following in press, web pages, journals, and books of all kinds from the latter phases of the twentieth century through to the present day, from academic theory through to teacher and parental guidance: *digital literacy, computer literacy, visual literacy, film literacy, information literacy, cultural literacy, games literacy, emotional literacy*, and more, up to and including *media literacy*. Aligned to this at a metalevel are ways of grouping and conceptualizing "literacies" and later sections will address examples of these—namely, *Multiliteracies* and *New Literacy Studies* (Cope and Kalantzis 2000).

One key aspect that all the areas share, even within their various different theoretical perspectives, is an attempt to describe a process by which meanings are both transmitted and received, as well as a sphere in which competencies are developed, demonstrated, and measured. This is because the term "literacy" itself is inextricably linked with competency in reading and making messages and, therefore, with learning itself. Literacy is something to be acquired, a set of skills and dispositions that lead a person to be "literate." The *Concise Oxford English Dictionary* (6th ed.) defines literacy as "the ability to read and write" (ed. Sykes 1979). To be a literate person is to be "educated" and "learned," these meanings originating from Latin derivatives and in use in these senses since the fifteenth century. From the eighteenth century onward, literacy becomes further connected in its meaning to the processes of learning itself, the step-by-step acquisition of knowledge of letters and how to use them (Hoad 1992).

For the many newer forms of literacy listed above, these competencies come in different forms for different purposes. Thus, apologists for "information literacy" propose teaching programs that place a high premium on reading, networking, and interpretive skills (November 2001). All of them, however, suggest a developing competence within the fields, which precede the word "literacy," although some go well beyond competency and emphasize the mastery of empathy and other life skills (e.g., as in "emotional literacy").

In recent years, further direct evidence of the connection between literacy and pedagogy came when "Literacy" began to supplant the term "English" as a subject in English primary schools. In 1998, a specific pedagogy was imposed by the government on primary schools in England, namely the step-by-step acquisition of a set of skills proposed in the National Literacy Strategy (DFES 1998). The Literacy hour prescribed teaching methods in primary schools which were intended to build sequentially, skill-by-skill, concept-by-concept, effectively atomizing learning about the processes of exchange and meaning making in all the constituent parts of National Curriculum English—namely, *speaking and listening, reading,* and *writing.* The result, although intended to be a comprehensive literacy program, was a greater emphasis on skills and metalevel analysis of text at the expense of active engagement with writing and publication by children. This continues in education systems at the moment and the various interventions aimed at stimulating creativity outside of narrow school systems is gaining ground in the after-school area, promoted by Dave Eggers in the United States and adopted here in London by some local initiatives (see, e.g., HackneyPirates 2012)

The burgeoning number of literacies listed in the opening to this section reflects many changes, not least among them are technological and societal changes that result in increased production and distribution in a variety of media. Alongside printed matter, across the developed world and in increasing areas of the undeveloped world, there is greater access to text, music, speech, video, and film on screens from televisions to computers to phones. There is more to be literate about and, because of the connection with pedagogy, more to educate about and more to be educated by. Literacy needs to be reframed as many have started to argue (Reid 2009).

In the late nineties, the New London Group proposed a collection of responses to the changing nature of literacy under the heading "Multiliteracies" (Cope and Kalantzis 2000), an attempt to describe and discuss the way literacy was moving in a world of accelerated change, together with plans for pedagogical responses to those changes within our education systems. They joined the tradition of linking literacy to pedagogy in their initial set of proposals:

> If it were possible to define generally the mission of education, one could say that its fundamental purpose is to ensure that all students benefit from learning in ways that allow them to participate fully in public, community, and economic life. Literacy pedagogy is expected to play a particularly important role in fulfilling this mission. (New London Group 1996)

Appropriately, these discussions, proposals, and hypotheses by Kress, Gee, Fairclough, Cope, Kalantzis, and others in the group were published as a collection in the millennial year, further underlining newness, change, and movement. The subtitle of the collection revealed the scope of ambition of the writers concerned, nothing less than describing "Literacy Learning and the Design of Social Futures." The focus throughout the collection was on establishing a semiotic basis for pedagogy and literacy, combined with a set of proposals to understand the impact on teaching and learning of new social arrangements brought about by significant changes in socioeconomic conditions. As a whole, in the introduction, the New London Group specifically addressed how changing conceptions of literacy were shaped by political factors. Some individual accounts in the *Multiliteracies* book (Cope and Kalantzis 2000) described a role for technology, particularly *networked* technology, in this process (see Ch. 2 by James Paul Gee). While others had a vision of practice in response to these changes that was rooted in social constructivism and social psychology (Crook 2001), this book proposed a theoretical and pedagogical reformulation of literacy as the major anticipated change in relation to new texts and new ways to make and exchange meaning in the world.

A further important near contemporary movement in the field, grouped under the term "new literacy studies" attempted to locate literacy within a sociocultural and anthropological frame. Preceding *Multiliteracies* by a few years, and similarly seeking to widen the definition of literacy, it was developed by a number of writers (Barton, Hamilton, and Ivanic 2000; Heath 1983; Street 1985, 1995). These early definitions were subsequently elaborated and developed alongside multiliteracies in the context of new media forms (Gee 2004a; Lankshear and Knobel 2006; Larson and Marsh 2005; Marsh and Millard 2000), of which, more will be discussed later.

Returning to the work of Brian Street, mentioned in the foreword above and revisiting the origins of new literacy studies in more depth, we find two potentially useful ways of (re)framing literacy. He proposed two operational models of literacy, the "ideological" and the "autonomous" (1985). He defined the autonomous model of literacy as one in which active engagement with literacy has naturally positive impacts on other social and cognitive practices; in other words, simply taking part in literacy activities confers enhancement of life chances and economic prospects. Literacy is seen as fixed and neutral in this model, operating outside of social and cultural factors and essentially immune to changes over time. In contrast to this, he defines the ideological model of literacy as one which

> offers a more culturally sensitive view of literacy practices as they vary from one context to another. This model starts from different premises than the autonomous model—it posits instead that literacy is a social practice, not simply a technical and neutral skill; that it is always embedded in socially constructed epistemological principles. It is about knowledge: the ways in which people address reading and writing are themselves rooted in conceptions of knowledge, identity, and being. (Street 2003, pp. 77–78)

"Literacy practices," as referred to here not only mean taking part in an exchange of meaning but also to the participants' concept of the process itself. In relation to reading and writing, Street defines literacy practices as

> not only the event itself but the conceptions of the reading and writing process that people hold when they are engaged in the event. (Street 1995, p. 133)

The ideological model is, therefore, a reflexive account of engagement with literacy events in which participant self-perception of their engagement in a practice are as important as their actual contribution.

These ideological and social definitions of literacy have been used by theorists such as Buckingham (1993) in *Children Talking Television* to support the contention that social and cultural forces are significant in shaping "television literacy." He employed the definition of ideological model of literacy as an important factor in shaping a "social theory of television literacy" which would

> begin by acknowledging that children's use of television is an integral part of the fabric of their daily lives…it would acknowledge that that the competencies which are involved in making sense of television are not equally available, but socially distributed, and that they are intimately connected with the operation of social power. (Ibid., p. 34)

Furthermore, Buckingham invokes the culturally dependent model of literacy as a way of accounting for changes in definitions of what it means to be literate through time:

> As media languages and technologies evolve, so do definitions of what it means to be literate—a process which is arguably accelerating at the present moment. (Ibid.)

In response to the proliferation of new media forms and technologies in subsequent years, others have invoked the sociocultural theories of Street and others to account for changes in literacy practices. For example, Marsh and Millard (2000) argued the importance to teachers and learners of an engagement with children's popular culture in literacy activities, in the context of new and older, print media; Haas Dyson (1997) proposed a method for engaging children in sustained literacy practices around their interaction with the superhero genre; Nixon and Comber (2005) looked at how two teachers worked with small-scale media production projects in early years classrooms in a popular culture context.

These examples have been followed by accounts that incorporate newer forms of media, including online activity, within "everyday practices" as well as classroom contexts (Lankshear and Knobel 2006). In turn, these follow formulations and develop concepts derived from the work of Gee (2004b). One of the most frequently cited concepts from this is the "affinity space," an online or offline space in which end users are sustained by a common purpose and, as a result, experience a high level of engagement and achievement. In this formulation of literacy and cultural activity, Gee raises the prospect of learner disengagement from traditional schooling with the attraction of new media forms as spaces for collaboration and "situated learning"; he writes that

> [learners] confronted with more and more affinity spaces...see a different and arguably powerful vision of learning, affiliation, and identity. (Ibid., p. 89)

The degree to which the productions under investigation in this book represent an affinity space and how much that is important to the outcome will be a matter for discussion at a later stage. For now, I want to focus more specifically on literacy in relation to moving-image texts.

Media Literacy

Media literacy, as will be seen below, is proposed as a central site for the reorganization of theories of meaning making and pedagogy (Burn and

Durran 2007). The definition of media literacy is contested in official government documents, academic papers, and books in this country and others. In Australia, one writer in the field has found the debates unhelpful and has even sidestepped the issue, preferring the term "media competence" to "media literacy" (Orr Vered 2008), although ultimately this notion risks a functional reductivism in practice, however subtly argued and nuanced it may be.

Media literacy, as we have seen, is often defined in relation to developing a critical understanding of the media. However, other important definitions are more expansive and explicitly include production. This is encapsulated in the definition by the UK government regulator Office for Communication (OFCOM), namely, "the ability to access, understand and *create* communications in a variety of contexts" (OFCOM 2005, my emphasis in italics). In this book, the aspect of the definition of literacy that is represented by the word "create" is central.

The version of media literacy offered by Burn and Durran (2007) widens the scope from OFCOM's focus on communication and its disinclination to encompass both semiotic and cultural theory. They detail a program that encompasses both of these aspects and propose a "cultural-semiotic model"—an understanding of the processes of meaning making that attempts to bring together three central sets of principles. First, the work of Williams from the field of cultural studies in *The Long Revolution* (1961) is evoked in the conception of lived, selected, and recorded cultural contexts. Alongside this, they propose a program defined by a conception of the "cultural, creative and critical" social functions of media literacy. Finally, they establish a third set of principles based on an understanding of semiotic processes with equal weight in teaching and learning given to understanding "discourse, design/production, distribution and interpretation" (Burn and Durran 2007, see esp. pp. 6–9). This seems to me to offer a usable and holistic definition on which to base an exploration of children's video production.

The connection between literacy and pedagogy has been noted above and discussions of "media literacy" and "media education" go side by side in many key texts. In Buckingham's *Media Education* (2003), cited by Burn and Durran (2007, p. 21), the emphasis is on establishing rationales for pedagogy that situate media literacy in contemporary cultural contexts. This book in turn builds on earlier texts such as *Cultural Studies Goes to School* (Buckingham and Sefton-Green 1994) to establish a case for the expansion of literacy pedagogy beyond the "functional" and into a productive relationship with culture and cultural theory. More recently, Buckingham has proposed that media literacy / media education should take a central role in school curricula, seeking to negotiate with the culture of its students within the contexts of new technologies, a role that Information and Communication Technology (ICT) as subject has not been able to fill (Buckingham 2007).

In the meantime, a further recurrent theoretical issue in media literacy is the analogy with print literacy. In setting out how a program of media literacy might operate, this analogy is often invoked (Buckingham 2003; Burn and Durran 2007; Lankshear and Knobel 2006; Larson and Marsh 2005; Sefton-Green 1998). This is not a comfortable or unproblematic fit and Buckingham sounds a cautionary note in pushing the analogy too far, in particular because of the lack of truly analogous grammatical terms between the two (2003, Ch. 3). However, as imperfect as the analogy is in many ways, he finds that the use of literacy in the context of media education makes an important and distinctive contribution, as follows:

> The emphasis on literacy reminds us of an element that is often neglected in media education. For literacy clearly involves both reading *and* writing; and so media literacy must necessarily entail both the interpretation and the production of media. (Buckingham 2003)

Earlier, Sefton-Green based some of his doctoral research into media production in secondary school settings on an examination of the "metaphor" of literacy (1998). From Barton's review of critical literacy studies, he found a useful definition that expands the reductive one quoted previously, to one which envisages literacy as a "set of social practices with particular symbol systems and their related technologies...to be literate is to be active" (Barton 1994, p. 32). Sefton-Green makes the connection between activity and practice, with what he calls "human agency—that is individual or cultural expression" (1998, p. 53). He makes explicit the connections between competencies and actions. For this book also, production, conceived as social action, is at the center of the understanding of the term "media literacy."

Previously in the literature review, the "production versus interpretation" debate was described, in particular how it has been played out in primary and secondary education and how some pragmatic solutions had been developed that described stages of development through which younger learners might move (e.g., Bazalgette 1989). For Burn and Durran (2007) developing media literacy in education involves a sociocultural engagement with meaning making in media texts, invoking two sorts of analytical frameworks to understand the process. First, there is the framework represented by the tools of semiotics, in order to interpret meaning making at a textual level; second, frameworks from the field of cultural studies are essential in order to situate learners within social and political contexts. Working with this in school means revealing what children already know and how this may be built on. They describe it in these terms:

> When children arrive at school, they bring with them highly developed forms of media literacy already. They have extensive *implicit* knowledge of how media texts work; and the semiotic approach can be used to analyse *what they are already able to do*. As importantly, however, it can be used to outline what we want them to be able to do in addition. (Burn and Durran 2007, p. 20, author emphasis in italics)

Two years later in *Making New Media: Creative Production and Digital Literacies,* Burn makes even more explicit the potential for linking different theoretical frames in the analysis of popular culture with an understanding of the ways in which children engage with media texts in educational settings:

> Kress and van Leeuwen's proposal (social semiotics)...connects texts with the social interests of their related signmakers: those who make them, and those who use, read, view or play them. In the context of education, it offers a theory of signification ready for synthesis with the work of scholars of children's media cultures, such as Buckingham, who provides influential research in how children engage with media texts as well as proposals for how the pedagogies of media education might be influenced by Cultural Studies. (Burn 2009, p. 2)

Elsewhere in his opening chapter, Burn adds "interpretation" to "discourse" and "design," "production," and "distribution" to the list of processes, or "strata," which Kress and Van Leeuwen (2001) propose for understanding how meanings are made in multimodal communication. Suggesting interpretation as an active semiotic process moves the agenda further still in seeking to close the loop between the analytical approach of social semiotics and the approach of cultural studies to the understanding of the production of meaning in media texts. Both are important; formal textual analysis seeks to understand the place of each of the different modes of communication and a sociocultural analysis adds an understanding of the affective relations between social actors, how and why particular roles in production were assigned, why certain shots were employed, why certain music was added, and so on. Both analyses enable a rich description of coherence in successful productions and potentially useful accounts of disruptions and fissures in less successful videos.

Intertextuality

Online video sites are full of parody and remix alongside original output. And in children's videos, there are, as in mainstream production, quotations, and appropriations from television shows and films alongside music and speech samples. In analyzing the form of these productions, we can use tools that help us to unlock each of the modes in production, adapted forms of multimodal analysis that allow us to identify and discuss textual quotations and appropriations within the finished productions.

The concept of "intertextuality," therefore, becomes an important additional frame through which to view media texts; the producer and subsequently the viewer make meaning from the juxtaposition of excerpts and quotations of media texts, which are in dialogue with one another. In this respect, the dialogism of Bakhtin (1981) and the subsequent repositioning of this in the light of semiotics provide ways into the apparent jumble of references and borrowings between these texts. There are echoes of the "mosaic of quotations" invoked by the semiotician Julia Kristeva to account for and define intertextuality (1980, p. 66). The apparent playful assemblages of texts are designed with the viewer in mind who knows the sources and how they relate to one another and is capable of making meaning from the intertextuality of these resources. They make different meanings through being read with each other.

Intertextuality in the context of media literacy implies what Fairclough describes as a "socially conceived" theory of media production. For Fairclough, any emergent theories of newer forms of literacy must incorporate both "language" and "discourse." He writes,

> In analysing the language of a text one is referring the text to a grammar or grammars, and seeing it in terms of rules (for some) or systems networks (for others). In analysing the text as discourse one is referring the text to an order of discourse or discourses...an order of discourse is the set of discursive practices associated with an institution or a social domain, and the particular boundaries which obtain between these practices. (Fairclough 2000, p. 170)

Negotiating these concepts of discourse is key to an understanding of media texts in the context of media literacy. Central to the design of a media text is its place in an order of discourse that incorporates the idea of quotation, remixing, and repurposing at its heart. Partly, this is bound up in the construction of the grammar, how shot-by-shot and edit-by-edit the meaning is made. Partly, it is revealed in how the collection of shots themselves reference other known examples of the discursive practices inherent in the form, and then, how these references work together to produce new meanings.

Fairclough claims intertextuality as the key differentiating concept in the application of textual analysis in the field of new literacy studies because it allows for the development of a method that maps properties of texts onto properties of "society and culture" (ibid., p. 174). For media literacy, this means mapping the properties of texts that "express pressures towards conventions and normativity, and pressures towards difference and change" (ibid.).

In this, Fairclough echoes and invokes Bakhtin who describes the ways in which utterances or "speech acts" have a duality within which they are in tension. The pressures, which Bakhtin calls "centripetal forces," are the ways in which speech acts must be subservient to the unifying organizing forces of the conventions of language systems. These are in continual tension with the "centrifugal forces" of the wider "heteroglossia," the varied and stratified wider systems in which all utterances take place. Bakhtin writes,

> Every utterance participates in the unitary language (in its centripetal forces and tendencies) and at the same time partakes of the social and historical heteroglossia (the centrifugal, stratifying forces). (Bakhtin 1981)

If we can substitute media texts for utterances, we can begin to reveal the ways in which media texts express this tension and play against it in their construction. Media literacy borrows from this model the implication of a developed awareness of the ways in which the texts speak to other texts while obeying the conventions of the form.

Such a conception leads back ultimately to a semiotic engagement with media production, with the methods required to look at texts within texts, modes within production. It does, however, contain a measure of social and cultural engagement that is absent in other analytical models. Burn suggests (2009) that semiotic analysis does one kind of work on a text while cultural studies provide a much needed further analytical dimension. Without a sociocultural frame, a focus on the features of design for meaning leads to an analysis of media texts that, at best, de-emphasizes aesthetic and affective response and, at worst, omits these aspects entirely. There are particular consequences for the study of identity in production that arise from overdependence on such tools. This view is expressed in other literacy studies focused on identity, for example, in Leander and Frank's critique of multimodality as a research methodology for studying youth production in online spaces (2006) where it is viewed as unable to account for embodiment or the aesthetic affects of texts and textual production. If the arguments about complementary frames of reference made above are true, then understanding pedagogy around production of the media texts *partly* depends on finding relevant and appropriate frames from cultural studies approaches to learning. This will be important in trying to reestablish the aesthetic and embodied aspects of the reference points, the wider heteroglossia. Since this study is also concerned with a specific new media form, the digitally edited moving image, it makes sense to seek theoretical models and propositions from cultural theorists who attempt to embrace these media forms. Henry Jenkins, for example, proposes a list of "new skills" to consider in thinking about media education in the paper, "Confronting the Challenges of Participatory Culture: Media Education for the 21st Century." Alongside some skills that are at the margins of relevance to this study (*simulation, multitasking, judgment, etc.*) are several more that are central to it—namely,

> **Play**—the capacity to experiment with one's surroundings as a form of problem-solving
> **Performance**—the ability to adopt alternative identities for the purpose of improvisation and discovery...
> **Appropriation**—the ability to meaningfully sample and remix media content
> **Collective Intelligence**—the ability to pool knowledge and compare notes with others toward a common goal
> **Transmedia Navigation**—the ability to follow the flow of stories and information across multiple modalities
> **Networking**—the ability to search for, synthesize, and disseminate information. (Jenkins et al. 2006, p. 4)

From the list above, the items of greatest relevance to short-form video clips appear to be, particularly in respect of quotation and repurposing, "appropriation" and "transmedia navigation." The uses of quoted and reenacted texts lie somewhere between remixing and working with "the flow of texts across modalities" (ibid.). One consideration in setting out the methodology, data collection, and analysis will be the extent to which this can be described and accounted for in the productions as a consciously applied set of skills by the younger people and how this is part of a set of skills that may ultimately inform pedagogy. The key to the deeper understanding of these issues is to amplify the word meaningfully in the definition of appropriation to explain further what it means to work with texts within texts. For this, we need to bring intertextuality into the frame, in the ways outlined above. We need to adapt appropriation as Jenkins defines it to include, "the ability to work intertextually with media content in order to make meanings" (ibid.).

In looking for ways to describe what is happening in the borrowings and appropriations in digital video production then, it is important to think about the purposes and practices of these new literacy skills. First, they may contribute to the understanding of what it is to be a skilled media manipulator, at a surface level, revealing the most competent authors as those able to roam freely through the various media references and repurpose them. Second, they propose at a deeper level that the authors are adept in borrowing the cultural capital of the original producer(s), either to signal distance or closeness to the original meaning, but in any case to align themselves with it as a reference point. Third, and deeper still, the juxtaposition of these reference points suggests that they are in intertextual dialogue with one another. In this area, we are close to Jenkins's concept of the "textual poacher," a fan, a consumer at play in the media assets they are obsessed with, taking them in as raw material with which to refashion and re-present their own contribution. In Jenkins's theory, the consumer has become the producer, not by stealth or simple quotation but by a process of reversioning, recombining, and repurposing their favorite raw materials to make new meaning (see Jenkins 1992, esp. Ch. 4, pp. 120–151). Adding intertextuality proposes a mechanism that suggests a deeper engagement with the material and a richer potential account of how the meaning is made, with consequences for an understanding of media literacy and how it might be developed.

Organizing Intertextual Spaces

The previous section showed how the selection of assets and their intertextual arrangements in the production are important elements in theorizing the overall authoring and design of a media text. A key part of the process, which allows both the form to take shape and the intertextual spaces to present particular meanings in dialogue with one another, is the process of *editing*.

One fundamental media literacy practice that is realized in digital video editing is the ability to organize different meaning-making resources onscreen and control their movement through time. This is control of an additional mode, proposed as "kineikonic" by Burn and Parker (2001). As they acknowledge elsewhere (Burn and Parker 2003), film theory has long considered the essential nature of editing in specific ways. They discuss Christian Metz who, in his conception of film "language" (1974) considered some aspects "cinematic" (just the filming and editing) and others "filmic" (dramatic action, music, etc.). Burn and Parker argue that a central aim of multimodal analysis of moving-image production is to combine these aspects together. In so doing, they invoke a particular way of thinking about the editing space onscreen:

> (The) elements are blended through the editing process, which we can imagine as a kind of multimodal mixing desk. Its function is not simply that of assembly but of re-design. (Burn and Parker, 2003, p. 23)

This conception of editing is important because it positions it as an active authoring and designing process, not simply the final part of moving-image production, which merely acts as an assembly point for previously organized resources. It becomes a process with its own organizing principles, a place wherein a key set of authoring decisions are not only taken but also enacted.

Of course, this agentive view of editing is not new in the world of film theory and criticism where film editors are venerated as being essential to the process and feted with their own awards. Indeed, Bordwell and Thompson point out the key role of editing within the "an entire film's stylistic system" (2008, p. 218), and go on to define it as "the co-ordination of one shot with the next" (ibid.). In their analysis of the process, they describe the contribution of specific cuts and juxtapositions of shots to the narrative arc of a film. Essentially, they are in the territory of Metz's version of the cinematic and are describing linear sets of visual relationships between one shot and the next. They are also describing a specialized craft skill within the overall canon of skills that are part of the tradition of filmmaking, and, as such, they are within a frame that privileges the cinematic and is much less specifically concerned with filmic modes such as gesture, music, and so on (for which theories of multimodality offer different analytic potential as Burn and Parker [2003] point out).

Even as such onscreen spaces were only beginning to appear, some authors were already identifying editing as a key feature of media literacy that pushed media production closer toward the analogy with writing. Bazalgette proposed editing as a new literacy skill in itself (2000), certainly for older children, within the context of the debate around English as a subject. In doing so, she invoked the time-based nature of film and alluded to the sorts of tools that were now bringing this under the control of a wider range of producer-users. At the same time, Sefton-Green and Parker (2000) present a writer's view of editing, building on earlier discussions such as those in *Making Media* (Buckingham, Grahame, and Sefton-Green 1995, Ch. 3), which acknowledge the changes being wrought by digital video technology, changes which bring the processes of digital video production closer to the metaphorical connection with print literacy, the construction of texts, moving things, copying, and pasting.

The metaphorical connection to literacy is strengthened by use of the term "inscription" in combination with the word "digital" (Burn and Parker 2001); their "multimodal mixing desk" is the digital tool which pulls a whole set of controlling principles and practices together into one virtual space. Here, it is certainly possible for the digital video editor to be cinematic and work with the relation of shot-to-shot, composing and trimming them on a timeline. However, it is also possible to be filmic in the wider sense, and be the sound engineer, the soundtrack compiler, the person who adds filters and effects, the person who adds titling and decides duration and juxtaposition for all the resources, and how they will work together intertextually.

The affordances, by which I mean the authorial possibilities inherent in this space, in this and similar entry-level video-editing packages, are represented by icons such as loudspeakers, camera, a music clef, and so on. The play head describes the kineikonic movement through time from left to right. The monitor window at the top right allows the editor-author to view the work in progress. The album in the rest of the top half of the screen contains thumbnails that represent clips to be dragged down into the timeline and placed alongside others. As Manovich (2001) has pointed out in his description of the differential features of "new" media, the dis-crete roles and crafts in "old media" film production are mimicked in the onscreen spaces of editing software, providing analogies with physical objects and older practices. In turn, these practices become available in the software in ways in which they have not been previously, allowing control of a much greater range of editing activity by means of the visual resources of icons and labels, timelines and waveforms (Sefton-Green 2005).

The visual metaphors and their affordances widen the potential access to these older roles and practices and raise the possibility of a new hybrid set of media literacy skills centered on control of all the modes in produc-tion in one place. It is important to remember that in addition to collaps-ing diverse filmmaking practices into one space, they also build on the wider cultural understanding of practices within software of many kinds, the understanding that a loudspeaker icon is present everywhere in virtual environments as a visual metaphor for volume, that a letter T stands for control of fonts and titling as it does in many other spaces, that a dustbin is where unwanted material will be "thrown" or mistakes erased (see also the discussion in Fursteneau and Mackenzie 2009, of Final Cut Pro). These aspects of mediated, productive, literacy activity, and practice are begin-ning to be theorized increasingly as aspects of sociocognitive action around editing spaces (Gilje 2009). At this point, the frameworks intersect with the discussion of creative, playful, fashioning activity with technology and are discussed in more detail below.

Play and Technology: Media Literacy in the Context of Provisionality

It is important to take note of a further possible representative practice in the context of digital video technologies. Not every video made as a piece of self-representation by children and young people ends up as the coherent, fully designed, literate, and realized use of meaning-making resources envisaged by some semiotic theorists. "Play," including a form of "roleplay" in front of and behind the camera, is also represented in the mutable and fluid possibilities in production, the roles in production on- and offscreen. Children are able to capture moments of their own play as it unfolds. It may be possible to observe this in the movement between roles and behaviors in front of and behind the camera. If it too is captured, it serves as a means of expressing a hybrid and fluid relation to a media literacy practice.

The juxtaposition of scenes and quotations with music and other audio may also be subject to different responses to the task of self-representation. These may not necessarily reveal themselves in the carefully controlled and elaborate referencing system of the media literate producer, working intertextually with the resources; they may simply appear to be "playful," experimental assemblages of resources. Sefton-Green and Parker found that children who were engaged in onscreen editing activities were often playful; there was a fluid and yet purposeful speech around the screen that enabled improvisation and, as they write, "Such active collaboration also has obvious parallels with children's fantasy play" (Sefton-Green and Parker 2000, p. 44). It can also be an aspect of self-representational video that allows for the play with developing identity itself to become the subject of the representation. However, in celebratory accounts what sometimes becomes lost is a critical focus on aspects of literacy, play, and creativity that allows these elements to be separated out and their interrelationship described. The arguments in this chapter aim to avoid overlap and underline distinctive features of these elements in producing a usable frame for analysis.

Sutton-Smith devotes a whole section of *The Ambiguity of Play* (1997) to a discussion of theorists who have made a causal link between the play and a developing sense of the self, in particular in the work of proponents of theories with identifiable, demarcated stages of children's development (e,g., Craggs 1992). Important distinctions are made here between a simplistic causal link and the actual practical relations within the setting. Sutton-Smith suggests numerous alternative causes for observable developmental and cognitive outcomes through play, not least in the changed relationship between adults and children. However, he also makes the point that the developmental and educational rhetoric around play usually seeks to make it safe and does not account for, or even always readily admit, its more challenging aspects in, for example, facilitating the construction of socially inappropriate forms of identity.

For Vygotsky, play represented an affective response to change or thwarted need; it is an exploration of what is possible and demanded in a given situation. The player applies active imagination to a given situation, and engages in play as "a specifically human form of conscious activity. Like all functions of consciousness it originally rises from action" (Vygotsky 1933). There are parallels between this conception and that of being active and agentive in a productive engagement with literacy (Sefton-Green 1998), as well as with previously quoted problem-solving qualities of play elaborated in the context of new media (Jenkins 2006).

For the reasons outlined, perhaps, the term "play" is often invoked when discussing digital technologies and young people not least in relation to the inherent quality of "provisionality," which they add to human action. If play facilitates the construction of hybrid forms of identity, some of them perceived as inappropriate, as noted above, then play with digital technologies records these forms along the way. Provisionality adds a self-referencing system to the process, which is open to the author to exploit. As has been presented in the first half of this chapter, the videomaker can place any number of modes together in different combinations before lighting on the version that fixes identity for that moment, for whatever particular purpose.

Perhaps, another way to approach the issue of play, facility, and even creativity with digital video production is to consider the ways in which the users interact for social and semiotic purposes with the technology as a set of tools. Loveless begins from the frame of creativity and works out toward the learners, proposing the inherent properties of the tools themselves as the affordances by which creative and fashioning activity occurs (Loveless 2002). However, this frame could be said to privilege the tools over the users in the setting and leads to a technologically determinist view of the activity, one which has been critiqued by a number of writers in the field of ICT in education (Fisher 2004; Mackay 1991). This would not be helpful to pursue in a frame that considers users in the context of multimodal productions in the wider media culture. Instead, joining these notions with learning theory in the form of flow theory (Csikszentmihalyi 1996) becomes more helpful, something which one of my masters students captured brilliantly in a dissertation analyzing youth media production, describing both the fashioning and the flow (Cannon 2011).

In seeking to theorize technology and education in a way that considers a more socially constructed notion of learning, other writers build on theories that consider the activity around tools as mediated action that leads to learning (Wertsch 1998); learners are seen to operationalize knowledge and skills in the social context of their interaction around the tools. Likewise, "Activity theory," which has sometimes been applied to technology in education studies and, specifically to digital video production (Pearson 2005), suggests that our experience of the world is mediated by cultural and social organization around related artifacts. For computers and technology in educational settings this means that our understanding of pedagogy and technology is deepened by taking into account the structures that surround artifacts and how the activity is mediated by the artifacts themselves (Engeström, Miettinen, and Punamäki 1999). Pearson, for example, uses activity theory in his study of children engaged in digital video production (2005), because of the way the theory allows for an account of the "interactions between human subjects, the mediating tools they select, and the object of their endeavours" (ibid.). In this, he reapplies and adapts work on ICT tools conducted during previous studies of ICT in educational settings (Bottino 1999; Somekh and Mavers 2003). These interactions around activity theory perhaps represent the closest match with theory coming from the media production side with its concern for interaction around production, although with its continued emphasis on "tools" and "solutions" this is a far from perfect match with a cultural frame.

Nevertheless, the emergent frames of analysis will need some way to account for the interactions around the tools as evidence of how they influence the experiences in the production, the use of semiotic resources in the representation of the self. The suggestion above in this chapter has been that editing is the key site for this activity and a number of writers have begun to explore this area further (Gilje 2009).

I also take the view that editing is of central importance in making meaning in moving-image production, facilitating the intertextual use of resources, as discussed previously. Users scan the screen with its arrangement of resources or assets in the form of clips, sound files, still images, titling, and effects, and place them alongside, between, and after each other. They add them to the timeline and fashion the arrangement in pursuit of a form for carrying the meaning they intend to make. This is a literacy process and those engaged with it are learning how to be literate in the form. In order to understand how pedagogy might operate and facilitate this process, we need an understanding of how the media text works in the relation between the form of what is said (the lexis of the moving image) and the ways in which that form is assembled and arranged (the grammar of the moving image).

For some, this has entailed thinking about how we might bring a metalanguage that describes these processes into the classroom (Unsworth 2008). For others, in practical classroom settings with older children where this has already been attempted, pedagogy is predicated on using editing software itself as a tool of analysis of, and play with, existing productions that leads, through discussion, to an emergent metalanguage around meaning making with the moving image (Burn 2009; Burn and Durran 2007).

Summarizing Emerging "Literacy" Themes

Each section above in the discussion of organizing principles in media literacy contributes something to the emerging picture of meaning making with younger learners in digital video production. I would like to use this concluding section to draw out the key issues before moving into the domain of identity.

First, the changing conceptions of literacy reveal a need to engage with the expanded versions of the term; a need, in other words, to engage both with multimodality and with the notion of new literacy studies in the context of digital video production. This proposes an engagement at the level of semiotic resources, understanding how meaning is made from all of the assets in short video pieces, the music, the speech, the gesture, the quotations, and so on. It also means attempting to get to the heart of the sociocultural circumstances around the productions, not simply the world of the school, but also the world of the children themselves and their relationship to media culture in their productions and to their practice of media literacy in relation to that culture.

Second, intertextuality and the ways in which video editing allowed intertextual space to be organized became important frames through which to examine a form that depends on appropriation, playfulness, and juxtaposition for its meaning-making potential. Think of the memes and playful videos that depend on this for their viral effect and how this multiplies through the spaces of YouTube (Burgess and Green 2009).

Third, in a related but different approach, this aspect of playfulness was developed in the context of the possibilities inherent in the medium of digital video itself, in particular the notion of provisionality and how this might in a Vygotskian sense reveal imaginative, conscious action in the productive engagement with a mutable form of literacy; in a celebratory mode, this is sometimes offered as an unproblematic way of being "creative." I would like, however, to emphasize the distinctive features of play and creativity that arise in Vygotsky. Play as an aspect of human development is bound up in the process of "internalization," in the way that structures and components of language are internalized in inner speech and become constitutive of understanding (Vygotsky 1978). At the point at which the inner speech becomes accessible to a listener, it may contain context-dependent, internalized talk and features that do not make it fully formed or fully communicable. In his thinking about creativity, Vygotsky addressed the issue of how "the process of artistic or intellectual creation may be considered the antipode of internalisation" (Kozulin 2005, p. 111). This is because the internalized speech cannot take its place in the culture, become widely understood, until it becomes externalized; at this point the inner, context-dependent thought gradually unfolds its meaning as "symbol-for-others"; it is creative, rather than playful at the point at which it is assimilated within a culture as a "literacy event" (ibid.). In a related argument about development, Vygotsky also proposed a play and creativity model, which essentially placed them on a developmental continuum. In younger children, play, or what Vygotsky's translators refer to as "fantasy," is an act which is dependent heavily on immediate, rational contexts and its susceptibility to emotional outbursts, coupled with intense experience, renders the younger child incapable of critical judgment (Vygotsky 1994). As children get older and enter adolescence, their thinking becomes more conceptual, less bound in rational objects:

> Adolescent fantasy appears creative when it is compared with children's fantasy, but by no means can it be considered productive in comparison with adult fantasy. This is because the creative character does not become an inherent part of it until adolescence. (Ibid., p. 280)

And it is the resulting ability to think in concepts that sets later developments apart and defines them as creative activity. Vygotsky goes on as follows:

> The essential change which the adolescent's imagination undergoes, is the external rapprochement with thinking in concepts...the adolescent imagination experiences basic changes and it becomes transformed with the aid of a new infrastructure under the influence of thinking in concepts. (Ibid., p. 281)

We might begin to think of ways of looking at media production by younger children through this frame. This gives researchers a way to analyze and give value to structural incoherence as an inherently necessary developmental stage. The "playful" aspects of the work in question are apprehended only by the members of the immediate group, and sometimes, only by the children themselves. The externalization that has taken place at the point of publication of these is, as mentioned elsewhere, a version of recorded play. We might also argue for the distinctiveness of the medium in being able to reveal facets of play and development that were previously not recorded.

Fourth, I am proposing the organization of assets and their assembly in production as a new active literacy skill in new media, that of curatorship. I will return to this theme in the closing stages of this chapter as a way of connecting up all of the explored themes. For now, however, and in order to facilitate this linkage at a later stage, it will be important in the next chapter to say more about theories of identity in the context of media production.

Finally, and before engaging more with identity, I would like to connect these themes to a model of media literacy that is circulating widely and is the theoretical basis for the Media Literacy Charter (Media_Literacy_Task_Force 2005). The 3 Cs model, in a way that is also echoed in the OFCOM definition mentioned above (OFCOM 2005) proposes that Media Literacy "emphasises *cultural, critical* and *creative* functions" (Burn and Durran 2007, p. 11). In this section, I have outlined versions of media literacy that will be useful in conceptualizing the work in the projects that embrace each of these; in particular, the focus on the setting and the *cultural* context of the young people engaged in the productions (and this will be a major feature in thinking about identity in the next chapter). As seen previously, I am also interested in what a *critical* version of practice may look like in the way it operates in the primary school. At what level, and to what degree, will it involve and engage with the metalanguage of media grammars? How will these projects situate such issues in relation to the children's understanding of form and function in what they are making? For the *creative* aspects of the work, to what extent is it possible to make a useful distinction between play and creativity in the ways proposed by Vygotsky? At what point do the productions assume an externalized state and enable an audience to make meanings? How do the children respond to this in the context of self-representation? These questions move away from literacy toward a discussion of identity and this is where the following chapter comes in.

CHAPTER 3

Identity and Storying

I would like to turn, in this chapter, to some of the sociocultural theories of identity that are helpful in thinking about autobiographical digital video. I will set these out in three sections. The first of these, "Storying the Self," looks at potential contributions from sociology and cultural psychology in developing theories of identity in relation to media production. The second, "Learner Voice in Production," looks at how identity links to the notion of "authenticity," which is often claimed for youth production. The third and final part looks at ways of framing identity in production in relation to "Location and Memory."

Storying the Self

Buckingham observed in his introduction to the MacArthur Foundation series on "Digital Media and Learning," that "identity is an ambiguous and slippery term" (2008, p. 1). Definitions abound in sociocultural and psychological theory either in relation to the self or in relation to performance of the self in wider society. He described the relationships between many of them and how they may be applied to learning with digital media, in particular in relation to adolescence and identity formation. He identified a key concern—namely,

> how these media provide young people with symbolic resources for constructing or expressing their own identities. (ibid., p. 5)

We have seen in the preceding chapter that we might look for the use of such "symbolic resources" in the analysis of videos that reflect high levels of appropriation of existing media. In discussing organizing principles in the videos, we can use multimodal and intertextual analysis to look at the elements and hypothesize on the use of form. For the actual choices themselves, we need to look at sociocultural and psychological factors in performance, identity, and storying, and at narrative construction.

Whatever else we do, we need to be aware of how identity construction is, for very many people, a facet of taking part in lived media culture. Self-representation in new media, for those who engage with it, means choosing to take part in one aspect of the lived culture of the day; it is made up of the negotiated codes and transactions in writing and reading the produced self. This is not unproblematic and in many self-produced videos, including by some of the young learners in this study, we see examples in which these codes are not as well understood or used as in others.

One account of identity construction in lived culture, which is often quoted, is Goffman's *The Presentation of Self in Everyday Life* (1990). This offers an account of the imperatives around the process. In the book, Goffman proposes that throughout our lives we move through a series of different contexts, each of which requires a different kind of "performance" to manage our appearance in the world, for reasons of personal gain and achievement (ibid.). The context shapes the way we respond and manage the presentation of our image. There is an emergent literature on social media that sees such online spaces as a prime example of this aspect of performed identity, often with a focus on younger people (see, e.g., boyd 2007). The ways in which the facilities of social networking sites allow for their users to manipulate the publicly shared image of the self appear to bring Goffman's notion of performance into the era of new media.

Where there isn't a direct match between new media and the conceptual framework of Goffman is in the fact that the performances are recorded and available for public display across contexts and across time. What gets selected at the point the media text is made remains fixed in time as a marker of identity. This has of course been problematic for people who record a media version of an aspect of drunken behavior to gain status with their peer group only to find that it is accessible to gatekeepers of a different kind of stage of life—university authorities or employers.

Records and representations of the self exist on mobile phone video, digital video and in the many media texts, pictures, and audio files in the context of social media spaces. The owners of those pages have some rights over access and, in most cases, though not all, can delete the whole record; but, nevertheless, once it is out there in the public domain in a media form it becomes a shared aspect of that person's identity, regardless of whether they wished to be identified at a later point in time with that set of behaviors and appearances.

The video projects described later in the book were never intended for exhibition beyond the peer group and the children's parents and carers, except in cases of academic dissemination and research. Nevertheless, the issue of being fixed in time in both negative and positive senses may well be something that occurred to more than one member of the production teams.

In fact, the children were made aware not only of the shared and performed but also negotiated aspects of identity throughout, and of the limits of their own individual input and their resonances with each other. They knew that their video had to capture elements of their life at school over time, that it had to stand for them in some way when they were no longer there, and that it was a chance to preserve their relationships and their accrued status and social capital within the group up to that point. In the case of performed identity for the camera and the editing screen, what is important to capture may have been the essence of the performed self in the context of school.

Goffman's concept of "front" may be important in analyzing this aspect of the experience. Writing about the relationship of front to "performance," he states,

> I have been using the term "performance" to refer to all the activity of an individual which occurs during a period marked by his continuous presence before a set of particular observers and which has some influence on the observers. It will be convenient to label as "front" that part of an individual's performance which regularly functions in a general and fixed fashion to define the situation for those who observe the performance. Front, then, is the expressive equipment of a standard kind intentionally or unwittingly employed by the individual during his performance. (Goffman 1990, p. 32)

Clearly, front is a whole way of being in the place, within the group and its social arrangements. During the analysis of representational videos, it is important to look for the recorded front, those aspects of the self that, following Goffman, appear fixed in the production, represented throughout by reference to song, patterns of speech, and, through each of these, a desire to record relationships and feelings as they were expressed during their time at the school.

Giddens provides some contrasts and contradictions with this view. In *Modernity and Self-Identity* (1991), he takes issue with one of the key derivations from Goffman—namely, that there are as many different versions of the acted out self as there are situations to act out in. Giddens sees the end result of Goffman's argument as being a view of the self in modern life as inherently fragmented and even conflicted. Turning the argument around, Giddens proposes that it is possible to see fragmentation and management of the self in different circumstances as a marker of modern identity itself. In essence, he seems to argue that this is what it means to be alive in late modernity. He contends that for those of us in this potentially fractured state, "contextual diversity" does not in fact promote a "fragmentation of the self" but rather a "distinctive self-identity which positively incorporates elements from different settings into an integrated narrative" (Giddens 1991, p. 190). For Giddens, this narrative aspect is an important component of the self-reflexive project of identity in late modernity and contributes to the idea of a trajectory of the self.

On the one hand, in preadolescence and adolescence, this "integrated narrative" may not yet be a feature of self-representation and self-expression as revealed in media production. On the other hand, it may be possible to locate evidence of the quality of self-awareness that Giddens describes as "reflexively understood by the person in terms of her or his biography" (1991, p. 53). It could be argued that the children in the productions in transition from primary to secondary school have a developing sense of their life trajectories, possibly for the first time (though this depends very much on a range of other factors to do with their personal situations). People speak of "moving to" a new school, a suggestion of a life-course or a life-journey. Whether or not individual learners perceive it in quite this way, it is still a major life change, and the videos themselves shot around this time may represent a personal way of accounting for their development to that point. It will be a feature of the analysis to look for negotiations with life narratives and trajectories among the children and this will form the basis of some of the discussion later in the book. Certainly, it is a phenomenon that has been noted in connection with identity construction in new media more widely (Davies and Merchant 2007) and from which, for example, Merchant developed the notion of "transient" and "anchored" identities, mentioned earlier in the foreword, to express the ways in which people move on a continuum between representation of the self in relation to fixed or anchored aspects of the self (culture, religion, and upbringing) and transient aspects, which he defines as

> change over time, being influenced by maturation, changing cultural conditions and peer group affiliations. These identities are defined in relation to media narratives, ideologies, popular culture, iconic objects, social activities and networks. (Merchant 2006, p. 239)

I will return to these ideas, particularly in relation to the work in one of the project schools in discussion and conclusion in chapters 6 and 7, respectively.

In the meantime, narrative and identity were identified as key to one important aspect of the camcorder culture research described in chapter 1. In the project, the construction of a set of home videos recording everyday life appeared to provide their makers with a sought-after stability, through a constructed narrative of the self, chiming with concepts derived from Giddens in the previous paragraph as the quotation demonstrates. Videos made in the project with the purpose of recording everyday life, showed evidence of

> wanting to build and hold onto a coherent narrative of one's life, which would provide stability in what otherwise felt like a fast-moving and chaotic world. Drawing on Giddens' (1991) notion of "ontological security," Silverstone et al. (1992) argue that as part of the domestication of technology, households create narratives which sustain a sense of their own stability. (Buckingham, Willett, and Pini 2011, p. 56)

This idea of "life as narrative" is also present in cultural psychology and the work of Bruner, who maintains that representation of the self by "autobiography" as a project is "a continuing interpretation and re-interpretation of our experience...so autobiography (formal or informal) should be viewed as a set of procedures for life making" (Bruner 1987, p. 105). Furthermore, for Bruner, the telling of the life is the making of the life. In the same article he writes, "I have argued that a life as led is inseparable from a life as told—or more bluntly, a life is not 'how it was' but how it is interpreted and re-interpreted" (p. 111). This notion that in storying the self we are simultaneously making the self is very close to the version of "reflexivity" proposed by Giddens, the construction of a life narrative from the trajectory of the self (1991). In looking at the use of both video and still image in social media, we see this idea of life constructed as told and this became an important frame to place over the work in the videos by children described in subsequent chapters.

Bauman also proposes a constructivist view of identity, which may be apposite in a discussion of the uses of media in representation. For him, the identity project is a puzzle without a final picture. The "making" process produces the picture from the assembled resources of lived experience. He writes,

> In the case of identity...You do not start from the final image, but from a number of bits which you have already obtained or which seem worthy of having, and then you try to find out how you can order and reorder them to get some (how many?) pleasing pictures. You *are experimenting with what you have.* (Bauman 2004, pp. 48–49)

Clearly, there is some analogous potential in this description of identity construction. Video editing itself is a search for a correct ordering of previously collected clips and resources. Just as in Bruner's assertion that the telling of the life is the making of the life, storying makes the story. In the case of the video productions, the editing of the resources into the whole is simultaneously a search for meaning at the same time as the construction of that meaning. Bauman goes on to invoke semiosis in his conclusion to that section of the book as follows:

> The job of an identity-constructor, is, as Claude Levi-Strauss would say, that of a *bricoleur*, conjuring up all sorts of things out of the material at hand. (Ibid., p. 49)

To an extent, the job of an editor is similar, collecting resources together in a way that makes sense. The children in the productions were positioned in the same relation to the videos they were making from the resources of their own captured shots and chosen music. These too were resources based on memory and transactions around shared experiences in the setting.

In *Acts of Meaning*, Bruner argues the case for a study of "Folk Culture" as the main transactional medium through which meaning is made. It is a case for the values of cultural psychology over what he refers to as "computational" psychology. Bruner makes a plea for such analysis in order to understand that experiences and acts are shaped by intentional states and that these intentional states are informed by an immersion in the symbolic culture (Bruner 1990, p. 33). It is in the interchange between people who recognize the symbols and signs of their culture that meaning is made.

These symbols and signs in a culture also have analogous possibilities in connection with "memes," described by Lankshear and Knobel in the context of new literacies as

> contagious patterns of cultural information that are passed from mind to mind and that directly shape and propagate key actions and mind-sets of a particular group. Memes include popular tunes, catch-phrases, clothing fashions, architectural styles and so on. (2006, p. 128)

Memes are derived in the text above from the work of Richard Dawkins in *The Selfish Gene* (1976). In its original sense, the idea was to describe small units of information, analogous to genes, which are passed on and undergo natural selection in their propagation. Although developed subsequently in many disciplines including the biological and psychological sciences, Lankshear and Knobel outline a sociocultural understanding of the term (see their discussion in 2006, pp. 210–244) in which "an idea is not a meme until someone replicates it by passing it on to someone else" (ibid., p. 213). In this way, cultural information in the form of a meme undergoes a process of natural selection. For digital video analysis, this means looking for memes in the form of cultural touchstones, genres, and media reference points that recur, are passed on, and form the backdrop to the dialogue and are woven intertextually into the productions to make meaning within the group. Memes could form a useful way of understanding the "affective" nature of production and will be returned to as a theme in later chapters.

Returning to Bruner at this point locates another version of the connected, transactional nature of narrated identity in his elaboration of "Folk Psychology," when he writes, "The central conception of human psychology is meaning and the processes and transactions in the construction of meanings" (Bruner 1990, p. 33). He goes on to quote the anthropologist Rosaldo in support of the assertion that "self" and "affect" are shared constructs and arise out of the group. She writes that they

grow not from "inner" essence relatively independent of the social world, but from experience in a world of meanings, images, and social bonds, in which all persons are inextricably involved. (Rosaldo 1984, p. 139)

This is in somewhat different territory from some of the individualized conceptions of identity and storying discussed earlier. It may, however, be pivotal in discussing some of the possibilities inherent in group digital video production with its many complex interrelationships and social acts in the meaning-making process, such as collaborative planning, shooting, editing, and exhibiting. Given that the videos were made by a subset of a larger group to be viewed by their peers, it would be likely that each group would establish a performed version of identity that provided markers of their place in the peer group, the class, and the school.

Learner Voice in Production

Because of their assumed authenticity, projects centered on media technologies are often built around the idea of getting closer to the thoughts and opinions of young people, in particular those who are marginalized or disaffected. This was, for example, identified as a key finding among the media productions described in "Being Seen, Being Heard," a report by the National Youth Agency and the British Film Institute (Harvey, Skinner, and Parker 2002). In the case studies reported here, the idea of motivating disaffected learners through media production was a key factor from the school side. Authenticity is perhaps too often claimed but difficult to prove in this connection. Nevertheless, for the schools in this study, it was assumed that there was a quality inherent in media production that fostered greater engagement on the part of the learners in the process, particularly because the content of the work was closer to a self-set agenda.

There are further examples of writing about self-representation in this constructive and positive mode that relate specifically to self-representational accounts drawn from educational settings through early life into adulthood and autobiography (see, e.g., Kearney 2003). In the opinion of some writers, following Bauman, Giddens, and others, all storying of the self is predicated on construction (ibid.). What is chosen as the aspect to be celebrated and remembered beyond the experience of the making of the media is a construct. In telling the story, the selective and selected identity, as we have seen, is being made. In the digital video productions, using the modes available to them, the children would perhaps select relevant memories, versions of memories, curating a set of media quotations, self-produced sequences, and other external sources into a whole. We can know something about the music they liked, how they wanted to be seen in relation to their peers, what media productions they took as inspiration by looking at the constructs they made. In discussing the videos and the processes around them it will be important to show how these different frames impact on the videos produced and how that was interpreted by the learners themselves.

This is a version of the critical participation in media production (as proposed by Buckingham 2003, p. 84); working with subject matter that is closer to the lives and feelings of students themselves. If they care at all about what is being said about themselves, by themselves, in the video, it is possible that the producers will develop a far more engaged stance in relation to the meaning-making process inherent in media production. Viewing and evaluating the outcome allows them to question their success or failure at expressing those views and, by extension, with appropriate pedagogical input, the success of their media composition. Later, it will be seen that for the children in both schools, but particularly in school B, this was a focus of production and evaluation. This is perhaps because finding ways to express their voice also necessarily brings students into micropolitical conflict and negotiation with peers and authority figures in the wider school community. These tensions are reported in other studies of life as narrative cited above, such as Chris Kearney's *The Monkey's Mask* (2003), which, nevertheless, concludes positively with a plea for the reconstitution of the school curriculum as a site for dialogic activity in which narratives and conversation about identity are the essential basis for progress on both social and pedagogical fronts.

In some recent education research projects, there have been attempts to elicit qualitatively more authentic responses from learners, in order to hear the "learner voice" more clearly. Some were designed with this in mind from the outset (Selwyn, Potter, and Cranmer 2010) particularly since the questions being asked, in that case, are about the lived experience of media technologies. This attempt to hear learner voice in research projects derives its background theory from different sources, in particular, the work of Michael Fielding. Writing about what he calls "Student voice," he proposes four stages of movement along a continuum in pedagogical activity in school settings from "student as data source," through student as "respondent" and "student as co-researcher" to "student as researcher" (Fielding 2004).

More recently, critics (Bragg 2007) have identified in the available literature some useful caveats for researchers, having detected issues in methodologies that claim to be hearing an authentic "voice." For example,

it is disingenuous to see children as finding, discovering, or being given a voice, as if we can simply access their authentic core being. What they say depends on what they are asked, how they are asked it, "who" they are invited to speak as in responding; and then, in turn, on the values and assumptions of the researcher or audience interpreting their "voices" (Connolly 1997). (Bragg 2007, p. 20)

Nevertheless, we can detect in the work of Fielding a sense of how pedagogy could be operated as part of a more participatory culture in schools. This has been mapped onto the design of research activities themselves, with learners being positioned as active participants in projects. The caveats quoted suggest that the designed structures and outcomes of such projects should be elaborated robustly to account for researcher effects in seeking to hear the voice. While there are serious questions to be asked about this, and only partial success to report, there is no doubting that this is part of a trend that has been long established of using media as a way of unlocking and revealing "authentic experience."

"Self expression" is a close relation of authenticity and is sometimes equally claimed to be a key characteristic of video production. Yet, this is an equally problematic term. Chitat Chan, for example, finds a relativistic definition of self-expression in his examination of youth media production, one in which authority establishes a critical distance while appearing to give value to youthful output:

Young people are [assumed to be] competent enough to express themselves creatively and proactively, but they may not be mature enough to express themselves properly or correctly. (Chan 2008)

Chan points out the tension at the heart of youth media production, a contradiction in which competence is somehow bound up in the notion of self-censorship and control. What the young people actually would like to say in production is positioned as an act of immaturity and a lack of proper self-control in their use of the medium.

Likewise, as the CHICAM project found (Children in Communication about Migration), media production projects neither confer instant nor uncomplicated authenticity and nor do they, of themselves, represent

> an unproblematic vehicle for dialogue between cultures...children use and appropriate media in diverse ways, in light of their needs and circumstances. (de Block and Buckingham 2007, p. 197)

The debates around authenticity, self-expression, and judgments of value pre-date media production and have some analogous connections back to print literacy in, for example, *Un/Popular Fictions* by Gemma Moss (1989). This study looks at the use of popular fiction for influencing and shaping student writing in secondary school English, and unpicks the structures and judgments that underpin this activity. In responding to texts produced by children, teachers can

> condemn children's writing based on popular fiction by describing it as derivative, a judgement whose negative value depends on an underlying assumption that good literature is the product of the individual's unique vision. (Ibid., p. 36)

This judgment echoes the "proper or correct" expectation of Chan's authority figures in respect of youth media production above. The assumption is that creative, authentic, and challenging self-expression can be stimulated by the use of popular cultural forms across modes but that the outcomes are not straightforward. The authentic value in production may not be apparent; children will not act in expected ways in producing texts, which tell their stories. They will appropriate and use sources in diverse ways and they may say things in their authentic voice that adults may not wish to hear and to which they will not necessarily ascribe value.

Even with the caveats, the attempts to create spaces for telling authentic stories of the self resonates with a strong theoretical tradition in cultural psychology, particularly in the work of Bruner who sees self-representation as an active, constructive process in which the storyteller literally makes their own identity with each telling and retelling of their story, as we have seen previously (Bruner 1987).

Location and Memory

The children's videos discussed later in the book were produced within specific contexts. In both schools, they worked in situations in which the usual curriculum arrangements were relaxed. In both cases, it was suggested in the brief that aspects of identity in relation to the physical spaces of the buildings, the playground, and so on, could form a part of what was recorded. Since the majority were also made during the final phases of their time at primary school, it was also emphasized that aspects of personal memory in the spaces could also form a part of the finished product. This meant that, in addition to locating appropriate theory from the fields of identity and voice, it would be important in interpreting the videos to find sociocultural frameworks that might account for choices in relation to memory and, also, to location.

The first of these frameworks is drawn from the work of Pierre Bourdieu, in the form of the concept of habitus. This is understood as the internalized schema through which the world is perceived, negotiated with, and lived in (Bourdieu 1986). In this study we see, in the multimodal construction of their video texts, the possibility of revealed, internalized schema in the videos produced by the children.

The second key concept used as a framework is described by Foucault in an interview with Paul Rabinow as the "hypomnemata," and is derived from writings from ancient Greece about a system for recording life events as material memory or as an externalizing process, which gave the writer a repository of the "self" on which to draw in times of stress or change (Foucault 1984, pp. 364–365). Giddens echoes this with his conception of "ontological security" (1991) and further links will be made to this idea at a later stage.

A third related and useful concept in this regard, and sometimes invoked in discussions of new technology (Van der Velden 2006; Yancey 2004) is the notion of the "palimpsest," a record created as a trace in particular location, displayed, and then wiped and remade over the original. This concept which is used to express the ways in which an individual lives and moves in a space is derived from de Certeau (1984) and will be useful combination with the habitus and hypomnemata in understanding the nature of the process of representing identity in relation to the immediate location.

Beginning with habitus, as derived by Bourdieu, it is possible to see it as an important concept in relation to video and performance in particular settings. In *Distinction: A Social Critique of the Judgement of Taste* (1986), he proposes societal structures and spaces as the "field" in which social actors operate in particular ways in order to maintain access to the resources of a particular class and status. As a result of prolonged, learned ways of being and living, members of a society develop dispositions that generate meaning making in the ordinary ways of being, the things acquired, and the means of acquiring them; this includes the ways life is spoken about and how it is constructed in the necessity of ordinary, daily existence. Bourdieu puts it like this:

> The habitus is necessity internalised and converted into a disposition that generates meaningful practices and meaning-giving perceptions; it is a general, transposable disposition which carries out a systematic, universal application—beyond the limits of what has been directly learnt—of the necessity inherent in the learning conditions. (Bourdieu 1986, p. 170)

For the children in the school years, the ways of being are internalized within the structures of the school day, the physical appearance of the space, the arrangement of the buildings, the school curriculum, the regulatory structures, and codes of conduct. They are further internalized in the performed and ritualized interrelationships between groups of children and teachers. Added to this are the ways of being circumscribed by approaching adolescence in a school community in a wider sense; the performed and lived ways of being with regard to choices of popular culture, clothing, and other markers of identity. This is, of course, circumscribed not only by school but also by the wider social and cultural background of the children in their respective families. What is available as a resource for authoring about the self is the way in which these markers play out within the class over a number of years, how they become habitualized. Indeed, in freely authored video texts made by children exploring their memories and feelings about their place in such a social arena we would expect to see that revelation of habitus is an aspect of performed, embodied experience played out in gesture, speech, and chosen media quotations or parodies. This is not the only frame of reference in regard to ways of being at school and making videos about aspects of that experience. Nevertheless, because it is a theory of actions on the part of social actors within a field, Bourdieu's conception of habitus provides a useful basis from which to begin to look at self-representational video work by young learners.

What is selected by the children in their attempts to make meaning can sometimes contradict traditional narrative forms and editorial continuity, carrying significance in ways shared only by those in the community around the production. This makes some videos difficult to interpret at first sight where the weight of the representative oral act overwhelms the ability of the producers to tell the story coherently in a manner that will be readily understood by an outsider. Understanding these texts means finding representations of ways of being that are part of the culture of the school, and of the habitus of the pupils there. Some of these markers related to habitus may not have been revealed before in the school setting. They are possibly not there in some traditional curriculum subject-based forms of self-representation. One of the possible outcomes for the research is to propose that in these forms of text is an opportunity to explore the previously unseen, but only if the children themselves can exercise some control of their embodied representation of the spaces in which they work.

The visual and performed record in the finished video productions may indeed have been intended to make meaning from the resources that constitute the habitus of those children. Noyes (2004) made use of this framework in approaching a different research question focused on transfer to secondary school, collecting video diaries from children in the final year of primary school (see Ch. 2). Following Bourdieu's (1977) theory of practice in constructing an interpretation of habitus and field relating specifically to the school setting, he proposed that

> an analysis of the (video) diary entries can map types and quantities of (cultural, economic and social) capital, the dispositions of the habitus and thereby examine the structuring effect of the three fields: school, family and youth culture. (Noyes 2004, p. 195)

In children's self-authored video, we may expect to locate evidence, in the choices and orderings of resources, of the structuring effect of learned behaviors and responses to the school setting, of the children's habitus, and way of being through their time at the school.

If habitus represents one useful frame for interpreting the video productions, the concept of hypomnemata may help to deepen understanding of their purpose and the children's engagement in them. The idea of the hypomnemata is derived by Michel Foucault from writings from ancient Greece about a system for recording life events as notes, as material memory, and as an externalizing process, which gave the writer a repository of reflections on which to draw in the future. This system employed one of the new technologies of its time, that of writing. The inscribed notes were not intended to be a diary as such, more as a record of how the self was developing in response to certain situations. In an interview, given in 1984, Foucault explains as follows:

> The point (of the hypomnemata) is not to pursue the indescribable...but on the contrary to collect the already-said, to re-assemble that which one could hear or read, and this to an end which is nothing less than the constitution of oneself. (Foucault 1984, p. 365)

This process of assembly of the "already-said" has parallels with the process of editing in the video productions, and with the notion of intertextuality. As they are assembled on the timeline of the video-editing software, editors work with the already-said, manipulating their own quotations of their own autobiographical representations. This is a complementary but qualitatively different dimension to the process already described in relation to habitus. If the habitus gives rise to specific forms of movement, gesture, speech, and choice of sound—and this represents the "what" in the embodied, recorded pieces—then the hypomnemata with its emphasis on assembly and selection describes the "how" and the "why." Foucault proposes it as an active process of construction in meaning making, in pursuit of learning from lived experience and moving forward.

The notion of the palimpsest also contains something of a trace or record that describes a person's lived experience and is then immediately overwritten. We may conceive this as an alternative to the hypomnemata. Not all students may see the record as something to be preserved or as anything that contains a potential lesson learned. It is possible through the analysis that some of the children may see the description of the movement through the space of the school and the recording of their time there as enough in and of itself, and are aware of how the trace is ultimately wiped.

In *The Practice of Everyday Life* (1984), de Certeau described a series of overarching social structures and physical spaces as "strategies," the institutions by which power is exercised in a city, the physical layout of the streets, the ways in which routes are mapped, and the permissions granted to use certain areas in certain ways. Individual users of the space resist these by use of "tactics," taking their own routes and shortcuts that allow them to move and to live in ways that were not predicted or envisaged by the authorities creating the organizing structures. We may see traces of this activity in relation to the power structures inherent in a school, in places traditionally out-of-bounds captured, recorded, and kept as a record, but not necessarily displayed again; the users may have moved on and the frame wiped, and the resources reused and reinscribed. Nevertheless, at the moment in which these stories are told, following de Certeau, we might expect to see that space is used as a central organizing principle, that every story told is not just a remaking of the self (cf. Bruner 1987), but a performed spatial practice in the location, which in itself recalls the "tactics" of lived experience.

The proposal of this section is that habitus, hypomnemata, and palimpsest are all potentially important frames that determine how self-representational video productions are shaped. They require a set of tools for analysis that can take account of the many modes through which these may be expressed.

Emergent Themes from a Consideration of Identity

Just as for the "Literacy" chapter, I would like to summarize some emergent themes from the consideration of *identity*. First, "Storying the Self," presented contributions from the field of sociology and cultural psychology, which proposed that the narratives of the self, in some respects, create the self from the resources available. "Learner Voice in Production" went on in the next section to problematize some of the aspects of media production, which are sometimes glossed over, most notably the idea of authenticity in the representation of identity. "Location and Memory" posited three concepts from cultural theory as being potentially important to the study: from Bourdieu (1986) the concept of Habitus, from Foucault (1984) the hypomnemata, and from de Certeau (1984) the idea of resistance to structures through the individual's use of the space, the way they are in the world as they leave a trace in the practice of everyday life. Each of these is clearly connected to representational literacy practices and the following section goes on to elaborate a way of thinking about those connections.

Curatorship: Organization and Representation

So far, the short-form autobiographical video has been theorized using aspects of literacy and identity. For literacy, the emphasis has been on the changing nature of definitions in the age of multiliteracies and on the ways in which media production operates in a system of quotation, appropriation, and intertextuality. For identity, the framework has addressed negotiation and representation in the context of storying the self and constructing life narratives within specific sites, actual locations, and memories. I would like to propose a metaphorical frame in this final section for understanding how systems for organizing and representing the self can converge as a form of "curatorship" and that this, in turn can be seen as representing a new literacy practice. In setting out this metaphorical conception of curatorship, I am not positioning the study within the realm of "personal information management" as considered, for example, by the Digital Lives Research Project (Williams, Leighton John, and Rowland 2009). I am specifically addressing the issue of texts as media assets and their relation to a literacy practice.

First, I would like to return to an earlier section that described how literacy could be conceived as a set of social practices associated with symbol systems and their related technologies (Sefton-Green 1998, quoting Barton

[1994]). This can be brought into the context of digital video production by a definition of "new media" that explicitly addresses the social contexts in which users encounter new media as both consumers and producers. This frame is applied by Lievrouw and Livingstone in the form of a definition of new media as follows:

> The *artefacts or devices* used to communicate or convey information; the *activities and practices* in which people engage to communicate or share information; and the *social arrangements or organisational forms* that develop around those devices and practices. (2006, p. 2, author emphasis in italics)

Video making and exhibition are taking place in a time of accelerated change in the nature of each of the three component parts of the Lievrouw and Livingstone definition. The "artefacts and devices" are different; digital video production is changed by access to tools that are ubiquitous and simpler to use than in previous years (Reid, Burn, and Parker 2002). The "activities and practices" are also changed; digital video alters and expands roles in production and postproduction for a wider range of human agents. Finally, the "social arrangements and organisational forms" are altered by the changed possibilities of production and organizational processes onscreen and offscreen.

One consequence of these changes in the social arrangements and forms with respect to assembling media texts is the extent to which the manipulators of media quotations are also in some respects the "owners" of those assets, or, at least, believe themselves to be. This latter point moves the theoretical framework in a different direction. In the changed arrangements around production, which new media presuppose (after the Lievrouw and Livingstone quotation), children may also be positioned as "owners" of media for constructing new texts, or at least as collectors and curators of media, self-produced or otherwise.

If we accept that part of lived experience of being productive in new media implies a curatorial relationship with media assets we could look on the processes of editing, assembly, and remixing. The processes of selection and recombination are themselves a set of skills and dispositions found in cultural anthropology, in, for example, the collection and display of important personal possessions. In *The Comfort of Things* (Miller 2008), for example, we find a proposition that relationships to possessions collected over time reveal important aspects of lived relationships with others. It could be that media assets fit for quotation and for repurposing are analogous to possessions in this respect, and that their selection and appropriation reveals important aspects of lived experience. In this way, it could further be claimed that productive media literacy practices are converging with cultural practices and that to be engaged in this activity is to be engaged at a high level with lived media culture, certainly with those aspects that pertain to the representation of the self.

I would like to conclude the theory chapter by drawing the two frames of organization and representation together and propose that curatorship is a useful metaphorical formulation for describing a new literacy skill of representation of the self in digital video production. Initially, then, the two frameworks emerge as a way of addressing the question as shown in figure 3.1 in which each subsection emerging from each of the main nodes retains the potential to be part of the other. For example, *location and memory*, while theorized in preceding sections under the aegis of *identity*, have equal potential in understanding the overall organizing system of a self-representational piece. An example from the other side of the diagram locates *intertextuality* as a way of understanding organizational principles and possibilities in the productions.

In figure 3.2, in suggesting a way of theorizing the research question that brings the two sides together, I have moved *Curatorship* to the center as an active skill or disposition of new media literacy, offering a way of understanding the uses that learners make of the meaning-making potential of owned media assets and quotations.

This interconnectedness of the two areas of literacy and identity outlined in the preceding sections and the potential overlap in understanding and employing them has a theoretical precedent in the overall conception of "new literacy studies," which has its background in literary anthropology and already discussed earlier (Street 1995). I am specifically locating this as a

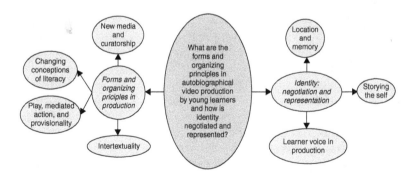

Figure 3.1   Theoretical frameworks.

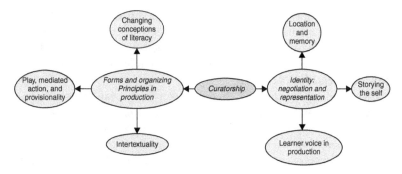

Figure 3.2 Revising theoretical frameworks.

"literacy practice" and not as an issue in the management of personal archives, which has been the subject of a recent study (Williams, Leighton John, and Rowland 2009). In the conception presented here, the social relations are a determining factor in the literacy practices within a group; to be literate in this sense is to negotiate cultural and social identity (cf. Buckingham 1993). A further related overlap is in the appropriation and remixing of the material of life from which narrative is constructed. From Bauman (2004), in discussing identity, came the notion that the person constructing their personal story was a *bricoleur*, conjuring a narrative "from the material at hand" and from Bruner (1990) the idea that there is a transactional, connected nature to construction of identity; both of these conceptions are important in the context of digital video production, as we have seen, with its spaces for organizing multimodal assets and re-presenting them for interpretation by a viewer. Bruner's notion of interconnectedness through the exchanges of shared signs and symbols within the culture is, as noted above, aligned to the concept of memes as described by Lankshear and Knobel in *New Literacies: Everyday Practices and Classroom Learning* (2006, p. 128).

From Giddens (1991) came the notion of identity in late modernity as an essentially fractured state in which the presentation of self is not quite as straightforward as a reading of Goffman (1990) might suggest, but which nevertheless is organized throughout as a form of project or "trajectory" of the self. The changing conceptions of literacy find an echo and an overlap in this in the concept of intertextuality with assets and modes in narrative, layered and organized in the editing space onscreen and provisionally available for reorganization and exhibition at any point.

The discussions in preceding sections on location, memory and identity reworked and developed conceptions of *palimpsest*, *habitus*, and *hypomnemata* (Bourdieu 1986, ; Foucault 1984; de Certeau 1984 respectively).

In each case, some aspect of collection, inscription, and personal trace was involved, which can be characterized as an act of self-curatorship. In the context of new media technology, and as set out in the opening chapter, one of the aims of the enquiry will be to conceptualize this self-curatorship as a new literacy skill; the organization and exhibition in these productions of assimilated assets (Robinson and Turnbull 2005) into new formulations using the tools of digital video editing.

There have been studies that have attempted to look at the ways in which children and young people organize their immediate environment or represent their "collections" of artifacts. In an ethnographic study in three London homes, Kate Pahl (2006) found that very young children's framing of their own photographs of their toys suggested heightened awareness of collection, containment, and display, including in one example, a child-made display case. Roberts (2008) wrote about the ways in which children made use of photosharing to give salience to objects and artifacts that were important to them. The ways in which children mediate and make certain aspects of their collections salient was previously discussed in Mitchell and Reid-Walsh's study of children's bedrooms (2002, Ch. 4) with their arrays of cultural artifacts signaling a buying into and appropriation of the culture. Curatorship as I am representing it in the study builds not only on some of these aspects but also on the conceptions of literacy and identity outlined previously, to suggest that it is an active practice in which the productive use of new media plays a key part.

This conception suggests the notion of curatorship as an organizational act at the point of exhibition construction and display. In a museum or art gallery, the collection is grouped and arranged with a narrative arc in mind by those in overall charge of layout, descriptive text, path through the artifacts, and so on. As Parry reminds us in *Recoding the Museum*, curators are authors at a metalevel of a story based on selected fragments and artifacts:

> Before we even begin to tell histories we have to make some decisions, *as authors,* about history-making itself. Any history—including those of museums, and of digital media in museums—requires a number of assumptions to be made about how history-writing works. The moment we choose to look back, to reflect upon the past, we find ourselves making choices... not only do we privilege and select narratives and theses based on the sometimes (fragmentary) evidence available, but, subsequently these are filtered further by the medium through which we choose to convey those histories. (Parry 2007, p. 3, my italics)

I will argue later that the children in the videos are selecting and filtering their stories through the medium of digital video and conveying those stories using skills and dispositions of new literacy as outlined above in, for example, the organization of intertextual space. What they produce depends on particular readings that are also fixed in a series of self-referential moments in the same ways as a gallery show so that reading depends on being able to make something from the resources on offer. That this is contingent on a series of cultural as well as cognitive processes is demonstrated by two examples—one from an art gallery exhibition and one from a national museum in negotiation with its collection in attempting a narrative of the past.

The book opened with a discussion of Grayson Perry's *Tomb of the Unknown Craftsman* (2011). In a further example of active curatorship of physical artifacts, in 2009, the artist Mark Wallinger curated an exhibition in the Hayward Gallery on London's South Bank, which was dependent for the success of its narrative arc on an understanding of several cultural touchstones, or memes. The title was "The Russian Linesman" and the works selected all had some connection with boundaries, lines, borders, juxtapositions, and misunderstandings. They depended for their effect as a whole experience on the understanding of the "Russian Linesman" as a framing device, famously the official who controversially awarded an England goal in the final of the football World Cup in 1966 when the ball bounced from the crossbar down onto the line, thus securing the team a path to the trophy. At the time, and subsequently, this has been much debated and its meaning negotiated. Elsewhere, the exhibition placed work dependent on visual tropes and jokes alongside one another and there were pieces of serious intent concerned with borders, Diasporas, and alienation. As the Hayward Gallery website explained, the Wallinger exhibition was

> concerned with the liminal, a concept with physical, political, metaphysical meanings. It signifies the dissolution of boundaries and fixed identities, and is associated with rituals and rites of passage, transitional states characterized by ambiguity, openness and indeterminacy, during which the normal limits to thought, self-understanding and behaviour are relaxed, opening the way to something new. Where necessary the artist will show his own work, along with objects that fit the manifesto—whether they are aesthetic, scientific, political and social or anthropological. (SouthBankCentre 2009)

Each of the works was an assimilated asset arranged by the artist-curator as author of the show; and the whole space was open to interpretation or misinterpretation, successful at making meanings for some and not for others. One of the ways of viewing the productions might be to look for these arrangements, moments of success as well as failure, and to try to account for them in terms of the literacy practices outlined in the first section of this chapter and the ways in which identity is represented in the second section.

A further example comes from a more culturally resonant case, closer to a literacy practice in the sense in which Street, as anthropologist, constructed it. As I have described in the Wallinger example, resources can be used in many different ways to make different meanings in the ways that they are arranged, described, and presented. In the Melbourne Museum, a collection of cultural artifacts from indigenous tribes is arranged in such a way as to

> reflect the various views of significance that these collections have for the individuals, communities and cultures from whom these collections originate, and for whom the collections continue to resonate with meaning. (MuseumVictoria 2009)

This is a retelling in the twenty-first century of one version of the story of part of Australia, a culturally problematic and culturally sensitive practice relating to the cultural identity of that nation. When the objects were first acquired and displayed in the nineteenth century a completely different narrative was made from the same resources. The Bunjilaka Gallery in the museum, for example, now frequently constructs a very different narrative from artifacts, one that is concerned with returning them to the indigenous peoples and, where this is no longer possible, even invokes a technological solution to the narrative drive around reparation for past misdeeds in the present handling of indigenous artifacts:

> The records, artefacts, photographs and films that were removed from Anangu Pitjantjatjara Lands, South Australia, are now too fragile to be returned.
> The Ara Irititja ("stories from a long time ago") project began in 1994. Over 35,000 historical and cultural items have now been digitally returned to the Anangu communities, via a purpose-built electronic archive. (MuseumVictoria 2005)

It will be important in analysis and discussion to think about the resource of self in the making of the narratives and exhibitions, to describe how the analogy of curatorship works as a functional and operational new literacy practice as well as to test its limits.

Themed exhibitions are frequently criticized for a functional incoherence in the telling of the story and where this breaks down in video production we may expect to see dissonances and a fracturing of meaning. We may also expect to see some response to "versioning" akin to the concern about authenticity and voice outlined previously. This concern is echoed in museum studies in the context of new technology; Parry refers to this as "recalibrating authenticity" (2007, Ch. 4, pp. 58–81).

Miller's *Comfort of Things* (2008) again provides an example of how the analogy might operate as a practice in the context of recorded life events as new media assets to be managed. Miller and (his student) Fiona Parrott's project was a series of interviews with people in their homes in a London street outlining their relationship to their possessions, in a project that attempted to show how this relationship was a marker of wider sociocultural and familial relations. In the sixth portrait, one of the residents of the street described how possessions, relationships, and experiences were organized in his laptop, as media assets, cataloged, organized, in an active fashioning process that goes beyond the "self-archive." Miller puts it like this:

> Digital media compress all the sensual objects of the world and reduce them to an other-worldly domain, where they remain a virtual presence. But that other world has its own order and aesthetics. It is not merely an alternative medium for the creation of self-archiving. Digital media creates its own sensual field, of text complemented by visual materials and sound. It can respect the larger integrity of connections between the media it incorporates. (Miller 2008, p. 71)

It is the idea stated above that "it is not merely an alternative medium for the creation of self archiving" that lies at the heart of reconceptualizing organization and composition in digital media as an active literary practice analogized in the word *curatorship*. Miller writes about the "sensual field" and the "integrity of connections between the media"; these are analogous to certain practices of literacy and identity in the context of multimodality and cultural studies, which I have outlined in the opening sections of this chapter and to which I will return in the later chapters analyzing specific video productions.

To summarize then, I am interested in the idea that when multimodal self-representation becomes possible in a new media form, curatorship becomes a useful metaphor for the resulting new literacy practice. This is because the range of collected assets are appropriated and held by the end user who shapes them, or a selection of them, using the tools available; these assets may be in the form of digital video clips self-created with the overall purpose in mind, or they may be in the form of collected pieces of music, or still images suggested by the existing organizational arc of the piece they are making. In either case, they sit in the software, represented as thumbnails, waveforms, or files, on a virtual shelf, awaiting assembly, organization, and distribution. Because they are digital, substantially the same resources can be endlessly reused and recombined to give new meanings for different exhibitions, just as a collection of artifacts or art works can be stored, brought out, laid out in new ways, and stored again. The multimodal mixing desk is the metaphor for the onscreen space in which the versions of the representation are assembled and formed (Burn and Parker 2003). The museum-curator metaphor accounts for the collection, selection, and exhibition process as a practice in itself.

If the areas described above in this chapter represent a response to the *cultural* and *creative* aspects of video production, it is also worth noting, following the 3 Cs model (Media_Literacy_Task_Force 2005) that a *critical* dimension is also necessary and that the pedagogy that develops around media production should also be predicated on developing that critical dimension. For teachers, this means addressing centrally the tactics and strategies that young people employ in their organization of media assets, understanding their developmental paths, and thinking about the ways in which they could perhaps facilitate the processes which lie behind this kind of work. Developing their own critical engagement with media production has sometimes been a strategy for introducing teachers to digital video production (Potter 2006) and this will form part of the reflection and discussion of the work in relation to teaching and learning at a later stage.

Each section preceding this one provides an important element in trying to understand the whole picture. The "Media Literacy" section, in chapter 2, adopted the concept that the form and function of children's literacy practices in new media are bound up in the conditions in which they live and that any engagement with meaning making in those practices must be connected to the cultures in which they are produced. This means designing activities that allow participants to be reflexive and demonstrate their relationship to lived culture, its affiliations and artifacts.

From the theoretical and into the pedagogical, the section which followed also positioned the research within the context of the school, the development of the media literacy curriculum, and its links with two major theoretical frames—namely, multimodality theory and cultural studies, both of which contribute to its overarching development as a subject connected to cultural production and new literacy practices.

From the "identity" sections came frameworks derived from different sources, including that of Giddens and *the project of the self* an important concept in the study of representative practices, particularly in the light of the form and content of the videos being made by the children.

The *curatorship* metaphor proposed toward the end of the theory chapter assumes a relationship to critical, cultural, and creative literacy practices on the part of the children. The movement from inward-facing production to display and communicative exhibition will be a major part of the reflection based on the videos discussed in the later chapters. For now, the following chapter will provide some of the background to the discussed video projects.

CHAPTER 4

Research and Voice

B efore going on to describe in some detail the video productions by some of the children, it's important to set down the background, and I will approach this under three headings below. In the first of these, I will look at the place of digital video (DV) production in education, including some of the major research projects that have shaped thinking about them to date. In the second section, I will outline the background to the videos, the kinds of schools involved and the sorts of settings in which they took place. Finally, in the third section, I will describe the approach to analyzing them, which is drawn from thinking about the various theoretical perspectives outlined in the preceding chapters: what to collect, how to collect it, and how to analyze it in order to explore and research the areas of media literacy and identity mapped so far.

Studies of Video Production by Younger Learners

While there are useful studies of shorter-term projects in the United Kingdom and elsewhere, much of the literature on student DV production focuses on older children possibly because there are subjects in the curriculum in which to locate these: Media Studies and Film Studies. The relevant research and writing in the field on younger, primary aged children, between 5 and 11, frequently positions them as readers of media texts, writing about and problematizing children's engagement with them as consumers of popular culture across screens and settings. There are some exceptions to this, which really do take a sophisticated view of practice and theory and describe for teachers and learners how a productive engagement with new literacy might work (see, e.g., Burn and Durran 2007).

While DV production is not always preeminently the medium of cultural production under investigation with younger learners, there are areas that have touched on it as part of a wider engagement with media technology in education. Some writing has positioned it as an instance of "creativity" with technology while other intersecting thinking coming from the discipline of Media Studies has sought to connect it with literacy practices. Casting the net wider leads to literature around technology in education in the subject of Information and Communication Technology (ICT) or, in its more international version, Information Technology (IT). Part of the issue in that subject is that DV production has been sidelined by a whole raft of technologically determinist research around more ubiquitous devices and associated themes currently being debated, for example, on United Kingdom–based mailing lists such as the "ICT Research Network," which frequently debates such issues as "Interactive Whiteboards," "Virtual Learning Environments," "Personalised learning," "Mobile Learning," "Social software/web 2.0 for learning," and so on.

The sociocultural aspects of video production, coupled with the ways in which younger learners first meet handheld, phone or video cameras, and editing spaces in primary schools make it a difficult subject to untangle and research in this context. A further problem is the fact that video appears to be a "known quantity," a medium which has a long tradition—namely, that of film and screen studies and the historical tradition of interrogating and interpreting moving-image texts. A senior member of a major technology research funding body once told me that projects involving DV were not attractive to forward-looking organizations because we "know all about that" already. The implication was that moving-image production was a known and well-understood quantity, extensively written about in the traditions of film studies alluded to above. I would contend, however, that it is equally important to understand DV production by children and young people, not least because in each of the areas listed above, in education and in the wider, lived culture around it, there are vast amounts of moving images, some of them self-produced, being made by children. Of course, these owe much to the traditional culture of the moving image but the shorter digital production is also a distinctive form, full of personal reference points and motivations, its nature different now not least in the ways of distribution, production, and even communal critique. Much of this has happened outside of the school system on DV cameras, mobile phones, and other devices. We need a way to understand the nature of this production and its immediate impact and effects on younger learners as they develop in the emergent media literacy curriculum and as they go about their lives outside school.

In the following sections, I will review of some of the existing research on DV production under the following headings:

Precedents and antecedents in digital video research: A brief historical survey of the field

Recent projects in the earlier years of schooling: A review of some key projects in the field in the primary age group, children in between the ages of 5 and 11

Production as research: A review of some texts that use DV production as a tool for other forms of research

Digital video, technology, and pedagogy: A review of texts relating to the uses of technology in school as it is relevant to DV production, particularly as it has been invoked in writing about creativity with new technology

Storying, identity, and roles in production: A review of texts that consider the social worlds and social purposes of DV production

Emergent themes: A concluding section, which outlines some of the less well explored, emergent themes in the field.

Precedents and Antecedents in the Field

Even before video production became more widely affordable and accessible with the advent of digital technologies, moving-image production in education was an area of development and debate in the context of Media Studies and other, related subjects, such as English in secondary schools.

Sefton-Green (1998) described the historical development of production in Media Studies within the context of the tension between asserting an academic status for the subject over a vocational one, while at the same time acknowledging the indivisible nature of the theory and practice in the field. He cited the differing levels of emphasis given to production in Media Studies examination syllabi throughout the 1980s and into the 1990s as evidence of debate within the subject around its relation to production. He also looked at media production in other subjects such as Art or English where there appeared to be a greater sense of its intrinsic value and where the academic status of the subjects was not contested.

In early guides for educators published by the British Film Institute and UNESCO (Greiner 1955; Hills 1950; Peters 1961), Sefton-Green found "a protectionist element" (1998, p. 22). He describes some of the early moral imperatives behind film education; teaching children about the terminology of film language and form in order to protect them from the supposedly more pernicious, dumbing down, effects of popular culture, giving students a way of repudiating its influence over their lives by understanding more of the mechanics of its production and of identifying aspects of higher-order culture within the medium. There is a concomitant protectionist stance toward the study of film itself, seeking to develop and promote its status as a higher art form, giving children the skills and vocabulary to identify moving-image texts, which have high cultural capital, some of which were said, at the time, to have an equivalence with other, recognizable "higher" literary forms, such as poetry and drama (Greiner 1955).

This connection with literacy and language issues resulted in a direct link with production through working exercises designed to introduce the form; the practical work proposed by these writers (e.g., Peters 1961) is concerned with using such exercises to develop a technical understanding of the subject at the expense of a wider, cultural one (see Sefton-Green 1998, p. 24). Others working in the field, however, doubted the need for any serious introduction of practical production as a tool for learning about film at all, whether centered on technical exercises or looser creative approaches. Masterman (1980), for example, argued for an emphasis on uncovering ideological structures in existing moving-image texts, equipping students with the ability to analyze media and identify the dominant ideology rather than make productions themselves. Both Masterman and, later, Ferguson (1981) believed that student production was low in both quality and sophistication and barely worth the time, trouble, and expense. As Buckingham has subsequently pointed out (2003), political arguments lay behind this disparagement of student work, with Masterman, Ferguson, and others believing that student productions merely imitated and reenacted popular forms and, that they were, therefore "an inherently unthinking process through which the dominant ideologies of media products would be simply internalised and reproduced" (ibid., pp. 124–125).

In the following years, however, the status of practical moving-image work in schools began to change as a result of curriculum development, theoretical reevaluation, and advances in technology. In *Making Media* (Buckingham, Grahame, and Sefton-Green 1995), the authors situate six case studies of different forms of media production from London secondary schools within these changing contexts. They reflect on the emerging Media Studies curriculum and place it within the contexts of other subjects, including English and IT. However, they are at pains to point out the importance of the dialogue between theory and practice throughout, arguing that it is "only on this basis...that more effective classroom strategies can begin to be devised" (ibid., p. 13). As will be seen in future sections, this dialectical relationship between theory and practice is a recurrent theme in the field in addressing areas such as media literacy, social practice, and the construction of identity in media production.

One such set of strategies of relevance to the present study concerns group work in media production. The case study described in the fourth chapter of *Making Media* reflects on the claims for group work in media production, including perceived benefits beyond learning film language—namely,

> a co-operative learning environment, which is based on small group work, will (it is argued) make best use of the available class time, foster students' confidence and motivation to learn, and make room for more constructive and egalitarian relationships between teachers and students. (Ibid., p. 76)

Certainly, as will be seen in the chapters that describe the fieldwork in the study, the emphasis on the wider benefits of group production was key in persuading schools to take part.

In examining critically the claims made for groupwork in media production, Buckingham et al. reflect on a study by Lorac and Weiss for the Schools Council on Communication and Social Skills (1981). Their report claimed effects beyond the simple learning of media concepts on students' work and relationships but did not address the complex detail of democratically allocating roles and responsibilities or of decision making in an essentially hierarchical setting. As Buckingham et al. state, "Effective group work obviously requires considerable support and intervention on the part of teachers" (1995, p. 77). The nature of this intervention is one of the determining factors in the success or otherwise of media production.

The situation for primary aged children was not always directly addressed in these debates between advocates of production and analysis because, as noted previously, there was no direct primary equivalent to Media Studies; it was located in the margins of other subjects (such as Art or English). However, whenever it *was* addressed, it was strongly influenced by the twin themes of defining and defending media education as a discipline as well as by the protectionist arguments around developing critical capabilities outlined previously.

The emergent arguments around production in the late 1980s and the early 1990s (as video cameras became more accessible—though not, as yet, digital) came from attempts to create structured media education experiences which had the rigor, look, and feel of other subjects in the National Curriculum, established in the United Kingdom in the Education Reform Act (1988), combined with the perceived flexibility and creativity of the Arts and Humanities. In these respects, the debates and positions of previous years over Media Studies in secondary schools were reenacted for younger learners—namely, the aim to create a subject area of equal academic standing in relation to others and to equip children with critical and creative opportunities in working with moving images.

Recent Projects in the Earlier Years of Schooling

Although video making has a tradition within Media Studies in secondary schools going back to the 1970s (Buckingham 2003), it is only in recent years, as Burn and Durran (2007) point out, that the emphasis on a theoretical *critique* of texts in Media Studies has been more easily incorporated with *production*. The increasing access to the user-friendly and affordable tools growing in use in domestic markets has been a significant factor in this shift. While for some practitioners at the secondary school level the theoretical and practical elements have been bound up together from the beginning (McDougall 2006), for others it is really only with the emergence of accessible digital hardware and software that the possibilities for production in the Media Studies curriculum have begun to be realized (Fraser and Oram 2003). This has been further fueled by the proponents of the emergent media literacy curriculum, since its definition and scope in the United Kingdom from the Office for Communication (OFCOM 2005) explicitly includes acts of production.

In schools in the United Kingdom, media literacy developments were mainly led by cultural organizations such as Creative Partnerships, the BBC, and the British Film Institute (BFI) all of whom fund school-based projects or professional development for teachers. Indeed, the BFI has been a prime mover seeking to "reframe" literacy itself in schools toward a greater engagement with moving image in school contexts (Chan 2008). This is a wide-ranging initiative involving an attempt to influence the development of the primary and secondary curriculum in the interests of developing all forms of media literacy skills, including both critique and production. Most recently, this has seen the emergence of the annual partnership between the BFI and the Cinematheque Francaise in Paris, which has seen highly aesthetic film language and production explored in educational contexts, alongside the aesthetic analysis of filmmaking deemed to be of high quality (BFI 2010).

In the earliest stages of the emergence of DV, however, the revolution in home DV production was in its infancy and its potential knock-on impact on media production in educational settings, while certainly being felt in secondary schools, was far less well developed as a practice with younger learners in primary schools. Partly, this was because DV equipment was only slowly starting to permeate the primary phase in a number of different and disconnected ways. In spite of pioneering work by Bazalgette and Craggs

(1989 and 1992 respectively), which sought to establish such provision, there wasn't an equivalent of secondary Media Studies in the primary curriculum to form a natural subject-based home for these tools and practices. As a result, the DV cameras and editing software often arrived as part of a project based within a variety of subject disciplines, most often including ICT, English/Literacy, Art, or others. Once again, the BFI was active at that time in partnership with the more ICT-focused work of the British Education and Communications Technology Agency (Reid, Burn, and Parker 2002). Nowadays, the picture in England is even less well defined with the subject ICT moving more closely toward coding and programming and no natural home for media education emerging in a country that still regards only print literacy as a priority.

However, with the emergence in the late 1990s and the early 2000s of simpler production tools in the form of affordable DV cameras, handheld devices, and user-friendly software, moving-image production with younger learners in primary schools began to pick up some momentum. While still lacking a place in the primary curriculum within a discrete subject, DV began to enter schools through the frame of ICT, Literacy, or innovative creative arts practice. A number of projects emerged that had DV production at the center of the research activity with a specific mission to explore the synergy between new ways of working with moving images and the primary curriculum. These came from a range of different backgrounds including ICT in education, media literacy in education, and in one case, a social intervention project with a European dimension.

As has been previously explained, this technology often found its way into primary schools in the United Kingdom through an ICT in education route. As noted above, BECTA, the former British Education and Communications Technology Agency (since disbanded by the UK government in 2011) commissioned an evaluation of DV work across the curriculum in 50 schools in the United Kingdom (among them some primary schools) (Reid, Burn, and Parker 2002). The brief for the United Kingdom evaluation was to provide feedback on the ways in which DV production, using tools provided as part of the project, impacted on pupil "engagement and behaviurs" in a range of curriculum settings. Across the 50 project schools, the findings indicated that there were indeed benefits to be had in terms of higher pupil engagement, the range of possible learning styles that could be supported, motivational factors, and "the development of other skills, such as problem solving, negotiation, thinking, reasoning and risk-taking" (ibid., p. 3).

However, and not surprisingly, given the input from the BFI into the project, the report concluded that there was a need for more work that focused on the distinctiveness of the medium, the notions of creativity embedded in the practice of the teachers, and the longer-term nature of the effects. The authors, in particular, proposed a greater engagement with film language and, by inference, with techniques that would allow for developments in this area to be framed and analyzed (Reid, Burn, and Parker 2002). In this sense, the report was seeking to influence thinking about pedagogy with DV and to reframe it and realign it away from the purely technological into an engagement with media across the curriculum.

In Australia, two years later, a report was published on a project that researched student initiated video in the primary school years (Schuck and Kearney 2004b). It provided further useful insight into video projects located within school curricula. Like the BECTA study, Schuck and Kearney were engaged in trying to examine findings across a range of curriculum areas. However, the focus in this project was on neither technological innovation nor an emergent media education program. Instead, this project focused on pedagogy and student autonomy in relation to DV production.

The sample was smaller than for the BECTA project (only five schools were involved) and the focus, as revealed in the title, "Students in the Director's Seat: Teaching and Learning across the School Curriculum with Student-Generated Video," was on moving-image production in which the students had a degree of control over planning, shooting, editing, and disseminating their videos. In common with the UK findings, increased motivation was held up as an outcome. Further findings of positive engagement across a range of curriculum areas were identified and attributed to student autonomy and pedagogies of what the authors referred to as "active learning" (Schuck and Kearney 2004b). The authors focused on the overarching pedagogical features, which were exemplified in their findings. The conclusion remained similar to the BECTA study, however, in as much as they called for further research in the field, although the perspective of these authors was rather different, claiming significant advantages in general conceptual understanding arising from working with DV. In their concluding paragraph, they wrote as follows:

> Findings of significance were the following: the authors saw clear evidence of student-generated digital video strongly enhancing pedagogy in the area of student engagement and autonomy. We noted ... that student voice and ownership were key factors in enhancing the learning process. A suggestion arising from the study is that more emphasis is given to the development of conceptual understanding through the use of DV, and that this area is researched further. (Schuck and Kearney 2004b, p. 8)

The CHICAM project (Children in Communication about Migration), funded by the European Commission, was a third piece of research into DV production from around the same time as the previous two from the United Kingdom and Australia discussed above. The project report presented evidence of the uses of DV production in a variety of informal educational settings across Europe made by young people who had migrated to European host countries (de Block, Buckingham, and Banaji 2005). CHICAM was framed by an explicit political and social purpose in its exploration of the use of video by the students involved and maintained a different emphasis from the previous reports and their concern with technical innovation, media literacy, and pedagogy. These elements were, of course, still present but because of the setting, the subject matter, and the political agenda of the project, they were more subservient to the processes of representation themselves than the previous reports. Reflecting after the project, two of the team wrote that

> we wanted to...know more about how children learn to use media technology and how they use the "languages," generic forms and conventions of media to create meaningful statements or representations. We also expected that this process would tell us a great deal about how these children interpreted and made use of the complex media environments in which many of them lived. (de Block and Buckingham 2007, p. x)

CHICAM had an agenda, which was framed by its wider social purpose of discovering to what extent media production had a part to play in representing voices that were not usually heard. The outcomes connected to media literacy and production itself were similar in nature to the other two studies above, but more complex due to the cultural differences in the settings. Overall, however, the report recommended, along the lines of the BECTA findings, that serious consideration be given, in particular, to the ways in which teachers could be made more skilled, more aware of the creative uses of technology in relation to identity (de Block, Buckingham, and Banaji 2005). This was certainly an overarching idea in the work described later in the book.

Creativity is often discussed in relation to DV production and features to a greater or lesser extent in all the reports discussed so far as well as other reports (de Block, Buckingham, and Banaji 2005; Lord et al. 2007; Pearson 2005; Reid, Burn, and Parker 2002; Schuck and Kearney 2004b). The term "creativity" is itself certainly problematic and the many interrelated definitions are complex and discussed in more detail in a subsequent chapter. For now, for some, there is a need to account for creativity in terms of the special properties of the tools of production (Loveless 2002), and of the affordances of the technology itself. In this case, the term "affordances," itself often difficult to define, is invoked to describe the latent possibilities of a medium or an environment (Gibson 1977). Thus, the tools themselves are still very much in the frame and occupy a privileged position in relation to the texts as key mediators of authorial design.

The authors of the BECTA report discuss the ways in which DV appears to free up the relationship between creativity and the curriculum. However, the case studies in this research suggested that a new set of constraints appear that require accounting for and operating with. These are accounted for as particular skills in the making of the film and learning media language (Reid, Burn, and Parker 2002), around timing and subject matter, or, following Loveless (2002), to do with possible misuse, or misunderstanding, of the ways in which the technology operates.

For Schuck and Kearney the important creative act in the productions leads them to introduce a discussion of "new literacies" (Cope and Kalantzis 2000), of how the projects allow for the formation of new ways of being literate through autonomous production. Their emphasis is on freedom from constraint. Indeed, the issue of constraint versus freedom recurs in much of the literature around case studies of DV production (de Block and Sefton-Green 2004; Reid, Burn, and Parker 2002; Schuck and Kearney 2004b) and is discussed in relation to the schools in this study at a later stage. Further discussions in the field by a number of writers (e.g., Knobel and Lankshear 2007; Lankshear and Knobel 2006; Marsh 2005) connecting these issues to an account of new literacies will be outlined in the next chapter.

Developing media literacy in learners through an engagement with a media production is also seen as a desirable possibility inherent within developing technologies, taking children beyond their position as media consumers and enabling them to become media producers (Buckingham 2003). The authors of the BECTA report find evidence of a gradual permeation of technical vocabulary into the projects over time (Reid, Burn, and Parker 2002, p. 56), almost as a necessity to develop a metalanguage in order to operate in the field.

The case studies from Australia further support the idea that DV production has immediate benefits in the teaching of "media literacy" even if this emerged in a nonspecific way during the work. Children in the project schools became able to evaluate and improve their work by reference to a range of models drawn from both their making and their watching of a range of media. In one Melbourne school,

> students developed rubrics so they could indicate the features of "great video" and they used these rubrics to guide their own work. (Schuck and Kearney 2004a, p. 59)

While these self-generated rubrics are useful and interesting in their own right, there is still a gap in our understanding of how the production side of media literacy operates in a progressive way, from the work of younger children on up through the curriculum within formal settings. A rare example of a research project that attempted to incorporate common themes across key stages from very early learners upward is provided by the "Special Effects" project, run jointly by the BFI and the National Foundation for Educational Research (NFER), and commissioned by Creative Partnerships (Lord et al. 2007). The aim was to assess the effects of moving-image work on children's learning and their general disposition toward school. It was carried out on behalf of Creative Partnerships in an attempt to provide an evaluation of their scheme to place animators, filmmakers, and artists in schools. I was employed as a field researcher and member of the steering group. The project ran for a year, during which researchers made three visits to projects in schools from the reception age group up to the higher end of secondary school. In the school I visited, I interviewed children before, during, and after an animation project centered on the local area. I took field notes and observed an animation artist working with children in key stage 2 on a number of occasions. The project found, across all projects in all age groups, that

> the most frequently and strongly reported effects on pupils from the moving image case studies were: enhanced enjoyment, film knowledge and skills (especially film skills and techniques), and social skills (especially teamwork). (Lord et al. 2007, executive summary, p. ii)

Here, we find echoes of previous studies even from the earliest years that reported on improved teamwork and social skills as a benefit of moving-image work (Lorac and Weiss 1981). However, it is important to note that these projects were focused on specific projects and interventions by creative professionals in the context of moving-image work. Certainly, in the primary phase projects, the authorial voice was not necessarily that of the children themselves. They had input into the projects at a low level, but were not engaged in the choices of topics or form although they were engaged and motivated by the work as evidenced by the outputs noted above.

Two further main differences between Special Effects and the fieldwork for this study are evident. The first was that for the primary age phase participants in the Special Effects study, the work was almost exclusively animation, a medium with a related but qualitatively different set of affordances and outcomes from live video work. The second major difference was in the curriculum mapping of the work that was onto specific goals and targets in subject areas; this is not to say that other, affective outcomes were not considered, just that they were not foregrounded. Newer research aims to look more closely at these issues in funded research in three locations in the United Kingdom in 2012 with three kinds of moving-image production in each, the formal aesthetic approach of the BFI / Cinematheque Francaise (London), mobile phone filming (Sheffield), and working with "machinima" as a form (Cambridge)—in all cases attempting to negotiate between instruction in media literacy and the incorporation of the agency, interests, and cultural capital of the youth involved (LKL 2012).

Across projects, findings about the enhanced enjoyment, knowledge of media language, and team working is borne out in writing about youth media practice, where the research has been conducted with older students in a range of formal and informal settings. Although outside of the scope of this study, such findings are often used alongside others such as creativity to enhance a project bid and interest teachers and students in project settings to take part. In a comprehensive survey of the field of youth media production, Chitat Chan (2008) identifies archetypal constructions of youth media production practice in the United Kingdom and the United States. These constructions position youth as finding in media production a space in which to articulate aspects of identity that appear to resist the dominant culture. For the authors of one report in the United Kingdom, for example, "Being Seen, Being Heard," produced in partnership between the BFI and the National Youth Agency, the authors found that media production projects allowed young people to develop

> not only a voice but...a language that other young people are likely to be interested in and which, by their very existence, stand(s) in contrast to other representations in the dominant television culture. (Harvey, Skinner, and Parker 2002, p. 93)

However, for Chan this and similar assertions posit further questions and responses of relevance to research in the field, in particular the linkage made between the institutions, the students, and the pedagogy in the setting. Chan points out that, in youth media production, the

> respective shaping of young people's positions can also be seen to reflect discursive practices that belong to a broader socio-cultural context. However, is it justified to say that young people's voices are merely the reflection of those ideological and institutional conditions? Do young people just naively assume positions assigned to them? How do they experience and negotiate with these positions, and on what occasions?...

> Youth media is not just about youth development and media technology; it is also about power, institution and pedagogy. (Chan 2008, p. 78)

This and other assertions about the positive impact of video as a social tool, its motivational properties (through linkage with popular culture), and its potential for celebrating diversity and inclusion and for being student-centered, were all part of the background to the thinking behind the research theme and the methods used in the field work presented in later chapters in this book. The major differences from the work of Chan and others who have looked more closely at these issues in the context of youth production were to move down through the age groups to see what the nascent use of this technology was like, to work inside formal structures (albeit unconventionally and quasi-informally in the end) and to record as far as possible the sociocultural processes in production for a different group of learners in a different setting.

Although, as previously noted, there is a lack of research into self-authored DV production by younger learners themselves, there have been projects that consider DV material as an asset alongside other classroom resources to be used in teaching and learning. The BECTA report into production (Reid, Burn, and Parker 2002) was followed by a project that looked at teaching with DV assets, which were not necessarily self-authored (Burden and Kuechel 2004). This was in turn followed by a project funded in the United Kingdom by the National Endowment for Science, Technology, and the Arts (NESTA), called New Directions in Digital Media (NDDM), which looked at the impact of DVD authoring as production by teachers in school contexts (Pink 2006). In these projects, among the many examples of repurposing video texts were sources as diverse as Channel 4 television and mainstream film, there were a small number of videos made by the learners themselves. In the later NDDM project, these were directed mainly by the teachers concerned and used as examples of pupils informing each other about such things as Spanish vocabulary, simple math. problems, in literacy strategy ideas, and so on. A quick scan of the project DVD results in the sense that the children themselves were not actively involved in structuring the video assets. The form of the video productions is skewed toward actual interaction with the national curriculum itself; neither is it concerned with any articulation of the students' personal experience, nor is it concerned with the use of the technology, students learning media language, or any of the other aspects under investigation in this book.

In Ireland, the FIS project attempted to build connections across the curriculum as a result of sustained engagement with Digital Video (DV) production. From its inception in 2000, it was concerned with some of the themes that drove the very earliest studies in the field around positive social and curricular impacts (Lorac and Weiss 1981). The evaluation report (McNamara and Griffin 2003), published by Ireland's National Centre for Technology in Education, approaches the subject from the direction of ICT in education; it was not a media literacy driven agenda, but one that, at least initially, began from the perspective of DV production as a techno-logical innovation and gradually moved into a more sustained engagement with media literacy issues. It was important because of its range and scope, running from 2000 to 2003 in 26 primary schools in Dublin and Cork, and driven by the idea that technological innovation based on DV pro-duction could support curriculum innovation, particularly in the creative arts. Findings were generally positive when reported for the media literacy activities and less so on the technical side, suggesting perhaps that some form of sustained engagement around the moving image itself, its forms and principles for organization would be the most successful model for work in this area.

From the project reports I looked at, there were a number of themes that suggested further investigation. This was sometimes directly expressed, as in the case of the BECTA project, which concluded that more research was needed that focused on the distinctiveness of the medium, the notions of creativity embedded in the practice of the teachers, and the longer-term nature of the effects on pupils (Reid, Burn, and Parker 2002). From this point onward, it should be obvious that projects with some kind of progres-sive, longer-term recursive and regular production work are rare but have inherent value. This was the premise behind an animation project in three local authorities in England, which aimed to explore the link between writ-ing poetry and creating animation by younger learners (Bazalgette 2010). FIS in Ireland reported some positive outcomes for similar curriculum-based activity (McNamara and Griffin 2003). Nevertheless, the unexplored domain here seems to be the self-authored video text, which lies outside the normal curriculum focus. This is where the videos in this book come in, and they will be described in detail in the subsequent chapters. For now, it is interesting to consider the use of video in research.

Production as Research

The use of visual data in research is the subject of a number of commen-taries and handbooks for researchers (Buckingham 2009; Kress and Van Leeuwen 2006; Rose 2007; Van Leeuwen and Jewitt 2001), many of which have relevance to the present study and will be discussed further in chapter 4. The distinctiveness of the moving image as a form, however, demands substantial adaptation and presents particular issues and problems for researchers (Buckingham 2009; Burn and Parker 2003). Nevertheless, video exerts great appeal for those researching in educational settings, partly because of the increasing ease of use of the technology used to gather the data and partly because of its perceived usefulness in generating apparently rich and "authentic" data. One such project, involving literacy lessons and the use of DV production concluded that

> it may be useful to explore teaching and learning around alternative media such as still and moving images, live theatre and storytelling, digital technology and the arts. Although some teachers are making good use of these media, the potential of these media for providing inclusive literacy experiences could be further developed. (Orr Vered 2008)

The implication of such enthusiastic writing is that the moving image as a medium is inclusive because it is central to the wider cultural experience of the children; this can then be used to generate rich data and approach any number of research questions.

As Buckingham (2009) points out, however, the use of video as a "creative" method, rich with possibilities, presents researchers with a series of further issues and questions that need to be addressed. Authenticity, for example, is often claimed in such techniques, but, Buckingham asks, whose voice is actually, authentically represented? Pink (2006) suggests that authentic, objective truth is not, in fact, represented in any simple way by the use of images in research but, rather, that new knowledge and critiques emerge from the process.

An example of a project that was based centrally around video data generated by participants comes from Andrew Noyes who introduced children to video diarying in pursuit of learning more about their fears about Mathematics learning in transfer from primary to secondary school. The major difference in this case was the research being guided by a question that was external to the video production; Noyes wished to learn more about math. and secondary school transfer, not about the media production itself. Although interesting findings emerged around the experience of making the videos, the major purpose of the piece was not to understand those processes of composition but to use them as a means to unlock and interrogate a different issue, namely the dispositions toward learning of the children involved (Buckingham and Sefton-Green 1994; Deci and Ryan 1985).

Noyes, as principal researcher, acted as an editor in the process and used the cultural phenomenon of the "video diary" as a vehicle through which to apply a particular ethnographic method, as revealed in the following passage:

> As the editor, I have a privileged view and see the whole interplay between child and camera/audience. Furthermore, when the video diary data is compared with complementary ethnographic data the simulations of the diary room can be analysed as dispositional improvisations within my theoretical framework. (Deci and Ryan 1985, p. 134)

This research strategy is very different in form from the nature of the engagement with video proposed for this study, where the children themselves are in control of the final, rendered outcome, navigating the virtual editing suites onscreen. There are certain similarities in the application of triangulating data and the use of other techniques but the intention is different.

Of much greater relevance to this study is the work of Andrew Burn and David Parker (Burn and Parker 2001, 2003b, 2003a). In these accounts, actual self-authored video by learners forms the basis of analysis and research. They look at how such video texts may be examined using visual semiotics as a way of understanding the use of multimodal resources to make meaning.

This has certainly been useful in other projects that have employed self-authored video as a research tool such as the Learners and Technology Project 7–11(Selwyn, Potter, and Cranmer 2010), to which I will turn in the following section.

Video Production alongside Other Tools as Research in Accessing "Learner Voice"

Involving younger students of primary school age in their own learning at the level of choice of strategy and content has a tradition in English schools from the Plowden report (1967) onward. Throughout the educational reforms of the 1980s and 1990s, however, there was a politically motivated and concerted effort to reverse progressive teaching of this kind and encourage teacher-directed pedagogy, particularly in the national strategy for literacy (DFES 1998), which, while no longer perceived to be compulsory as a model, still exerts a strong influence. This and other teaching guidance also appeared in different versions in secondary school classrooms and the system in England, bounded by complex but narrow assessments and simple league tables of exam scores, enforced on all participants by a punitive and performative inspection regime. Thus, in many classrooms, while good teachers abound and new methods are introduced in pursuit of higher and higher standards, the educational experience has been exposed to the risk of fossilizing around the traditional transmission mode of pedagogy in classrooms dominated by "teacher talk." This has been concomitant with a narrowing of the curriculum, although there is wide recognition of the need to broaden the experience of children and to explore new curriculum models, such as those proposed by the thorough and well-researched primary curriculum review published by Robin Alexander and others (2010).

The attempt to hear the "learner voice" on these issues in one recent project in England (Selwyn, Potter, and Cranmer 2010) was based on a democratic, participatory, and emancipatory view of research design using models of learner involvement in curriculum activities proposed by Michael Fielding (2004). He suggested that there were four stages of learner engagement with the curriculum. In the first of these stages, learners are used simply as a data source, assessed against normative targets. At the second stage, we think of learners as active respondents to questions with teachers able to listen and analyze the responses they give in particular settings where they have the freedom to discuss aspects of their learning. The third-level positions learners as coresearchers with increased involvement in the learning decisions taken by teachers. Finally, with learners as researchers themselves, partnership is the dominant motif in activities, with the "learner voice" leading the way. It was felt that, in using methods that had an accordance with these views on participant involvement, we might get closer in our research to hearing a more authentic "learner voice" and, subsequently, closer to an understanding of new literacy practices in this age group as they moved between uses of technology and media at home and at school.

The methodology we chose in the end was fairly complex, with interdependent elements running in parallel, which, nevertheless, yielded extremely interesting results about the interrelationship between children, their self-reflexive views on their uses of technology and media at home and at school. We decided to involve pupils in collecting the qualitative data by setting up focus groups in which children would record interviews with each other using simple handheld audio devices. We would listen in and eventually join in with adult-directed questions afterward. We would also collect drawings of future uses of technologies in places of learning in the final section of a pupil questionnaire. Finally, we would encourage the filming by children themselves of short commentaries in school about the spaces and practices there and at home. Our research had, therefore, a triangulated focus on agentive and self-determined ways of using technology (as opposed to being used *by* technology) and remained cognizant of the factors that come into play when young people are engaged in techno-literacy practices, which are also techno-cultural practices. We found that recording their own voices and their own response in media with which they are familiar builds on children's existing and developing skills and dispositions in new media.

Our sample size comprised primary schools in five settings in the England from children in the upper age range, between the ages of 7 and 11. The wider findings have been reported and published elsewhere (Selwyn, Potter, and Cranmer 2010). The focus of this article is on commenting on the salience of the video data in which children recorded views on new media literacies at home and at school while *simultaneously* using new media artifacts and making new media texts.

Most of the short interview clips made by the children were filmed with handheld devices and in midshot or close-up. They frequently featured a child or pair of children, with the questions asked from behind the camera. This had the effect of freeing up dialogue between children familiar to each other as well as allowing researchers to look for other key markers in gesture and choice of framing. In order to do this, adapted frames for multimodal analysis were applied to the moving-image texts (see Burn and Parker 2003; Kress and Van Leeuwen 2001).

Five videos in particular proved useful to the triangulation of agency in the study as a whole. By themselves, they may sound trite and obvious; weighed against the survey returns, interviews and drawings, which the children also made, they came up time and again as useful markers of young children's views on the issues of technology in school, in particular recurrent findings about a wish to have more control over their uses of new media, to be more playful with it, and to use their autonomy in these activities for more learning by moving the locus of control closer to themselves. It is important to note that this is still not about technology itself but about the situated practices at home and at school.

In the first of these five videos, however, a young child who expressed her doubt that anything useful would be found out in the research project gave a more prosaic, but nonetheless real, response. She is framed in midshot, seated at a table while an older girl asks her whether anything can be learned about children's technology use in the home that might be usefully applied to school uses of technology. She answers "no," casting significant doubt on the enterprise in one sense, but reinforcing our key finding overall that, for the learners in this school, there is a well recognized and understood gap between media and technology uses in the home and those at school. It is recorded on this clip during the eight long seconds it takes for the girl to think it through. She does not give the expected answer; neither does she give an automatic response. Her gaze and her gesture at least suggest the performance of thinking the issues through.

In this and in the other clips, it took control of the camera to free up the learner-researchers to provoke deeper thinking on the subject. Pupil-led talk on the subject of home-school links was rich in many of their pro-ductions with children frequently moving off-script and being confident to follow a line of thought. This helped to create a series of "fly on the wall" documentary-style productions, which allowed the interviewers to assume the role of investigative journalists.

The videos that examined more closely the issue of home use took the form of focus group discussions, led by pupils. They used some of the techniques employed by the researchers, building on answers in the style of a semistruc-tured interview and, in most cases, allowing for discussion to take place. In the second example, the main topic of conversation concerned the different uses of websites and social networking and alluded directly to the subver-sive nature of the activity at home compared to school. Although there was a knowing moment of performance in which one of the speakers at least suggested that banned sites could be explored in either setting if you knew how to keep it concealed. The speaker acted the concealment in embodied form by covering his mouth as he revealed himself to be a regular user of the social networking site, Piczo, which was blocked in school and discour-aged at home. The speaker was well aware of the fact that the research video was being made in school by his friends and could be seen by teachers and researchers. He was keen to reveal his use of this site, yet in the gesture of partial disguise of his voice, he was signaling that he was aware that doing so is effectively transgressive. He showed awareness of the watching children, teachers, and researchers and of his position as a particular kind of subver-sive, social actor in the setting.

The third example showed a girl in one classroom in extreme close-up, criterial in filmmaking for suggesting that confidential information is being shared. In this segment of film, the child's gaze is directed only at the ques-tioner as she ponders the ways in which it is possible to access sites beyond the suggested age limit. A long pause ensues in which the interviewer moves things along with the word "Anyway" and the girl responds, smiling in agreement with "(yes) Anyway" in the sense of "moving along," a familiar linking technique in television presenting. Awareness of form coalesces with the knowing curatorship of the moment. Just as the Piczo example above, the children suggest they know way of being that matches their motivations and attentions as social actors regularly traversing the space between home and school in their Internet use.

If sophistication or perhaps a knowing subversiveness is suggested in the previous two clips, the fourth example shows that there is much to be done in the way of understanding certain cultural-literacy practices as poten-tially dangerous. Two girls are seated side by side in mid–two-shot being filmed by a third. As the interview progresses the girl reveals that at home she will "talk" to anyone on the Internet using her real name and answer any questions that strangers ask her. This answer in a school setting which prided itself on a successful e-safety campaign revealed a staggering mismatch between assumptions on both sides of the semipermeable membrane between home and school. It also further underlined the usefulness of being open and communicating in research in ways that are as close as possible to the learner voice. New media texts and artifacts in this clip and in these circumstances were revelatory of hidden practices in this and in many other examples.

In a more techno-celebratory mode, the fifth example clip filmed somewhat more conventionally than others showed an older girl, aged about ten, eulogizing her mobile phone. This device and the practices around it were the most pleasing and, to her, most easily integrated way of working with technology between home and school. It seemed obvious to her that this should be so. She could not see any disadvantages to this but alluded to the potentially most prosaic finding of all, which was that running out of charge was perceived as being the only downside to mobile phone use. As in life outside, so in life inside the school.

Data from the videos were analyzed alongside the initial survey returns across all five schools, the children's drawings of new technology use across the divide between home and school (see Selwyn, Boraschi, and Özkula 2009), and audio-interview focus groups in which the children were trained as facilitators and left to work on their own. Across all available artifacts and media, there was, as reported elsewhere (Selwyn, Potter, and Cranmer 2010), much unsurprising evidence of the disconnect between home and practices with technology (not least the expected regulatory effect), but much also revealed about the ways in which the young people positioned themselves as agentive, able, and knowing in both settings. Particularly evident in the evidence collected using these new practices, as well as in the drawings, was a desire for change and a plea for greater integration into school of new literacy practices that allowed young people to break free from the constraints shaping the social and pedagogic functions of the school. Pupil engagement with the process suggested that they had a sophisticated understanding of the ways in which the social spaces operate and how their new media use differs in the context of home and school. The desire for change did not appear to spring so much from wanting to engage less with the formal curriculum, as might be imagined by following the "digital natives" argument (Prensky 2005), so much as from a wish to bring some of the skills and dispositions developed in technology use and media consumption outside school across the membrane boundary between home and school, back into the educational setting.

The findings from the "learner voice" project in the first did, however, suggest a deeper need to develop forms of curriculum organization that fit better with the cultural and literacy practices of young learners. This rather prosaic and reductive finding nevertheless conceals some important detail about the ways in which digital media culture is becoming a field in which skill sets and dispositions are developed by younger and younger learners outside school. In the project, over time, in their expressive modes in the video output they provided, the texts, practices, and social arrangements of recording and capturing ideas became a facilitator of richer, qualitative data comprehensible by unlocking the many modes that underpinned both the form and content of what was being said. In bringing this forward in their work, the children were thoughtful, articulate, and constructive, demonstrating perhaps that they merit a genuine participatory role in the access to media technology in the settings of their formal education.

But where does DV production fit in primary schools and how has this been expressed in practice? It is to these issues that the next section will turn.

Digital Video, Technology, and Pedagogy

As we have seen previously, DV production as part of a "subject" discipline has frequently been without a natural home in primary schools, unlike in secondary schools, where the cameras and editing software are often accessible by, if not under the control of, teachers of subjects such as Media Studies, English, Drama, or Art. Instead, DV cameras and editing software often arrive in primary schools under the aegis of the subject of ICT. From this point, depending on the context of the school, it might be possible to introduce the technology into other subjects and we have seen, for example, that there is a potential home for it in primary schools within the overarching context of primary English, particularly as this develops and broadens in the direction of media literacy. At the same time, larger numbers of teachers in training in primary education, for example, are being introduced to DV production as an instance of "creative" practice with technology within their ICT sessions (Potter 2002; Sharp et al. 2002). This means that many initial assertions and assumptions in relation to pedagogy involving media and technology have entered the primary phase from a different direction, outside of media literacy debates. Of course, there is a blurring of this view as several disciplines overlap and interact with one another. The cameras may arrive in a primary school in a cross-curricular setting as peripheral ICT devices but, if the context is truly collaborative and up to speed with recent developments, they may fall into the hands of a literacy coordinator who has been working with the BFI in the ways described previously in literacy contexts (see also Lord et al. 2007) and find wider uses in the school.

Media literacy, information literacy, gaming literacy, and others are terms that are being used in technology and education contexts to try to capture a range of responses to the ways in which technology is shaping our experience of the world and our understanding of literacy, as seen in the foreword above. Theories of how children learn with, and interact with, media culture through, for example, video gaming (online and standalone) have recently begun to inform educational debate for primary aged children. Researchers are asking why do learners devote so much time, concentration, and effort to gaming or social networking activities and so little time to the equivalent, traditional educational experiences (see, e.g., Gee 2004b, Selwyn, Potter, and Cranmer 2008).

We can trace in these questions and debates the emergence of an overlapping world of theory and practice in the wider field beyond debates about media production. Indeed, as technologies converge and computers become televisions, video-editing suites, library portals, gaming consoles, and communication hubs, it has become possible to see similar convergence and overlap in the academic world in terms of the theoretical perspectives on offer about education and technology (though this is seldom unproblematic).

Discussing technology in education, some writers now assert that technology is part of material culture, used by learners and their teachers in many aspects of their lives (LeCourt 2001). And writers in the field of the sociology of new media point to the changing nature of social arrangements and practices around new media artifacts and texts. Increasingly, individuals experience and interact with learning through their consumption and production of digital media. This experience, mediated by tools and artifacts and their relation to each other, changes the ways in which knowledge is produced, understood, shared, and accessed in fundamental ways (Lankshear 2003). One result of this is an apparent potential shift in the locus of control of learning between formal and informal structures and sites of learning, moving the thinking about the uses of ICT in the direction of greater learner control; sometimes this is referred to as learner "agency" (by, e.g., Cuthell 2002) although, again, this is contested by others as a fanciful notion in which technology is in fact seen as the dominant motif and determinant of human action (Buckingham 2007, 2011).

Loveless discusses technology in the context of the learner's experience of pedagogy (2002). She argues that problematic issues and key differences in learner experience with technology arise from the varied ways in which teachers frame their understanding of children's learning itself. Loveless explores ICT related pedagogy as a learner experience following several observations of children and their teachers in primary classrooms. She has written about technology in relation to the curriculum as it is described and structured, in schools in England, retaining a focus on the learner as the center of activity. Frequently, creativity is a theme with which she is engaged, and for Loveless, there are key properties of the medium of ICT in schools, particularly relating to productive tools, which foster creative practices by learners. These properties include those that allow learners to make and change decisions rapidly or to model a variety of hypotheses before deciding on a solution to a problem. She often invokes the concept of "provisionality," a factor that allows the user to test hypotheses and make changes at every stage, altering fundamentally and irreversibly the role of the teacher from that of instructor to one of mentor-facilitator. This change is not always easily accomplished and sometimes not recognized as necessary, particularly where the overall rationale for the use of technology in places of learning is so diverse and diffuse.

For primary educators, thinking about DV production through the ICT frame positions it as one example of pedagogical change brought about by technology itself rather than through a wider and changing engagement with media and cultural production, which is, in fact, simply enabled by the technology. This is further complicated, of course, in education systems with no clear pedagogical consensus on the uses of technology more widely in schools (Cuban 2001; Selwyn 2002; Twining 2002a, 2005). It may also explain the lack of joined-up thinking in relation to DV production where use is so patchy in schools; there is no simple match between the ICT frame of reference and the (media) literacy frame. The answer may lie in looking for social and cognitive theory, which brings the tools of technology into the cultural frame, and this is one possibility presented in this book in the following chapters. For now, this chapter continues with a consideration of a different branch of theory, that of identity.

Storying, Identity, and Roles in Digital Video Production

Representation of learner identity has been aligned with new media and DV production by a number of writers (e.g., de Block, Buckingham, and Banaji 2005). The sociocultural dimension of this activity and how it has been accounted for in "new literacy studies" as an engagement with "affinity spaces" (Gee 2004b; Lankshear and Knobel 2006) is also important and an idea to which I will return. For now, it is useful to note additional perspectives drawn from Bruner and others, which allow the discussion to move further in the direction of identity in new media (Bruner 1987) and into issues of pedagogy. Of particular interest here is the idea of new media as a social practice through which identities are represented in different and potentially more compelling and complex ways than with traditional forms, in particular, relating the issue to the previous section, how the medium allows for this to occur through the control by learners of a variety of media resources in production.

A number of different writers have commented on work that sees representational practice as being important in the reproduction of identity. Researchers in a national project in Chile see "new media" incorporation into learning as a way forward for a whole society, using it as an organizing principle for (Hepp, Hinostroza, and Laval 2004). Also in South America, Grossberger-Morales lists the properties of digital media that match her requirements in creating a multimedia representation of her identity:

> The need to tell my personal history in my own (bilingual) voice
>
> The ability to take advantage of every aspect of multimedia technology: digitisation and integration of moving and still images, video, sound and words. (Grossberger-Morales 2000)

The idea that the control of multimodal properties of the medium, in particular the mode of sound, could be important is prevalent in many project reports on identity and DV production, in particular the CHICAM project where music is cited as a key marker of authorial intent in self-representation (de Block, Buckingham, and Banaji 2005). The CHICAM project was set up to

> explore the ways in which media production and communication might allow refugee and migrant children to share, compare and express their experiences of migration. (de Block and Sefton-Green 2004)

The medium of DV, combined in CHICAM with communication between project members over the Internet, was used by the project workers and the children with whom they worked, to make short representational pieces of video connected to themes of daily life, school, friendships, family, and peer relations. As noted previously, the project had a sociopolitical objective; the use of the media would be a form of political activism, giving voice to marginalized groups. A video on the project homepage featuring Liesbeth de Block introduced the project as being about children

> creating their own representations of themselves and their lives... Technology now makes it so much easier for them to be in control of the image and the message... they can bring new voices to debates that concern them, their own voices. (CHICAM 2004)

These aims notwithstanding, the team later reflected on the project in more qualified and cautious terms, in particular the idea that there was a simple mapping of one set of experiences onto another, rendered universal by the properties of the medium of DV. In fact, in appraising each other's productions in the early phases of the project, children

> were looking for information about the other places and children involved in the research. Here again the film did not speak of their lives in the present or connect visually or aurally with any shared culture: it felt too distant, too much like somebody else's narrative. (de Block and Buckingham 2007, p. 162)

This idea of complicated reception and disconnection is important, even though the project videos in both schools, which feature later, were made within an apparently shared space and shared culture. In spite of the problems raised by the project, the authors found in the "participatory media work" that there were "possibilities...less easily available using other methods" and that such activities could

> begin to equalise the power relationships between us and permit young people to represent themselves in their own terms. (Ibid., p. 176)

The act of storying, or taking control of a self-narrative, is further theorized in relation to contemporary notions of identity by a number of writers concerned with power relations in self-representation (Finnegan 1997; Kearney 2003). In the case of all the learners, whether younger or older, this is negotiated within a number of defining parameters, including their position in the curriculum and their social position in the class or group.

There is a growing interest in the ways in which learners use storying as an active method of constructing their identity, not merely representing it. Hall, Bruner, and others are quoted in this regard in "Consumption and Everyday Life" (Mackay 1997). The latter, in particular, sees autobiography as an active, constructive process and there are other examples of writing about self-representation in this constructive mode, making the self with each retelling of the self (Bruner 1987; Kearney 2003).

For the "cyberkids," about whom Holloway and Valentine (2002) write, negotiating their use of the spaces from the physical, embodied use of the computer in the home through to the spaces on the Internet involves repeated engagement with the concept of identity. At the same time, they are in tension with adult perceptions of childhood, which seek to both romanticize it and then direct and control processes in areas that they perceive to be potentially harmful. In their research, Holloway and Valentine found that nowhere is this truer than in the area of new technology. Adults in their study often direct children toward activities in new media that are academic and "improving" in nature, using online encyclopedias or focusing on reference material, which helps them, on one level, to understand their place in the world. Production, interaction, and play are seen as essentially lower-level activities. Increasingly, of course, both adults and children are at play in the worlds of identity online and many of them are using video and images to represent versions of themselves in online spaces (Garfield 2006).

Other writers who have researched ICT, digital media, and identity include Chris Abbott and Julian Sefton-Green who, along with Rebecca Sinker, have proposed that evaluating children's creative output in new media requires a new language in order for it to be fully appraised and understood (Abbott 2001; Sefton-Green 2000b; Sinker 2000). This is a concern I share that led to some of the formulations outlined later in the book.

Several studies have noted that DV production occupies the space between formal and the informal settings of education and even between these worlds and the home (de Block et al. 2004; Sefton-Green and Sinker 2000; Schuck and Kearney 2004b). The difficulty emerges when these worlds share some sort of space with the formal legal elements of both the taught curriculum and the informal curriculum and there is a genuine tension here. Some writers characterize this as a clash of cultures, of school cultures with home or popular cultures and move the debate toward a definition of popular literacies and how these may be brought usefully within the school setting across the boundary described earlier (Haas Dyson 2006). This is not so easily managed in the handling of sensitive issues around autobiography and children's own cultural capital and interests, as we will see.

Emergent Themes

Summarizing the sections above, we find several emergent themes. The first of these is the need for more research that examines the place in the curriculum of DV production that is cognizant of the structures and changes in educational settings and recognizes its place in the life of those moving between outside and inside school cultures. Almost all the project reports called for some sustained, longitudinal engagement with moving-image production particularly in how this related to questions of identity. Where this had been useful in the research described in the "Production as Research," the following section described locating self-representational work as a useful starting point combined with some appropriate analytical tools.

The section on "Digital Video, Technology, and Pedagogy," identified ways in which DV production had been aligned with technological change when it was introduced into primary schools, particularly in relation to creative practices and pedagogy. The emergent theme here was the lack of an easy match between the frame of reference provided by subjects in the curriculum, such as ICT, and that provided by a media and cultural inflected frame.

The final section, "Storying, Identity and Roles in Production," considered the social worlds and political purposes of DV production in some relevant research. Against the backdrop of increasing access to moving-image production, this book aims to explore younger learners' self-representational practices and organizing principles in DV production. Gathering some of these emergent themes together helps identify some of the gaps and opportunities for work in the field in future.

First, much of what the production process means for the learners themselves in the primary years goes into the margins of the various studies when other concerns come into focus, such as curriculum innovation or technological change. One of these largely unreported aspects is the reflective response of pupils in terms of organizing practices and principles in production. In other words, what aesthetic and affective judgments of their own work do pupils make relating to their own critical experiences of media texts and what does this reveal about their knowledge of organizing systems in video production, or indeed wider conceptions of literacy?

Second, an area touched on but not explored fully for younger learners in the wider literature, is an account of the spaces, social worlds, and circumstances in which DV productions arise, based on a detailed understanding of the setting. As a consequence, one aim for this book and for the work featured in later chapters is an account of the part played by memory and association in choices of location, music, and performance. How were these aspects organized in production in such a way that they represented the social worlds and identities of the performers and producers at specific moments in time? What are the reasons behind the choices of multimodal assets in particular moving-image compositions and how do they contribute to making the meanings that the children wish to convey?

Third, given that the tools of moving-image production are becoming ubiquitous in many children's lives inside and outside formal settings, and that so much of the available literature in the field focuses on older students, more needs to be done to understand the place of production in the earlier years of education. What do younger learners know already and what do they need to know about the language of the moving image? What is the innate, but unrefined, nature of their media literacy as revealed in composition and where this might be taken in the future? Finally, what kinds of existing theory might be useful in getting underway with these questions and how may it usefully be repositioned?

In the following sections, I will present the background to the videos made by the young learners in the project schools, how it took place, and in what context.

The Schools in the Project and the Brief

Two primary schools were chosen as sites for the short-form videos, which the children would make. In the first school, the video production was linked to ongoing work about moving from primary to secondary school. The videos that they were going to make could represent the children at that moment of transition and communicate aspects of their life to their peers, parents, carers, and, potentially, their new schools. In the second school, the project was linked to work with children with special educational needs who were withdrawn from the mainstream for an afternoon a week, mainly for behavioral reasons. Their project, in a similar way to the first school, was centered on how they could communicate aspects of their life to the wider school community, their parents, and carers using a short-video piece.

Children used small handheld cameras and downloaded the footage for editing into a simple software title for editing, which provided the children with a user-friendly interface, allowing them to manipulate the ordering of individual clips, the transition between the clips, the use of sound (including the importing of music from home), and titling (including the use of visual effects and rollovers).

Technical instruction for shooting was limited to a brief introduction to the camera during the filming stages and the connection to the laptops for the editing stages. The editing was also introduced in a brief session and backed up with support sessions at particular moments around adding sound and transitions using a projector and screen arrangement. In both schools, children were given materials in the form of planners, which incorporated a version of a storyboard, a to-do list, and a shooting log. The emphasis was on the "unmarked" nature of the logbooks (the children were not to be subject to corrections of any kind on their work), the personal ownership by the children, and the fact that they could take them home. The message here was the partnership between the formal and informal settings and the location of the work outside their normal curriculum activity.

School A was a mixed gender, nondenominational community primary school with 470 children on roll, situated in an area of South East London with a very wide range of social and economic backgrounds. The children who worked on the videos here were aged 10 and 11 and were in the final weeks of the final year of primary school and just about to move on to secondary schools. There were 28 in the class and they produced ten short video pieces in mixed friendship groups, numbering between 2 and 4 people. The time of year, the summer term, was chosen to ensure maximum, off-timetable, freedom to complete their productions in school time. The children had just completed their final SATS (Standardised Assessment Tasks and Tests) and were beginning to do some activities usually associated with the end of the school year: a school journey, cycling proficiency test, and a leavers' show. The video project fitted in alongside this set of activities and allowed a degree of freedom from constraint for both themselves and their teacher. The timescale in the study was, however, relatively short in these circumstances and the pace was fast. Only 12 days spread through second half of the summer term were available.

School B had many similarities to school A. It was a also a mixed gender, nondenominational community primary school with 430 children on roll, situated in an area of not only mixed social housing but also close to a very expensive area. The children in school B were members of a nurture group, a Friday afternoon off-timetable activity for children with certain special educational needs. Within the system in place at the time in England, these children were recorded as being at "school action" level (see DFES 2001, section 5:43). That is, interventions were designed within the framework of the school, funded by the school, and provided by the school. A specially trained learning support assistant worked on Fridays with them on issues to do with their relationships with other children. The 12 children, drawn from throughout the key stage 2 age range (aged from 8 to 11 years) had difficulties in dealing with the formal activities in the curriculum at the school. They were unable to take full part in the daily subjects of literacy and numeracy in the morning and science and arts activities in the afternoon. They behaved in a disruptive manner or in a mute, withdrawn manner. As a result, many of them were often in trouble, excluded from activities and generally marginalized within the school community. The video project here was designed with a flexible framework, as in school A, allowing a degree of authorial freedom as an indicator for successful pedagogical design and one in which the rhetorics of "learner voice" and "creativity with new technology" could be used as touchstones for analysis (among others previously described).

In school A, the brief given to the children was to make a video about their time at the school in any form they felt to be appropriate. In school B, children were encouraged to make a video that could stand for them and tell someone at a distance something about their lives. In both schools, the video could consist of a series of sketches, interviews with former teachers, interviews with friends or younger children, drama activities, dances, or talking about site-specific scenes around the school.

A time limit of around 3–5 minutes for each video production in both schools was given, although the children frequently pleaded for more time. They were motivated by working without major constraints on the content of their productions but were, at the same time, very aware of the need to remain focused and organized in their learning about and working with media production. As a result, they were asked to plan their videos in the form of a mind map on A3 paper, recording as much of what they thought they knew along with what they had to do to make the project succeed. These were used as the starting point for their efforts and information was then transferred to a form of storyboard (although deviations from the plan and improvisation were expected to play a large part as well).

During the day, in each school the working method was to meet regularly as a group and consider where they were up to in their videos. The electronic whiteboard was used to display work in progress, to share opinions and to suggest ways forward for each other. For a variety of reasons to do with local geography and the proximity to several county boundaries, children in both schools had friendships they would be losing since they would be leaving to go to several different secondary schools. In school A, given the fact that it was the last time that these children were going to work together on a project, an additional authentic imperative of celebrating and commemorating time, place, friendship, and identity was formed. For school B, the imperative was similar but quite complex because of the nature of being a mixed age group. From the ten completed videos produced in school A, I chose four examples for further analysis, and from school B, there were two from among the four that were finished—mainly because with these videos I had the most complete trail from paper planning through to final version and postproduction interview, of which more is discussed below.

Toward a Framework for Analyzing the Videos

For a comprehensive and meaningful analysis of the videos themselves, theoretical frameworks were required, which took account of them as literacy events, as outlined in the two chapters preceding this one. This required a way of looking at how the many modes of speech, image, gesture, sound, and visual narrative were combined and to what effect. The starting point for a method for looking at these videos was that of "multimodal communication" as articulated in the work of Gunther Kress and Theo Van Leeuwen and as reinterpreted by Andrew Burn and David Parker in relation to media texts (Burn and Parker 2003a; Kress and Van Leeuwen 2001). From this perspective, the act of making meaning in video arises from how the writer-performer-editors combine text, speech, music, image, and gesture. If we analyze the choices of different modes in the videos and the relationship between them, it may be possible to achieve an understanding of how and why self-authors make use of the available resources to make meaning.

Multimodality formed the core of the analysis and I drew up a grid to annotate and capture the different modes and resources employed for making meaning in the videos. However, I decided to record some additional elements that are not always present in formal multimodal analysis. Critics point out that in its purest form it does not, in itself, enable an account to be made of other key cultural and social elements. Leander and Frank, for example, writing in the context of online presentation of youth identity, point out two ways in which purely multimodal analysis does not allow the whole picture of aesthetic production to emerge:

> First, in striving to posit an expansion of media resources in new media practices, the multimodal perspective elides important differences between types of medium. Linguistic, visual, audio, gestural, spatial, and multimodal resources are grouped together as "resources" for meaning making and for rethinking pedagogy, rather than adequately distinguished as involving distinct social practices (New London Group, 1996)…secondly…multimodal perspectives often place much more emphasis upon meaning-making than on affective or aesthetic attachment. The relations of persons to texts are strategic and rational, involved in "design" and "work," including the "design" of "social futures" (New London Baugh and Lloyd 2007) rather than embodied, sensual, and involved in personal attachments and cultural affiliation. (Sefton-Green 1998, pp. 185–186)

It was clear that for youth production and performance in digital media, as Leander and Frank put it, "affective or aesthetic attachment" (ibid.) was important. Different frames were needed to look at those concepts alongside the modes and how they made meaning together. These frames were also required to look at the different social practices emerging around new media (as previously discussed in relation to Lievrouw and Livingstone's definition above about changed practices and arrangements around new cultural artifacts).

I constructed a long form table to annotate the sequences in between editorial cuts that not only took account of how the modes worked together but also attempted to convey the relation of the parts to the whole as well as to other aesthetic factors. These were the elements included in the long form of the analysis:

Scene: This was where the number and timing of each scene was logged.

Scene description: Some simple narrative was provided here that gave a basic overview of the scene.

Genre/direct media reference: This allowed the media elements, direct quotations, or nonspecific genre parodies/appropriation to be identified and contribute to intertextual analysis.

Element within video: This allowed for elements within the overall organizing system of the video to be identified.

Camera/technical: This category was used to describe particular issues that arose in the shooting of the scene, identifying shot types or technical difficulties.

Action/gesture: Particular forms of gesture that accompanied the speech, sound, and shot types were described under this category, including performance movements of particular kinds (elaborate or encircling movements, "street" gestures conveying particular sorts of cultural significance, anything that changed or underlined overall meaning in relation to the other modes).

Speech/sound: This was used to record all sound, diegetic and nondiegetic, including transcriptions of all speech in the productions.

Style/identity/ways of being: This was used as a way of recording performance and embodied meanings within the production, referring to what the performance revealed about the "habitus," the way of being within the setting (after Bourdieu 1986, p. 170). This became "memories/references" in the shorter version of the grid and provided the additional elements needed.

Transition to the next scene: In this section, any relevant transitions were noted, particularly in respect of what this revealed about competence or otherwise with the software. I also created a short-form analysis that provided a single thumbnail per scene and a shorthand description as a snapshot of each video production. These shorter descriptions, as will be seen later, were aligned in the shorter grids with the following headings:

Scene and timing
Scene description
Element within video production
Memories, references
Genre / direct media references
Camera work / technical
Sound

Interviewing the Makers of the Videos

Having collected the paper trail of the children's storyboards and planning logs, observed the filmmaking, and used an adapted form of multimodal analysis on the videos they made, the remaining work to be done, which might conceivably prove useful in working with these videos, was to talk to the children themselves.

The design of the postproduction interviews was based on the principle of the semistructured interview, which followed a small set of defined areas through which the conversation could move. Each of these was accompanied with a set of *possible* conversation prompts and was designed around a set of themes that asked for immediate reflection on the process in relation to as many of the theoretical frameworks as possible. I used questions with the major themes of literacy, identity, and pedagogical design in mind, centering on production issues, grouping, and the technology. The areas covered and sample starter questions in the semistructured interview are shown in table 4.1 in block capitals and italics, respectively, though conversation ranged far and wide in the event.

Table 4.1 Interview questions for filmmakers

Area of question	Link with frameworks
AUTHENTICITY FOR THE CHILDREN / PERSONAL ENJOYMENT *Sample opening questions: Have you enjoyed the video project? What has been the best thing about it?*	All, but especially the following: Identity and storying Play, mediated action and provisionality
COLLABORATION / WORKING METHODS *Sample opening questions: Have you enjoyed working with other people on it? With whom and why? Were their any difficulties about things, like sharing decision making, etc.?*	• Storying • Learner voice in production
PLANNING / WIDER MEDIA INFLUENCE / CULTURAL AUTHENTICITY *Sample opening questions: Going right back to the beginning and the planning of it, did you find that it was useful to think everything through first? How did you plan it? Did you stick to your plan? What happened when you started using the camera? Did you find yourself thinking about any TV shows or films for your ideas? Which ones do you think influenced you most?*	• Media literacy • Changing conceptions of literacy • Intertextuality • New media and curatorship

I also decided to record the interview on video with the help of two people who were outside of the project so that the "researcher effect" might be diminished and children would not always seek to give the answers they thought might be required. The interviewers in both schools were to sit out of sight, behind the camera, and to record, from one side, the responses of the children. This was set up to give the opportunity for analyzing responses that were inclusive of more than just the mode of speech (see Auchard 2007, esp. pp. 10–13). The video interviews functioned as multimodal texts themselves with further useful possibilities for triangulation of any assertions and findings, watching how the children maintained their roles even in postproduction.

This chapter has outlined the ways I went about examining the videos made by children. In the one that follows, I will describe the kinds of short-form videos made by children and will look in more detail at two of the productions from one of the schools.

CHAPTER 5

Video and Performance

In school A, the children produced ten videos. They ranged from playful but incoherent excursions around the space of the school through to comedic, carefully edited parodies and, in one case, a quiet and reflective piece about time spent in the place and a deep friendship. All of them placed original footage alongside quotations and appropriation from favorite media, some of it on the sound track, some acted out for the camera. Improvisation and performance in the spaces of the school became hallmarks. Each video was a montage of modes and clips intended for reading by their classmates and families, markers of time spent in the school in different friendship groups or, in a couple of cases, as an isolated person.

"Right, let's get on with the show" and "This is where we used to sit," made by two boys and two girls, respectively, offered a really interesting and contrasting approach to the task, and they generated a huge amount of useful data that was captured using the approach described previously. I intend to discuss these in more detail in the subsequent sections. For now, as an instance of the range on offer and a snapshot on the varied groupings of the children, here is a list of the eight other productions:

"Do not try this at home" was a collection of parodies, walks around the school, and interviews with teachers and with children. A group of four girls, high achievers in the class, who approached the production with a clipboard, detailed notes, and shooting schedules, made it. There was a degree of improvisation and play involved throughout and mildly transgressive behavior, hurtling up and down the school hall on mats.

"Me and him are close," made by a mixed group of girls and boys was a similar collage of faces and names, including a long sequence during which each child in the leavers' classes was named alongside a spoken, off-the-cuff, biographical sketch. A favorite teacher was pursued round the school paparazzi style looking for an interview.

"In the ball pool," made by four boys, was a chaotic journey through places in the school, which featured rooms and favorite spaces, which were normally out-of-bounds. The project gave them license to roam with the camera into the "ball pond," a sensory area for children with special educational needs. Once they were in there, a great deal of playful anarchy ensued.

"Dance with me," made by a mixed group of boys and girls visited many of the outdoor areas of the school including an exercise trail. There was a great deal of movement of the camera, some handheld interview shots with very much younger children, recalling time spent in the spaces lower down the school.

"My walk around the school," made by one girl who started the project late, did not join a group and realized her own production was a single viewpoint representation of play in the spaces of the school and, as with "Me and him are close," featured an extended chase of an adult around the school looking for an interview.

"On their bikes" was another solo production, also by a boy who started the project late, after the groups had formed and similar in style and feel to the one above, though less idiosyncratic. It featured clips of the "ball pool" once again (see above), alongside shots of children completing their cycling tests (hence, "on their bikes"). Once again, it was important to capture and interview a favorite adult.

"The two of us," made by two of the boys was a record of friendship, which had some technical difficulty over the sound in the beginning featuring the two protagonists running across the backfield at the school. It went on to show a series of pratfalls and practical jokes with a continuous R. Kelly sound track playing.

"Walking in to the school" was made by four of the boys and featured the only shots that included the world outside as they approach and enter the gates. Once again, R. Kelly provided the sound track to the excursions around the "ball pool" and some interviews with each other that were parodies of documentary filmmaking.

In school B, the videos contained some similarities to those productions with four short films capturing and cataloging the spaces of the school and the experiences of the children therein, particularly with respect to their behavioral needs. Some more direct media parodies were in evidence in these productions possibly as easy well-known touchstones, which brought the different age groups in some of the videos together. They remained firmly under the control and within the world of the children and there were very few interviews with adults in the setting. In this school, all the children were in mixed groups.

"DJL" contained scenes of walking round the school in role as reporters, getting caught up in fictional film happenings, including some play fighting on "world book day," and some editing that allowed each child to have their favorite music as a cultural marker on the sound track.

"The Last Touch," featured explorations of the playground and some sophisticated sound mixing, with both nondiegetic and diegetic sound used.

"Our Amazing Clip," featured original sound track music played by one of the boys on the harmonica, complete with clips from favorite pieces, brought into the mix by the children alongside a long sequence in which one of the girls interviewed her classmates and teacher as a record before she left (this, of all the productions in school B, most closely resembled school A's work).

Finally, "Morning news" parodied both a school news broadcast and a dance routine in the school hall and included a joke wedding at the end.

Across both schools, there were both anchored and transient affiliations and representations, successes and failures in terms of coherence and even overall enjoyment (or not) of the process. None of it was unproblematic. But all the work, across both schools, yielded fascinating videos with much to think about in the light of the theories and methods discussed in the previous chapters.

In the following sections, I would like to offer a detailed description of two of the videos made by the children in school A. They offer interesting and contrasting approaches to the task but help to draw out the underlying choices and modes in production, which recurred throughout all of the videos listed above.

"Right Let's Get on with the Show"

In school A, two boys in the class made a video that was exceptional in terms of its impact and lasting impression on the children, other adults, and the many students who have encountered it. Their production is a collage of fragments of parody and media reference, combined with allusions to memory. Constructed from the planning, as will be seen, it was realized as a response to the task in which the boys took ownership of the project entirely. There was no interference or input from adults during its creation.

Keiron and Raymond formed a close partnership within the class group. They were not the quietest children in the class but they were by no means the noisiest or most challenging in terms of behavior. Their friendship was a mutual support system based as much on in-jokes and references to wider popular culture as it was on shared memory and shared locative experience. As will be seen in the following section, they approached the self-representational task and produced a video that not only drew on aspects of memory but, more than that, on shared cultural reference points, repurposing, and reworking media references through parody and direct appropriation. In this, they reflected their roles within the group as "class comedians" (as reported by the class teacher and head teacher at the school and confirmed by personal knowledge of the class).

Scene by Scene through Raymond and Keiron's Video

Raymond and Keiron's video drew on a wide range of reference points that dipped freely into and out of popular media culture (The *Matrix* movie, the *Johnny Vaughan* TV show, the music of the White Stripes, and so on) as well as to reference points from their own past (a previous school assembly, their role in the class as comedians, and so on).

Scene 1: "That's a Lovely Porsche Boxster" 00:00:00–00:14:14
As described in chapter 1, in the opening shot, and seen in figure 5.1, Keiron is some distance away from the camera but apparently sitting in the driving seat of a car and being questioned about it, where he got it from and how

Figure 5.1 Opening shot of Raymond and Keiron's video.

much he paid for it. From behind the camera, Raymond asks him for the details, gets an answer, moves the car, and it is revealed as a toy being held up to the camera. The dialogue, as seen in chapter 1, runs as follows:

"Oh hello Keiron."
"Oh hello Raymond."
"That's a lovely Porsche Boxster."
"Beautiful innit? Beautiful!"
"Er...how much was it?"
"About three quid."
"Where'd you get it from?"
"Round the sweet shop. It's a fakey."
"Nooooooooooooo!"

The opening 14 seconds establish the tone and structure of the whole production. It is a striking and funny scene that announces the main themes of the text. It makes explicit the idea that Raymond and Keiron are going to be performing fully in their socially constructed role as class comedians. It is clear from the opening shot that they wish to manipulate the medium in such a way that they are represented "in role," using their last opportunity to make a statement about their time at the school.

As revealed later in an interview with the two boys, the foreshortening joke comes from the popular TV show "You've Been Framed," which features accidents, jokes, and stunts recorded by members of the public. In fact, so certain were they that this joke would work, they planned to use this technique again at a later stage in the video (see below in scenes 5a and 5b).

By the close of the opening scene, we have information about the order of discourses within which meaning will be made. The audience knows that Raymond and Keiron will be playing themselves as the class knows them, driving the project forward with pace and with humor. They also know that they will use models drawn from media culture (the foreshortening joke as well as the satirical take on the interview to camera). At the same time, the roles of the two protagonists in relation to each other have been delineated. Keiron is in shot but some distance away. Raymond is behind the camera but his voice is louder. The fact that he is not in shot is compensated for by the status conferred on him as interviewer and director and announced by the louder voice. These roles, as will be seen, were to be reversed in the fifth scene of the project.

Scene 2: "Mama Took Those Batteries"—0:00:14:15–0:00:45:05
The second scene sees the boys positioned side by side in the center of the shot in front of a mural at the school. This scene operates at many different

levels and in many different modes, related to the discourses within which they occur. Gunther Kress and Theo Van Leeuwen define discourse, in a similar way to Fairclough (discussed earlier in ch. 3), as "socially constructed knowledge of (some aspect of) reality" (2001, p. 4). The discourses in this scene are rooted specifically in the shared knowledge and cultural experience of Raymond and Keiron's class inside and outside school. Not only do they tap into the shared experience of past events in the school but also they cast the net of references into the shared cultural experience of an episode of the Simpsons. Both are significant to members of the immediate audience for the piece, and both are interwoven to produce the meaning required for this particular project.

First, in terms of reference to the shared cultural history of the class, in an earlier year group, year 4, Raymond and Keiron had performed a song together, which remained part of the folklore of the class. It was well known as a shared memory and occurred in the earliest draft of their linear plan for inclusion in the video (see the fourth frame in the storyboard in the section above). The choice of situation, in front of a mural painted by the class in an earlier year was also a signifier recalling times gone by.

In terms of shared experience of media culture, the song also happened to be their own version of a blues song composed in "the Simpsons" by Bart Simpson in which he protested at his mother, Marge, removing his computer game batteries. This became "Mama took those batteries" instead of "Marge took those batteries." In this class, as in many others, the Simpsons were something of a touchstone and much of the children's play referred to episodes from the series.

This easy manipulation of reference points from their own past and their own media experiences was typical of their piece and added a further layer of structural complexity. They knew that their audience would be able to recognize both in what they had done. They were in a video in year 6, in front of a mural they had painted in year 2, and performing a song they had performed in year 4. In a few seconds of screen time, four years of their primary school life were represented.

There is a further mode to consider that helped to define the position of the boys in relation to class members. Not only were they two of the acknowledged comedians in the class, they also had their own musical choices to make. The musical form chosen by the boys for their song in the video—and in year 4—was the 12-bar blues, complete with a mimed harmonica part. This chimed in with their choice of music for the sound track and was a powerful indicator of their individuality. This form of music was, perhaps, also considered by the boys as being somehow adult, or semi-adult, in nature and, as well as demarcating them from the remainder of the class, suggested an "otherness" in terms of style and outlook. Raymond and Keiron's musical choices at this point and elsewhere reflected their "otherness" both in approach and in choice of sound track. "Mama took those batteries" was the first white pop blues on the sound track and it was to be followed later by borrowings from CDs by the "Red Hot Chilli Peppers" and "the White Stripes."

Scene 3: "This Brings Back a Lot of Memories"—0:00:45:06–0:00:52:00
A scene that lasts seven seconds follows the blues song. Up to this point, Raymond and Keiron had signaled that they were going to play with the format, that they were going to use it to express cultural differences and create resonances with shared discourses within the class. In this very short segment, they show that they are also capable of gently mocking the whole process of the video itself. They sit by the mural in a window seat. Both boys, but with Raymond dominant on the sound track, put on the voice of an elderly person saying, "This brings back a lot of memories." This bridging sequence is significant with both of them in shot and both of them clearly in control. They seek to bridge the gap between themselves and the overarching purpose of the video piece. By mocking the whole process of making memories in this way, on camera, they assert their control of the whole authoring process. They further indicate their participation in, yet separateness from, the rest of the class.

Scene 4: Breaking the Window—0:00:52:01–0:00:58:21
This scene shows both boys playing football in the middle foreground and appearing to break a window. Raymond, with his back to the camera, passes the ball to Keiron who kicks it out of the shot and to the right. The sound of the breaking glass was added from the software library. Both the boys then run away.

This episode has several reference points. The preferred activity of all the boys and many of the girls in the class was playing football in the area shown. Placing themselves in that place at the heart of the video underlines their place in that class at that particular moment. However, they are operating within their own previously announced constructed roles of class comedians. The visual gag that they represent is the breaking of the glass out of camera shot. It recalls a kind of humor that belongs in an earlier era, from "the Beano" or other popular but anachronistic comic reference points, a little like their preference for older musical forms.

The measurement of the breaking glass onto precisely the right point on the sound track raises the question of how the possibilities of the technology might have directed and affected the outcome. Both boys are taking part in a project that has allowed an editing suite to be created in their classroom. The normal curriculum is suspended and they can spend time working on their finished video. They know that there are possibilities within the software that will allow them to generate events "after the event." This is what they have done in "breaking the glass." We can see from the first minute that the two boys are able to control and assemble their work in a variety of styles in a range of modalities.

Scene 5a and 5b: Show Off—The Gorilla Fight—0:00:58:22–0:01:18:00
In this scene, Raymond fights with a toy gorilla and the foreshortening joke is revisited. Keiron holds a toy gorilla in front of the camera in the foreground of the shot. Raymond stands at the back of the hall appearing to be hit by the gorilla and hitting it back. Effects were added live (Keiron's fighting noises into the camera microphone) and afterward (a sharp blow, added from the software library, again the boys realizing their decisions by looking in the library of possibilities within the software).

For this sequence, as noted above, the roles are reversed. There is an interesting counterpoint to the allocation of roles in the opening scene. Keiron is behind the camera and Raymond is in front of it. Keiron gets to make the comment in the final section of the scene. He reveals the joke by throwing the gorilla the length of the hall and calling out "Show off!" to Raymond who makes a comedy fall.

Scene 6: Basketball, Break Dancing, and Hall Sequence with Sound track 0:01:18:01–0:01:31:00
The opening of this scene provides a graphical match with Keiron spinning on his back directly from the fade out of Raymond spinning on his back in the previous scene.

This scene, taken directly from the planning, incorporates break dancing and basketball moves. Many of the videos, particularly from the boys, featured these cultural reference points, alongside football and R. Carey. However, the choice of the music was, again, distinct, drawing not from the expected tradition (hip hop, rap, etc.) but from the boys' preferred musical form—the white pop blues—as espoused by the Red Hot Chilli Peppers (see the note of this in the original planning in fig. 3.1—the music being shown as RHCP).

Scene 7: Johnny Vaughan Show 0:01:31:01–0:02:19:00
A long "Johnny Vaughan" interview follows with Raymond slipping between a straightforward impersonation and a variety of accents. The whole scene is ad-libbed between the two performers (both commenting, "I didn't know

you was going to do that" in interviews afterward). This scene is also notable in the light of comments later in the interviews about how the camera "gives you ideas." At one point, the camera adopts the persona of Donald Duck and nods at the interviewer. In this case, the camera appears to be a character in the video itself. It is almost as though it was interjecting itself into the process, freeing the boys to improvise within the overall construction (see reflections on the interview with the boys in the following section below).

During this scene, Raymond and Keiron maintained their place in the discourses established in the previous settings and discussed above (summarized perhaps as media-aware class comedians). The range of accents used by Raymond, slipping from a South London accent into a kind of Irish accent, draws on the seamless shifting of roles in playground discourse. It also references presenters who slip between roles in popular television programs, featuring, for example, impressionists such as Alistair McGowan (featured at the time in the UK on BBC TV). Raymond attacking the camera who he says is "blanking" him explores their role in the social discourse of the class in the closing of this scene. Sometimes disputes are solved in this way in the playground and this reference point was particularly strong with the audience of the boys' peers.

Scene 8: White Stripes Video: The Matrix, Titles, Glimpses of Classmates 0:02:19:01–0:02:53:00

This scene adopts a different form, that of the music video (employing the more fashionable blues of "The White Stripes: 7 Nation Army"). Small segments of clips filmed around the classroom and school appear with the action sound tracked throughout. This is the first time that the boys choose to write on screen, naming some of their classmates and the class teacher.

This is also significant as the this is the first time they appear as "themselves." They are on the sound track, captured on the camera microphone in a separate sound file cheering and celebrating Keiron's version of the *Matrix*. In this most extreme reference to popular culture (mimicking the special effects from the *Matrix* at a fraction of the cost, by Keiron running up a wall), they choose to present themselves to the audience as knowing auteurs. They emphasize their "otherness" again accompanied by the music of the White Stripes.

Scene 9: This Brings Back a Lot of Memories: Outtake Sequence 0:02:53:01–0:03:01:00

Raymond and Keiron made virtually no mistakes in any takes. Yet, they were anxious to honor the tradition of the outtake, which is often added to the ends of videos and tacked onto DVDs. At this level, they were at one with the discourse of popular culture. They filmed a number of different versions of this scene but decided to incorporate Keiron getting the voicing of the line "wrong" when he says, "This brings back a lot of memories." This recalls the third scene above and recapitulates all of the previously discussed elements, particularly the "otherness" the boys feel. They proceed to play fight on camera and there is a fade to the end title sequence.

Scene 10: Can't Stop—End Title Sequence 0:03:01:01–0:03:35:00
This scene references the ending of the film *Dumb and Dumber* where the two characters walk away from the camera, pushing each other as they go. They disappear out of shot and then reappear running back toward the camera with a few seconds from "Can't Stop" by the Red Hot Chilli Peppers playing. The titles run through almost the whole of this scene and thank the teacher and the project coordinator "for letting us do this." The concession to permission having been granted for the boys to play and experiment in an otherwise structured and prescribed setting is revealing and sets the video apart from the world of the normal classroom. The locus of control has shifted toward the learners, and they recognize that they have been given power and responsibility in their roles as writers and directors. As the introduction finishes and the first words of the song are sung, the video ends. This ending is placed right on "Can't stop" and is the last of a series of perfectly timed visual jokes. They stop, and the whole video ends, just as the lead vocal sings, "Can't stop".

The Paper Trail: Raymond and Keiron's Storyboard

In all the projects in the study, the teachers were pleased to see a written or drawn element and the children, given the plethora of worksheets and tests in schools, were also on familiar territory sitting in front of a sheet of paper that required them to fill in information. So, in one sense, the use of the storyboards and the logbooks played along with the prevalent classroom models and the need to devise tasks that enabled children to be writing and busy, a feature of paper-based tasks in media education, which has been noted elsewhere (Buckingham 2003).

As it happened, Raymond and Keiron produced a planning sheet that was detailed enough to allow them to be accurate in setting out their key scenes, in estimating their needs, and the time that would be taken in shooting them. However, the sheet did not represent a reductive and rigid model for their production that left no room for improvisation. The longest scene, the "Johnny Vaughn" sequence, took one of the boys by surprise and emerged spontaneously. This was revealed in interviews after the production.

Even so, an examination of the storyboard does reveal how the production as a whole was conceived as a finished piece, with all of the major comedic and parodic scenes in evidence. It is very different from others, as will be seen subsequently, in its detailed use of the timeline, paying specific attention to the music to be used. The boys were thinking from the beginning about the different resources and modalities in production available to them and their potential for realizing their vision of themselves at that particular moment in time.

Raymond and Keiron's storyboard, shown in figure 5.2, represented the most accurate of all the groups its relation to the finished outcome, with Katie and Aroti's a close second, as will be seen in the next section. A key element here is the awareness of form, and of the need to entertain as well as inform. The boys' production faces outward toward an audience expecting to be entertained by two boys who, as classroom jokers and defusers of situations would be expected to take the viewer through several media references and parodies.

The storyboard signals awareness of form with the first and last boxes indicating the need for titling. In between the opening and closing credits, the storyboard plans for the car scene, the memories sequence, the blues singing (which a viewer may assume to have been improvised but which

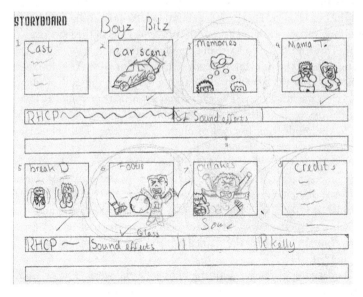

Figure 5.2 Raymond and Keiron's storyboard.

was included with some detailed and serious purpose exploring the multi-modal affordances of the medium), the break dancing, football and, finally, outtakes. The scenes that were added later fit with the overall intention, to provide entertainment, parody, and visual jokes. Thus, the foreshortening joke was added with the gorilla at the production stage. The scene with the chat show host was improvised and added afterward (a version of, at the time, TV presenter Johnny Vaughan). However, they stuck mostly to their storyboard using it as a working document that was important in shaping the production. The ticks under the pictures do not indicate a teacher intervening in the process. As noted previously, no adults marked the storyboards; they were considered to be working documents owned by the producers. The boys added the ticking when the various scenes were filmed and mirrored the onscreen software that produced ticks next to used thumbnails.

Aside from the drawings, the boys made use of the lines underneath the boxes to outline sounds they needed. "RHCP" on the top left stands for the American band the Red Hot Chili Peppers of whom the two boys were avid fans. More on the use of this particular musical form follows in later sections. At this stage, as can be seen under the final box, the boys also intended to use a song by R. Kelly, which was heavily quoted in other videos. They dropped that as an idea, preferring to use their own musical preferences as markers in particular ways (see below). The other sound identified under from the box labeled "Footie" was to be added from the audio library within the editing software itself. This was the breaking glass in the sequence where the boys pretend to kick a football through a window.

The style of the drawing is detailed and careful with the framing serving as an almost exact map for the framing used with the camera when the production was underway. The car is drawn with a rear spoiler as in a real Porsche Boxster. It is presented in the frame in a similar way to its appearance in the production (rotated through 180 degrees). The box is labeled "Car scene" as a marker (see fig. 5.3).

It wasn't until later viewing that the meaning of the frame labeled "Mama T" became apparent, as a reference to the song "Mama took those batteries away" (see discussion below). The framing in the storyboard is identical to the finished version with the boys' pretend harmonica playing and serious furrowing of their brows criterial to their acting the part of serious blues singers. Side by side with the frame from the movie, they appear as shown in figure 5.4.

The drawing of the scene (in fig. 5.5) with the word "Footie" above it escapes the frame and joins the text of the sound effect required—"Glass." The boys are joining the two modes in the planning, underlining, and

Figure 5.3   Car scene in the storyboard and in the video.

Figure 5.4   Mama T frame from storyboard and in video.

enjoying the effect that will be produced in advance. The expression on the face was not captured in the production but the effect was the same, that of a moment of chaos for which they would surely be in trouble. This picture most strongly echoes the overwhelming mood of the video and the misbehavior outlined within it, that of the kind of gentle anarchy in comics like the *Beano* (a long running children's weekly comic in the UK, published since 1938). You can also see clearly in figure 5.5 the tick which indicated that this scene had been filmed, using the boys' own meticulous record keeping system, which also mimicked how thumbnails were recorded in the software.

The outtakes were planned from the start because all movies were seen as having outtakes. This was at a time when a number of productions included them just before, or during, the end title sequence. The boys indicated on the planning sheet their intention to include these extras within their own video. The drawing shows a close-up on the two faces that was not actually achieved in the final shot. The boys clearly made use of it as a marker for

Figure 5.5   Breaking glass frame from storyboard.

Figure 5.6   "Outtakes" frame from storyboard and in the video.

their dispute, which actually involved Keiron trying to pull off Raymond's hat (see fig. 5.6).

An Interview with the Producer-Directors

The careful planning on paper, alongside the awareness of media production issues around the use of sound and framing, marked Raymond and Keiron out as media-savvy producers before they even used the camera or the editing software. This apparently innate ability with quotation and repurposing of popular media was explored in the interview afterward. The confidence in their ability carried over into the conversation with the researcher where the boys slipped in and out of the role as successful video directors, assuming the gestures and mannerisms of Oscar winners being interviewed by Jonathan Ross. They were acutely aware of the camera and that they were in fact still performing and played up to it accordingly. This was particularly true of Raymond while Keiron at least attempted to answer the questions with a degree of seriousness.

The boys sit side by side with the interviewer out of shot. As they settle themselves into the chairs and into the situation, Raymond looks straight at the camera and winks at it. Keiron, only too aware that this has happened, bites his lip and tries to keep a straight face. Throughout the interview, Raymond engages with the interviewer and Keiron half turns toward Raymond, willing and able to expand upon their feelings about the project and talk in the role of directors about their methods and inspirations, in particular their quotations and stolen ideas from popular media. As they sit down, they both signal their intentions, adopting American accents, and saying, "Well, alrighty then!" (borrowed from Jim Carrey's *Ace Ventura*). The mood of their video, irreverent, anarchic, and playful, continues into the interview.

As with all the productions, the opening questions in the schedule covered overall enjoyment and levels of satisfaction with the project as a whole. In answer to this, Raymond and Keiron both assert that it was hard work. Yes, they enjoyed it but stated, "I thought it was hard" (Keiron) and "I found it quite annoying" (Raymond). The engagement with the project was total from the two boys and it was not something they went into lightly, even though the lighthearted, anarchic, and comedic results belie this seriousness. The boys viewed video production as hard work, focusing, in particular, on the difficulties in editing the sound effects. Raymond uses gesture to underline this issue. "When you put in the sound effect (on the timeline) you have to put it right on the dot" (points with left hand to imaginary timeline in the air, miming fixing a sound clip to an exact location in the edit).

Asked whether any of the films or TV shows they knew had provided them with ideas they responded with a detailed answer about ideas borrowed from the "weird" section of *You've Been Framed* and from the BBC show *The Big Impression* (featuring impressionist Alistair McGowan) for a "Johnny Vaughan" interview sequence. There followed a number of film references, including describing how, because Keiron had learnt to walk up the side of the school, they should include a sequence emulating Keanu Reeves in the *Matrix*. Using the editing software, they paused him in midair to create a parodic reference to Neo's abilities in the film. Other direct quotations from movies included the walking away from the camera play fighting, borrowed from *Dumb and Dumber*, a further comedic marker of identity within the class.

When they were asked about the importance of planning, the boys acknowledged that this too was a key element ("Cos if you didn't plan it, it would come out...all rubbish"). They described the use of the storyboard sheets as being essential to the success of their production. This was not the case with very many of the other videos made.

One of the most significant sequences in the interview is when the boys are asked about the use of the camera once they had started filming and whether or not they made any changes to their plans. At this stage, they give the camera its own personality and refer to it as being like a third party involved in the production.

> *Keiron*: It (the camera) gives you ideas...in the end we had more ideas...
>
> *Raymond*: I don't know how you say it. It didn't like give us ideas like (*pause*) it talks to you...it gave us ideas like what you could do with it...
>
> *Keiron*: He changed his voice...I didn't even know you was going to do that...

The scene in question from their video is the interview sequence with Raymond performing as the interviewer in a range of accents, with the camera apparently personified as someone or something giving permission to improvise, as well as ideas for the direction of that improvisation. What seems to be important here is the notion that the activity itself became self-generating. Making the video helped to make the video. They confer agency on the camera in the exchange between themselves and the interviewer, and yet, what they employ in the production itself is their own agency, released from other, more usual classroom tasks, and subjects. As Keiron says near the beginning of the interview when discussing why the filming was the best part of the work, being active and mobile instead of passive and inert was the most important aspect: "Going round the school...instead of doing Maths and all that."

Play, improvisation, doing "fun stuff like the gorilla attacks" (Raymond), any kind of action seems to be key in their reflection on the process. They are not drawn into a discussion of their friendship so much as the activity around their friendship. For Keiron, it was natural to record some of the things he and Raymond had actually done together as real events "like in year 4 when we done the Mama took those batteries song." Nevertheless, it seems the two boys disagreed "most of the time" (Raymond) and a degree of creative tension appears to have been present all along ("He was bugging me all the time—I want this and I want that," Keiron). Again, the dynamic between the two of them in production, the batting of ideas backward and forward seems to have been important.

I will return to some to the significant elements in the Raymond and Keiron's video but for now would like to move on and contrast theirs with another of the videos from school A.

"This Is Where We Always Used to Sit"

Katie and Aroti were two other members of the class in School A, the first project school, who completed a video together. Their production, in common with all the "Children in Transition" project videos, was conceived as a commemorative piece for their time in primary school. Memories, interviews, and locations were central to the plan from the beginning. Both children were quiet within the class and occasionally troubled by events in the classroom and playground. They were regarded by their peers as a couple of "loners" without a range of relationships to draw on. As a result of this withdrawal over time from the rest of the class, the opportunity to represent themselves and their time at primary school on video was dominated by scenes and constructs that would enable them to underline their bond with each other as it had been formed over time within the class. As will be seen in the scene-by-scene descriptions that follow, it became a tour around sites of personal, mutual significance in the school alongside interviews with important adult influences, interspersed with memories.

Katie and Aroti chose to put themselves into the frame in a variety of locations, talking to camera, quietly and quickly, making an effort to record secret places around the school that were of special significance to them. Despite working in close proximity to the two boys, Raymond and Keiron, seen in the previous section, who were sophisticated quoters and manipulators of media, they both resisted the opportunity to use media-referenced humor or visual jokes. The tone of the video, far from the jokey and parodic nature of some of the others, was, for the most part, serious and restrained. It did not have many camera or editorial tricks and neither did it make use of musical quotation, except at the close when the credits were running and a song from the boy-band Blue is quoted.

Structures and Purposes

At first sight, their video seems artless and full of errors in sound recording and camerawork. Beside other productions in the class, it ranks in the middle of the range in terms of technical ability and on the day of screening, there was a degree of restlessness from those watching who wanted a more up-tempo and upbeat video to look at. The pace is slow and reflective; there are neither apparent major media quotations, nor attempts to play for laughs. The audio quality is frequently poor (which was also a problem for many other productions due to the lack of an external microphone). Nevertheless, the video production was a process and an activity that was seized on and engaged with fully by the two girls. It was felt by the girls themselves to be successful on their own terms and in their own way.

Closer investigation of the video and of some of the texts and artifacts around it, including Aroti's interview responses and some of the written plans for the production, reveal a more cohesive and subtle structure than is apparent at first viewing. Analyzed in this way and contextualized by knowledge of the girls within the class the video production is revealed as a purposeful attempt to meet the requirements of the original task concerned with identity and, in particular, to make something that relates their identity and their friendship to the environment of the school in both a temporal and a locative way.

The structure of the video is set out by Katie and Aroti in a series of ten mixed locative narratives, singly or gathered in groups, interspersed with four interviews, as follows:

- Location-based narrative 1 (together—playground)
- Musical section (which may not have been directed by the girls)

- Interview 1 (Ms. Carey)
- Location-based narratives 2 (together—first bench), 3 (together—second bench), 4 (Aroti—bridge), and 5 (Aroti—also on bridge)

- Interview 2 (Ms. Black)
- Location-based narrative 6 (Katie on chain swing on back field)

- Interviews 3a and 3b (Sabina with Aroti and Katie in turn)
- Location-based narratives 7 (Katie in the science area) and 8 (Aroti talking about playing Hopscotch)

- Interview 4
- Location-based narratives 9 (Under the shelter, by the mural) and 10 (together at the end, recording the names of the three different school halls)
- End titles

The only exceptions to this overarching structure of location-based narrative interspersed by interviews are during the musical section (which appears to have been adult directed) and the end titles—to which the discussion will return below.

There was no desire on the part of Aroti and Katie to attempt to follow other groups and subvert the structure or the subject matter with, for example, humorous interludes, parodies, and direct media references. The only point at which they deviated from this plan was in an animated sequence where the word "MUSIC" was spelled out on the whiteboard while they played a variety of instruments but even this break in the rhythm of their video was "serious" play with, as noted above, a strong adult-directed influence.

Aroti and Katie's authorial voices are heard in the cumulative effect of the recapitulation of the elements within the production. It has a songlike structure with the two modes, locative narrative, and interview, answering each other but taking forward the whole production. We hear in the interviews from four adults concerned with their care and education at four different phases of their time at the school (nursery, infant, junior, and present day). These are broken up by reflective, chorus-like narratives of locative memory and habitual behavior, which were, in themselves, places of comfort, enjoyment, and markers of identity in, occasionally, difficult times. Their production, supported by this structure, becomes, by design and organization of resources, a personal narrative of locations and emotions felt over time. Far from being haphazard, the elements are carefully placed and advance the story that the producers wish to tell.

Planning on Paper: Written and Drawn Artifacts

Speaking afterward, Aroti asserted that the planning, and in particular the storyboard, had been important to the overall success of the piece, even though in some respects the plan had not been stuck to. Initially, for example, there were 12 people to interview, yet the plan allowed them to see, written in front of them, the reasons why this could not be achieved in the time, and why they had to cut it down to 4.

Interviews with people in the school setting were highly salient in the storyboard (as can be seen in fig. 5.7). For the girls, there was a high level of importance ascribed to telling the story through teachers and other interviewees. The planning called for each of the figures to relate aspects of the girl's past at the school in each of the locations listed.

Each of the figures in the frames is drawn as seen by the children. The portraits of the girls themselves are shown virtually identical and interchangeable, arms rising or raised, long hair, big eyes, and smiling, with the same captions written inside the frames as can be seen in figure 5.7.

The four teachers are depicted in the storyboard in chronological order for the class teachers and end with the head teacher. The first, shown above

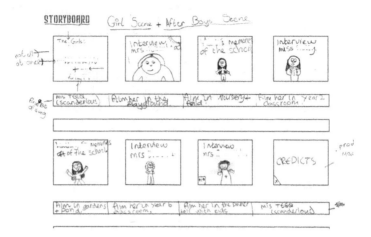

Figure 5.7 Storyboard for Katie and Aroti's video.

bottom left nursery teacher, is drawn full face, smiling under a sunny sky as she would have appeared to them as small children, the smile criterial in their selection of elements to represent her (cf. Kress 2004). The next, Ms. Carey, is drawn in the same form as for Aroti and Katie, big eyes, smiling, and same hair. This teacher, known for her empathy with the children, sense of humor, and for being "child-centered" is shown as more like a child than a teacher.

When she is interviewed, Mrs. Able is shown in a match to the design from the storyboard. When Ms. Carey is interviewed she is in a noisy classroom, much like the one that Aroti and Katie learned in during their early school life with Ms. Carey (two years at Key Stage One). The choices in production echo the circumstances in which they found themselves in those years. The style of interviewing is relaxed, open, and informal, reflecting both the memory of the class and the original production design.

By contrast, the other two teachers, the head teacher, and the year-6 teacher are depicted at distance in the storyboard, almost full figure and wearing stars as badges. The badge system as a reward for achievement is distinctive and a marker for authority and the more serious elements of schooling at Key Stage 2. Ms. Black and Ms. Roberts, although not pictured in an unkind light (they are both smiling), are viewed as a more typically *teacherly* part of Katie and Aroti's experience of school and therefore, distant from the children.

Asked later about changes to their plans, Aroti conceded that things changed as the filming took place. Ms. Roberts's interview was not included, for example. Others simply never took place. This was due partly to pressure of time and partly to the different things that occurred to them. As a result, Aroti recalls later, "We just made stuff up." The "stuff" that they "made up" is the other of the two twin cores of their production, the narratives of location carefully laid out between the interviews of teachers.

"Habitus" and Location

The focus on location is one of the two main elements that dominate the planning and execution of the video. The production opens with Aroti and Katie standing at the site of a recently removed tree, which had been there throughout their time at the school. When they speak, their voices are low, talking downward as they watch their balance on the logs. Their voices are partially drowned by wind noise on the camera microphone and partly by traffic from the road outside, visible in the shot through the railings. The dialogue in the opening is as follows:

> *Katie, lost, inaudible words*...places...erm...a big tree was here but then it got knocked down...it's also a really nice place...with big stepping stones (*moves off in circuit on the stepping stones around the perimeter and around Aroti*).
> *Aroti, realizing there is a gap and she should contribute, looks away, and her speech is drowned in the wind / traffic noise. But becomes audible again as she gestures round the circle with both arms*...and it's a circle. (See fig. 5.8)

Enclosing and encircling gestures and movement are used alongside the framing of the circle where the tree used to be to underline the togetherness of Aroti and Katie and to suggest their separation from the rest of the life of the playground. The choice of a recently removed fixture of school life in the opening scene is recapitulated in the penultimate scene.

The last scene with the girls in it, is a sequence where they move around the site and record the names and location of the school halls (see fig. 5.9). At the time the production was being filmed, major changes were being made to the school. Previously, and throughout their time at the school, the buildings were in three disconnected school halls. During the video production, building work had begun to join them together physically to make one complete structure. These building works feature in the background of many of the shots in nearly all the productions from School A. However, Aroti and Katie are the only two producers who make specific use

Figure 5.8   Aroti and Katie in the opening scene from their video.

Figure 5.9   Closing scene of Aroti and Katie's video.

and mention of the fabric of the building in this way. The production opens and closes with images of change and upheaval, which are salient in terms of the way in which they wish to represent themselves and the school before they too move on and change. The locative narratives mirror their own state of change, the imminent movement from one school to another, and the growing up it implies.

The visual construction of the shots not only emphasizes the changing landscape but it also emphasizes their embodied performance within it. The repeated form is the two-shot or the midshot in a specific location around the school. Couples, usually Aroti and Katie but sometimes one or other of them with an interview subject, dominate the shot list. The camerawork and staging emphasizes the two of them within the landscape, so, what is articulated in their composition is their representation of "two-ness" and their own interdependence, even symbiosis. There are almost no other shots of anyone else in the whole production and that is unique within the videos made for either project in this study. The mise-en-scène of the production is of a unit of two narrating or presenting to camera throughout.

The production visits many quiet areas of the school environment to capture places of importance to the girls. In an early scene, the girls employ a bench that Aroti describes as a place she would visit when "feeling sad or happy." This personal observation indicates a high degree of ownership of the video making process, seeing it as something during which they may take the viewer into confidence. It is also a significant way of expressing feeling in and about a specific school location, which is repeated as a motif (as noted above). The repetition of these key phrases suggests habitual or even ritualized behaviors.

The dialogue in the first scene at the first bench is as follows:

Katie: This is one of our favourite parts of the school because it is very…
(*Looks across at Aroti for an idea of what to say next…Aroti carries on and finishes the sentence*)
Aroti: …fun and it's got lots of wildlife…
Katie: It's very quiet. And this bench was given to us by Sylvia Thompson who was an old secretary of the school.
(*A pause follows while the donation plaque is focused on, broken by Aroti taking up the reason for the choice of location…*)
Aroti.: We always used to sit on this bench when we were sad or happy and we always felt better after a while…
(*Aroti looks across at Katie and raises her eyebrows, possibly indicating that Katie should add more, possibly that Katie should call the end of the scene.*)

At the next bench, the dialogue again underlines the use of the school environment as a record of past feelings and of ways of being in the world of the school, the girls' "habitus" (Bourdieu 1986). More than that, they come to be the principal ways in which actions and reactions are established by the subjects in the setting in which they find themselves. For the girls, their internalization of their performed "otherness," reliance on each other, and lack of connection with the rest of the world of the school is a key element of their production. They present themselves in this way as a representation of their learned ways of being at school.

These structures can be read using tools of visual semiotics; for example, this approach is useful in identifying framing devices such as the circles and the enclosed nature of the visual (within the system of "two-ness" identified above). However, this is not all that the medium affords the girls, in the same way as it is not the only analytical frame that can be applied to the work. Patterns of movement of gesture and of speech, recapitulated throughout the girls' production underline their desire to perform and record their way of being in the school. On a number of occasions, the girls gesture to each other or perform in some way within a closed system of their own making. As they label each of the school halls toward the end of the video, they frame the name of each hall between the two of them and gesture across the sign toward each other (see fig. 5.9).

When Aroti performs the hopscotch scene, she gestures back at Katie behind the camera with open arms (see fig. 5.10).

Finally, again toward the end, standing under the shelter near the open space at the back of the school, the open armed gesture returns with Aroti half turning toward Katie. The work of Merleau-Ponty may be important here in accounting for the performed aspect of living and being as it relates to places of learning (Engeström, Miettinen, and Punamäki 1999; Merleau-Ponty 1962); in particular, the idea that learning in an environment and a community is through embodied action and learned responsiveness to a given situation. The revelation of the layers of these meaning-making states in embodied performance is one of the distinctive features of moving-image work, seen throughout the productions made in this setting.

For the girls in this production, it becomes a matter of record that they place themselves in the various locations, using similar gestures and the same form of words over and over again in the same performance—locating themselves in places of importance in recalling and reperforming their habitualized experience of coping with living and being in the school community, as the following exchange illustrates:

> *Katie:* This is one of our favourite bits because...well, whenever I was upset Aroti used to take me to this bench and cheer me up always...

Figure 5.10 Aroti's gesture back to the camera.

Aroti: And...although this area is quite new...but we had lots of good
times and bad times here.

Katie: It's also very good and nice and shady for the summer...when it's
very, very hot.

The location affords them the opportunity to be together and to look after
each other in moments of stress and difficulty in other relationships at the
school. The "whenever" suggests that it was a regular occurrence, and further examples of this are outlined below. It is as important for Katie and
Aroti to record this aspect of their lived experience at the school as it is for
them to interview and remember key adults. This is because their interdependence is a highly salient feature of their life and times at school A.

The linguistic constructions, which the girls use, give a corollary to the
visual and gestural "two-ness" and recalled performance of being with each
other as outlined above. The passages below highlight words that suggest
this repetition and habitualized behavior, such as "whenever," "always,"
"used to," and so on, as italicized below:

Katie: This is one of our favourite bits because...well, *whenever* I was
upset Aroti *used to* take me to this bench and cheer me up always...

Aroti: And…although this area is quite new but *we had lots of good times and bad times here*

…

Katie: This is one of our favourite parts of the school because it is very…

Aroti: We always used to sit on this bench when we were sad or happy and we always felt better after a while.

As stated above, there are no recorded interviews or interactions with other pupils at any time in this video (other than a very brief transition after one of the interviews). The video is constructed as a way of recording repeated and habitualized behavior of school life at the same time as celebrating their shared experience and mutual dependence on each other. The cumulative effect is one of intense memory making through the locative narrative, which celebrates their friendship, even as it commemorates the spaces of the school.

One way of understanding the underlying motivation and purpose in this use of the medium is to see it as a version of the "hypomnemata." This concept, introduced in chapter 3, is derived by Michel Foucault from ancient Greece writings about a system for recording life events as material memory, as an externalizing process, which gave the writer a repository of the "self" on which to draw in times of stress or change (Foucault 1984).

This video has already been interpreted above as reflection of the girls' "habitus," employing memories of their performed, embodied experience, which not only their peers in the intended audience may be able to read, but it also has a purpose for the girls as a media equivalent of the hypomnemata, with notes and markers for themselves taken forward at a time of stress and change. The two girls, close friends for all their school life, will be going to different schools in a matter of weeks and this is their recorded response, a locative-narrative assembly of places and people, of responses and strategies for coping that they can take forward into their new life in the new school.

What becomes significant in this instance is the contribution of the material of the medium to the girls' performed and lived memories as inscribed on the tape. This is not to say that the medium is being employed simply as a diary record, in the same way as the hypomnemata itself was more than a diary. There are no specified dates and times in their production. The aspects of the past that are performed and recalled are actual reinterpretations of their earlier years at the school. They are reinterpreting the past and re-presenting it as a set of habitual and learned behaviors that defined their relationship and their way of being and living at the school, supporting them through difficult times. With their move to secondary school imminent, the digital inscription is used here as a reminder of how to live and how to survive transition by underlining embodied experience. For these girls, it is about withdrawing into quiet places, finding someone to empathize with in times of stress. The video production becomes an equivalent of the notes and records of the hypomnemata, intended to be viewed later and referred to not so much as a record of how specific events unfolded over time but as how life was lived during those experiences, what happened, and how was it dealt with.

"What Did You Think of Us?"—Reflexivity in Performance of the Interviews

The sections where the girls interview the teachers and the other, visiting adult are used as intermissions within the locative narrative. They break up the contemplative personal memory and note making of the shots around the school. And yet, in their direction and content, they support the over-arching purpose of emphasizing the relation of Katie and Aroti to each other and back to school life. Here too, where the overall impression is one of artlessness and a rambling style to the video production, closer viewing, and knowledge of the setting uncovers a structure to their choice of interview subjects in the finished piece.

In total, the girls interview four adults and each one represents a distinct phase in their school life. In the final piece, they move chronologically out of sequence, backward and forward through their experiences. They are organized chronologically in between the other scenes as follows:

1. An interview with Ms. Carey, a favorite teacher and a regular cast member across the videos made in school A. She taught them for two years of their school life in Key Stage 1 when they were aged between 6 and 7 years old.
2. An interview with Ms. Black, their year-6 teacher for the whole of their final year at school and during the whole period of the video project.
3. An interview with Sabina D'Alessio, a PhD student at the Institute of Education who visited the project during one day of the filming and helped some of the groups. She worked with Katie and Aroti's group and she was responsible for influencing the content of the section on "Music," the only part of the video in which it is possible to discern an alternative authoring voice from those of Katie and Aroti.

4. An interview with Ms. Able, their teacher when they were in the nursery and one of the longest serving staff members at school A. She, like Ms. Carey, was also interviewed in other productions.

Earlier in this section, the interview planning was discussed and drawings in the storyboard were analyzed to describe aspects of their relationships to the proposed interview subjects. The head teacher was also shown as a subject but she did not survive into the final edit. The emphasis was, in three of the cases, on adults who knew them well and a fourth adult with whom they were involved during the making of their video.

During the first interview, the first question, about the length of time Ms. Carey has worked as a class teacher, is used as an icebreaker. The key finding is the relation of the teacher to the girls themselves and the key question is about what made their class special above all the others she has taught, what will be remembered about them when they are gone. The constructions that find an echo in their own transcribed speech to camera in the locative narrative are those that report habitual memory, the sense of repeated lived experience (as italicized below):

> *Katie*: How long have you been teaching?
> *Ms. Carey, counts on fingers while smiling.* ooh, er seven years, eight years...seven, no eight years.
> *Katie*: What did you like about our class more than other classes?
> (*Camera operated by Aroti, moves from side to side to the speaker each time.*)
> *Ms. Carey*: *You were always so much fun.* I *always had so much fun* with you. *Always laughing and making jokes... and you loved doing some artwork* and *you loved drama...*
> (*Aroti zooms in very close to Ms. Carey's face at the close of the scene as she says the final words about fun and drama.*)

The retention of this interview in the final edit is explained by its easy sublimation into the overarching structure and mood of the piece, of remembered, embodied experience.

The second interview, with Ms. Black, takes a different form. Ms. Black uses the medium and assumes control to get her own feelings about the class across. Katie and Aroti push for the remembrance of themselves in the classroom in the same way as they have with Ms. Carey. Ms. Black has had a difficult time at this point, with the added complication of a video project and her classroom being rebuilt around her. She opens up in a humorous way with Aroti as interviewer because this is also the experience that both

Aroti and Katie have had some of the time in the class during their year 6. The "looks to camera" and the "looks back at Aroti" attempting to make her smile as she describes what the class is really like indicate a shared confidence about the people in the room. Its place in the overall scheme of the video is assured by its underlining of their experience of being with the class. It is not celebratory but it is a humorous moment in an otherwise solemn and low-key production; it is there because of the shared truth about relations between the social actors in the class:

> *Aroti*: What are your favorite things about our class?
>
> *Ms. Black*: That's a really hard one. I'm going to have to think about that one for quite a long time...come back in about ten years?
>
> *Aroti, smiling now but trying to concentrate on the job in hand*. What's your favorite thing about teaching?
>
> *Ms. Black, pretending to think hard but knowing the answer*. It's got to be...the holidays.
>
> *Aroti, as before—smiling and then pausing to be a proper interviewer again*. Have you anything to say about our class?
>
> *Ms. Black*: I've got lots of things to say about it but I suppose (*pauses to think*) I must say it's the noisiest class I've ever taught.
>
> *Aroti*: How many years have you been teaching?
>
> *Ms. Black:* This is my seventh year.
>
> *Aroti, now being prompted by Katie from behind the camera*. Did you enjoy working at your last school?
>
> *Ms. Black:* Yes I did. The children were fun and it was very nice.

The final question in the second interview looks at life outside of the school and prompts Ms. Black to think about happier times in her old school. When, during the third interview, they have the opportunity to question someone from another country entirely, an Italian visitor from Rome called Sabina, they ask questions that are mainly concerned with seeking out the feeling for habitual, lived experience in a place with the repeated "What is it you like about...?" line of questioning (italicized in the text below):

> *Katie*: This is an interview with Sabina who is from Italy... *What is it you like about it here?*
>
> *Sabina*: I like the people...I met so many people...like the students...can you hear me? And the people...
>
> *Katie.*: *What do you like about* your local environment?
>
> *Sabina*: Actually it's the same thing...the people. and I like to go to the seaside...it's about twenty minutes you know and I like to go to the

seaside it's about you know twenty miles... (noise of other children talking off camera)
...
Aroti: *What do you like about* our school?
Sabina: I like the way that you... uh... welcome me very well, you know I immediately felt part of the team, you know, part of the community... I felt as—you know... one of your friends... that was really nice... thank you.

No other children are interviewed in the production, unlike in others where the naming of names and the presentation of relationships with peers by members of the class is very important. The interview with Sabina survives into the final edit in the girls' video because it fits the impressions of remembered time but comes from an externalized view. The "fitting in" that she describes is something that is weighing on Katie and Aroti's mind as they contemplate new relationships but they see how it is possible to do that from the visit of the stranger into their own video production.

The fourth interview takes Katie and Aroti back to the familiar, and immediately precedes the trip around the school for the last time. The girls are keen to get to the heart of the embodied memory of the longest serving teacher at the school and to see what she takes with her in terms of her own memories and impressions of being a teacher:

Katie: .What's your favourite thing about being a teacher?
Ms. A: Favourite thing about teaching? I think because I've been here quite a long time—one of the best things is seeing the children as they get older... and just seeing how they are when they're older really... actually now seeing some children working in supermarkets and things... doing Saturday jobs—children who used to be in the nursery here... so that's one of the nicest things.
Katie: How many years have you been a teacher?
Ms. A: Well, 15 here... erm (*pauses to add it all up and looks surprised herself*)—26 years!
Katie, looks up at her and raises her eyebrows. That's long... (*Mrs. A laughs off camera*).

This interview possibly survives into the final edit because it looks back at lived experience and the longer view of life outside of the year-6 classroom.

The interviews break up the flow of the locative narrative but retain the mood and the emotional charge of the whole production by focusing on the overriding themes of memory and habitual behavior. They give Aroti and

Katie a perspective on their own movement away from the security of their relationship and their time at the school. This is recognized and noted in the final fame of the production. The image that they choose from the library within the software is of balloons, signifying a party, a celebration. The music, which plays, is the only nondiegetic sound in their production and the only time they provide a sound track piece. Again, the choice of lyrical content, from the boy band, Blue, released in 2002 on the Virgin label in the song, "One Love," is in harmony with the overall authorial direction, memory, reflection, and acknowledgment of change: "It's kinda funny, how life can change / Can flip one-eighty in a matter of days."

Interview with the Makers of the Video

Beginning with the conversation around the production, on the day set up for the interview, Katie was unavailable and Aroti answered questions about the production. Her comments were revealing in terms of both the means by which the production was generated and constructed and the underpinning subtexts layered into the structure.

Following the introductory question about enjoyment (answered positively), the interview moved into the area of why the experience was enjoyable. Aroti begins by expressing a view held by many of the other children that the process involved engagement with something "new." This was new for school and new to her. The "something to do" echoes the video's quiet revelation about how it is to be at the margins of school life and frequently bored (and this will be a theme that recurs in later chapters). Over and over again, this feeling is recapitulated in the production itself (see the hopscotch scene where Aroti says—"it gives me something to do!": scene 13 in main production above 00:05:08–00:05:18). In the interview, Aroti says of the video work, generally,

> [Yes, I enjoyed it because] ... you get to do something fun in school [lifts right arm up to point back at interviewer, raises eyebrows, and then gestures with an upturned hand] ... and something new ... because we don't normally do projects.

To Aroti, the act of video production is new, open, and untried, suggesting new possibilities for activity within school. For this production, this means new ways of staking a claim on the space, of making their mark in the school, in the world of the classroom. This finds echoes in the later discussion of learner voice.

Asked to select the best part of the project, Aroti singles out "the editing" before adding (after a pause) "the recording, all of it."

Partly, Aroti is articulating what she thinks the interviewer would like to hear. She is aware of herself as a social actor within a discourse around "project work." The interviewer is an outsider whom she would like to convince about the activities that have taken place. In her gestures and general demeanor, she expresses satisfaction with the work and is not concerned with further explanation. It is enough that the production got made, was shared with Katie, and is now a video, which can be viewed again and again.

During the interview, the focus on the editing is interesting because at other times during the conversation the editing would appear to have been a trial, with the girls having to significantly reduce the running time of the finished piece. In reality, the editing proved to be significant in spite of these difficulties, in pursuit of a different vision from the others in the group, dealing with a deep and complex relationship between people, buildings, and their daily life at school.

Considerations of friendship surface often in the interview and are equally seriously treated and equally revealed in her answers. The group had initially formed a larger one working on the same production as the two boys Raymond and Keiron. The split, which occurred between the boys and the girls in the production, was amicable and negotiated between the two sets of friends, each realizing that the other had a particular vision they wished to pursue. The boys labeled their storyboard "Boys bitz" (as seen in the previous section) and the girls labeled theirs as "Girls scene and after boys scene." At this stage, they were to work separately and combine elements of their work but after discussion, and mainly for reasons of length (they were both over the stated limit at that stage), decided to pursue entirely separate productions.

The interview moves into group dynamics and the friendship between Katie and Aroti is described as a "given" as an essential part of the school experience for her and for as long she can remember. Indeed, the four children in this group were two pairs of friends of opposite genders, as Aroti explains,

> When we got put together we were... friends already and Keiron and Raymond were two best friends and me and Katie we were another two best friends.

The decision to represent places was taken very early on and was reflected in their symbiotic relationship in production. Aroti remembers early conversations with Katie when, "She told me which places she liked and I told her." Their video has a definite location within the field of "place," with a location-based narrative giving equal importance to the interviews of teachers. Even in the latter parts of their production, the teachers' narrative reflection on their part in the school was as important as finding out about the teachers. A reprise of asking, "What do you remember of us or of your time here with us?" is common throughout.

While the two girls worked together, Aroti was happy with the level of cooperation, suggesting that decisions were shared but that talking and working things out achieved compromise. She mentioned that transitions were one area that had to be negotiated ("You know that bit where the scene changes"). These were selected and inserted at the final stages when the atmosphere was fraught and the deadline loomed with the need to cut the production down to the required length.

The interview moves into media influences on the work used by Aroti and Katie but she declines to make this a major feature of her work, saying that it was more a feature of Raymond and Keiron's video production (and she goes on to list the main influences on the two boys). She did, however, identify nature programs as an influence on the section in the pond area at the back. As noted in the video transcription on the framework above, there were other subtle influences discernable from children's television production, the style of interviewing and presentation, in particular in the sequence where they question Sabina, an Italian visitor. Apart from the section on "music," which may well have been directed by Sabina (at least partly), the tone of Aroti and Katie's piece is documentary in style, interviews and memories of place, voices of teachers, and quiet, reflective accounts of the importance of the places in their memory.

Asked if she would like to do the project again, Aroti stated that she would like to do the same project with new friends at the "big school" and she would use the same kind of production design again centered on interviews mainly, and presumably, equally distinctive in its overall style, focused on location, personal narrative, and quiet activities shared with close friends.

Commonalities in Performed Identity in the Video Interviews

One of the main aims of the interview analysis was to use the transcription to triangulate on themes around agency and identity, which appeared to be emerging in thinking about these videos in both schools. Looking back through the interviews as a set, it is also possible to identify some commonalities based on the children's performance during the interviews, looking at their gestures, the ways in which they addressed the camera and the interviewer. Some of this evidence has already been used in support of specific arguments above, but, taken as a whole, there were, once again, some emergent themes across the whole set.

First, to a greater or lesser extent, the children viewed the interviews themselves as a performance and an extension of the project. Having just come straight from either shooting or editing, children were acutely aware of the frame they were in as they sat and answered questions.

Second, gestures within each of the interviews mirrored the performances themselves within the editing and shooting. Similar relationships to each other, to the task itself and to the historic record of the event were exemplified in seating position, gesture, and addressing of the camera.

Third, the children often reflected the ways in which film and performance are discussed with hindsight in film review programs. Their experience of interviews with film stars, filmmakers, and musicians on television was reflected in the authenticity of their gestural behavior during interviews. They were playing a part they had seen played before. Examples drawn from each of the video interviews below will be helpful in elaborating these points.

In the interview with Aroti, focusing on the video in which the two girls explored their relationship to the location and to each other, Aroti sat on her own and looked back at the interviewer. Clearly uncomfortable at first, particularly since she was being interviewed without her partner, who was unavailable, she was very quiet and only drawn into the process by skilled questioning. Aroti's body language during the interview suggested that she was enclosed within herself. For almost the entire interview, her arms were folded, echoing the encircling movements used in the production, by which means the two girls delineated their separation, their otherness, and their togetherness. The posture she adopted throughout the interview suggested that, in the absence of support from her partner, Aroti was going to maintain the same authoring strategy as she performed herself during the interview.

For Raymond and Keiron, the two boys who produced the video that embraced media quotation, visual humor, and a huge range of role-play, the interview was an opportunity to continue to explore these forms. They gave serious and thoughtful answers to the questions but they never lost sight of the camera. Raymond frequently adopted the following gestures and poses: winking conspiratorially at presumed viewers, moving his arms into explanatory poses, struggling for the right way to perform the answer, particularly when thinking about the use of the camera, acting out the editing process, pinching his fingers into a small shape, and expressing physically how very, very difficult the sound editing was, even as he is elaborating it in speech. Keiron also performed, half turned away from the interviewer, half toward the direction of Raymond, the camera, and the watching audience. He made visual contact with the audience beyond the camera as well as with Raymond. Their gestures and ways of performing the interview matched the schemes and tropes of their production perfectly.

The pressing concerns for the mixed gender group at school A were recording of friendships and of group identity, including difficulties in relationships but, centrally, a concern to preserve names and record them accurately. Gesturally, their interview contained some elements in common with Raymond and Keiron, with looks to camera and between the two children being interviewed. Kyle seemed concerned that he preserved a cool look, sitting in a relaxed pose, and looking downward but aware throughout of the camera on him. He wished to project distance and seriousness. Just at the end, he added a further dimension, adopting a significant gesture, raising his hands, and splaying his fingers, addressing the camera, using a "street" gesture, a variant of "Westside" or neighborhood signifier, as a cultural marker. Annie was serious throughout and looked directly at the interviewer, only breaking eye contact and staring toward the camera as Kyle turned to make his own visual statement; this could be read as an attempt to make a connection with the viewer and provide counterpoint to the take on things that Kyle is providing. Annie is exploiting the possibilities inherent in the act of subverting the interview.

In the video constructed by the high ability girls in School A, in which play, and trying on new ways of being, were the dominant themes, their gestures and posture during the interview suggested that they had returned to the role of compliant high achievers. They attempted to please the interviewer but were clearly more interested in pleasing themselves, explaining some of the more difficult-to-understand passages in the production. With one of the girls absent, the three who remained sat side by side with the most dominant of the three in the center. Glances were frequently made in her direction by the two on either side while answering questions, perhaps checking that permission had been granted to say certain things in certain ways. As with Aroti's interview, the group was, to an extent, closed off from the outside, looking more inward. Their only real look at the camera showed them side by side, looking out at an audience beyond but with no sense of playing up or enacting the role of interviewee as Raymond and Keiron and, to a lesser extent, Kyle and Annie did.

The interviews in school B were conducted in the same way in the production groups. The children in the two groups did not so explicitly mirror their representational practices in production as in the first set of interviews in school A. There were, nevertheless, moments in which it was possible to see gestures and body language reinforcing certain aspects of their work.

In the interview with the Morning News video makers, the two children who made the long dance sequence in the middle sat side by side, emphasizing their separate role in the production. Heather, who played the role of the news anchor, sat some way back from the others and needed to be coaxed to join in. She did not readily take part and had to be invited by both the interviewer and the other children to contribute. Her shoulders were raised in a tense way throughout and she rocked back on her chair as though hoping to disappear from the frame. In the video production, as a newsreader, she was able to introduce a barrier between herself and the viewer, hiding (literally) behind the script. The other two were in role as successful filmmakers, confidently talking through the production. The boy sat with his hands on his knees and moved forward to answer. The girl in the center dominated the discussion with her interpretations of the video production. None of the children had any sense of difficulties with the video in terms of its impact on their teachers or peers.

The second group struggled with expressing itself in much the same way as they did on screen. They contradicted and talked over each other, three authorial voices who did not quite manage to produce their vision in the way they wanted. Of the three, the most comfortable, John, sat on the left in a relaxed pose, happy to talk and to explain. The boy in the middle, Denzil, and the girl on his left were more defensive, legs closed with hands together in the middle. Denzil was the most uncomfortable, both in what he said and in how he sat, somewhat defensively. Lily had a better outlook on the whole thing but was generally overwhelmed by James's responses.

The video production was still very much in the minds of all the children interviewed and perhaps, the most interesting aspect of all of these interviews was the ways in which the performance of identity continued to be elaborated. Having engaged in digital inscription and been at play in the onscreen world of editing the children were aware of how a version of the interview could be shaped. They were aware of performance, as might be expected, but also continued to reference themselves in the ways they described in their individual productions.

In the subsequent chapters, I want to outline the discussion that emerged from these investigations of the authorial intent of the children concerned.

CHAPTER 6

Editing and Coherence

In the next two chapters, I want to look back at the videos in both schools and describe how they led to the positioning of the new curatorship as a literacy practice in new media production. As noted above, this practice is theorized somewhere between media literacy and identity and I approached these in consecutive chapters earlier, chapters 2 and 3. I will move back into identity theory in chapter 7, "Location and Memory." For now, I would like to look at the more formal, textual elements in the videos under the overall heading of "Editing and Coherence."

Media Forms

In both schools, the children produced a range of media forms, from parody through to documentary through to personal storytelling. Children became characters, played with roles for themselves, improvised, planned, joked, parodied other media texts, switched voice, switched genre, worked with pace and timing, worked with no timing, miscued, timed things expertly, recorded audio badly, added music skilfully, made exceptional use of the resources, or left some unexploited and unexplored. This was a very time-pressured process, with little teacher-directed input and with the research effort directed at investigating nascent forms, readiness for video production through self-representational form. Notwithstanding all the inherent difficulties, in all cases, in all interviews, the children mostly revealed a high degree of satisfaction, alongside the frequently expressed regret that more could have been done. The sheer range of output across both schools, and evident in the two videos analyzed in depth above, demonstrated the ability to handle a range of expressive success with a variety of media forms. However, not all productions succeeded in equal measure or even in the same way. Some were challenging to a viewer and disappointing to their makers. While some undoubtedly managed to produce forms that conveyed specific meanings, even if only in short bursts, others became fractured and dissonant.

The forms and some of the surface features of the productions are recapped as below:

"Right, let's get on with the show" by two boys in school A with its jokes, slapstick, visual tricks, use of sharp editing, well-chosen music, and sound set the bar for their peers in terms of its construction and use of intertextual resource (see fig. 6.1).

Two girls at school A produced "This is where we used to sit." In complete contrast to the previous video, this was a piece in which the settings of school locations, such as the playground and pond, and the overall organizing frame of (occasionally painful) memory created a meditative, even somber, experience that had moments of quiet and an artlessness not in keeping with the celebratory mode of other productions (see fig. 6.2).

From among the other videos produced at the school come the following examples:

The confident, high achieving girls in "Do not try this at home" (School A), flew at the task and found it enjoyable, frustrating, fun, and just out of reach of their ideas of themselves and what it could be. Combining interview, documentary style, anarchic play, breaking down under the weight of ideas, and the need to represent all aspects of themselves in one space, it felt

Figure 6.1 Thumbnails of foreshortening jokes and two-shot.

Figure 6.2 Thumbnails of the two girls in "This is where we used to sit."

like a starting point and, at its close, the girls were all surprised at how little came across to a viewer and were beginning to see what more they could have done to make it clearer (see fig. 6.3).

The makers of "Me and him are close" jumped at the opportunity in a similar way to the previous group, with an ambitious program of documentary and anarchic playfulness. They ended up considering the medium as a record of friendship, describing this at times with similar words to those used by the makers of "Right, let's get on with the show" (see fig. 6.4)

In school B, children making "Sorry for the disturbance" recorded similar levels of anarchic play in spaces in a variety of forms, including news parody, a dancing session, and wedding sequence. Disjointed, rapid, comedic, and strange to an outside viewer they seemed to derive benefit from their attempt to wrest control of a form and from working with others with whom they did not usually work (see fig. 6.5).

Figure 6.3   Thumbnails of the girls in "Do not try this at home."

Figure 6.4   Thumbnails of the makers of "Me and him are close."

Figure 6.5   Thumbnails from "Sorry for that disturbance."

Figure 6.6 Thumbnails from "007 meets Dr X."

The makers of "007 meets Dr X" produced a montage containing many forms, from news parody, through to recorded play, dance, and play fighting, accompanied by personalized use of sound (one chosen representative track per filmmaker). The whole thing was perceived as a good effort and very interesting (by the main editor) and very displeasing (by one of the stars) in terms of how his mother would react to his part in it (see fig. 6.6).

With some of the similarities in form in evidence, including parody of news and interviews, or anarchic free play interspersed with more obviously narrative forms, there were clear distinctions in terms of the successful use of expressive qualities across productions. However, it is possible to locate aspects of Street's proposed model of "ideological" literacy (Street 2003) across all these practices, in the children's rich engagement with the medium in so many forms. Likewise, I found evidence in the videos and the interviews afterward that suggests that the video makers had internalized many of the processes themselves and become aware that they were engaging with a new literacy practice. Thus, Kyle is able to name teamwork as a key component in his vision of himself as a new literacy practitioner in digital video production; Raymond and Keiron give interviews in role as famous directors; Lily quietly describes her joy at finding herself undaunted in the many possibilities of editing when others couldn't cope. Equally, there are times where this awareness broke down or arrived too late in the day, as happened with Ellen, Hattie, and Siobhan's regret that they only saw the potential of the medium and their relation to it, after they had finished.

Gee's "affinity spaces" (2004a, pp. 77–89) in which people successfully take part and make meaning inside groups or networks has something to offer the discussion of the children as new literacy practitioners, certainly in so far as some of the defining characteristics of this concept are apparent in relation to the videos. Affinity spaces, which Gee suggests are usually found in networks outside of formal school structures, offer opportunities to access higher order thinking skills. Even though these video projects take place within school, as I have pointed out above, the aim was to provide something outside of the normal curriculum activity; perhaps, they illustrated a way to create the kinds of opportunities that Gee mentions, within the school environment. Affinity spaces have 11 characteristics in Gee's original conception and these projects exemplify 6 of them as follows (from proposals by Gee [ibid.] with each characteristic quoted in italics):

- A *"common endeavour"* is established in the brief at the beginning of these projects, with its high-stake emphasis on self-representation.
- There is no attempt to separate children into skill sets and to establish mastery of some over others, *"newbies and masters and everyone else share common space."*
- In the editing, of which more is discussed below, *"content is transformed by interactional organisation"*—the children bring in media assets to be added to the production and discuss their place.
- *"Intensive and extensive knowledge are encouraged"*—thus, children may value each other's ability to work *intensively* with a specialized part of the process, with editing, for example (Lily, Raymond), and at the same time as *extensively,* for example, by bringing in an idea for the overarching narrative (Keiron).
- *"Tacit knowledge is encouraged and honoured"*—such that even if not articulated in words, people's individual contributions are incorporated in the form of their tacit understanding of form and their generation of new ideas for content, even where this is sometimes hard to express (Katie, Aroti).
- *"There are many different forms and routes to participation"*—this takes account of the different roles in production in new media; the affinity space in production fosters engagement by a wider group across different skill sets for different lengths of time, at different times.

Some of these issues have also been addressed specifically in relation to younger learners (Larson and Marsh 2005; Marsh 2004), in arguing for a wide and inclusive definition of, and engagement with, new literacies, which takes into account the range of practices undertaken by young people with new technologies at home and at school, such as we have seen in these productions. Marsh, for example, notes that

> an insistence on the inter-relationship between literacy and other communicative practices is essential in the current social, economic and technological climate. (2004 p. 4)

She also points out that the necessary interdisciplinary engagement between these domains is still in its earliest stages, certainly where the youngest learners in the education system are concerned.

The next two sections will attempt to look across the videos to identify how literacy practices are operationalized in the productions, further identifying two key issues. The first of these is to do with editing and specifically the organization of intertextual space, the uses of onscreen editing in intertextual, multimodal production. The second issue is the way in which some forms of output are evidence of a continuum from play through to realized form in children's work.

Editing: Organizing Intertextual Spaces

Beginning with editing, as established in the analysis, Raymond and Keiron's video from school A was viewed as highly successful both by the performers and by the audience of their peers. The key to this appears to lie, at least partly, in the overt and relatively easily read intertextual organization of the elements in relation to one another. The boys' production built on years of appropriation of media into their embodied and lived experience at the school. Their humor—sketches and skits in the playground, in school assemblies, performed and embodied ways of being in the school—were all key resources. These were organized, layer-by-layer into the production and incorporated into parallel references to media texts.

This is the kind of activity undertaken by the "textual poachers" envisaged by Henry Jenkins: fans taking the media elements of their choice, reappropriating and re-presenting them in order to make new meanings (Jenkins 1992). The facility with which the boys were able to do this may have been unusual. The fact that they did provides pointers and possible templates for work with other learners by tapping into the potential interrelationship between performance and media appropriation. Certainly, they exhibited relatively developed levels of many of the skills that Henry Jenkins and others propose for the new media literacy, including

> the capacity to experiment with one's surroundings... the ability to adapt alternative identities for the purposes of improvisation and discovery... the ability to meaningfully sample and remix media content... the ability to pool knowledge and compare notes towards a common goal... the ability to follow the flow of stories and information across multiple modalities. (Jenkins et al. 2006, p. 4)

The ways in which Raymond and Keiron operated successfully at an intertextual level suggests that key skills in production are the ability to borrow the cultural capital of other resources of text, sound, and video from the "heteroglossia" (Bakhtin 1981) and align yourself with them, however fleetingly and in the context of the overall organizing scheme of the work. Thus, in their video, the White Stripes and the Red Hot Chilli Peppers are set on the timeline alongside and between textual elements of anarchic play, media quotation, and appropriation, which allows the shared knowledge and cultural experience of life inside and outside the school to be in intertextual dialogue with one another. This depends on knowing where these resources are in a collection of media assets and how they may be repurposed in juxtaposition with one another.

This successful intertextual play also finds echoes in other productions that did not communicate their meaning so immediately to audiences. There were examples throughout of nascent aspects of this facility with media, unformed and incoherent as it sometimes was. These were aspects that could potentially be revealed and developed in later experiences in digital video production, after adapting pedagogy (see the discussion below and in ch. 7). I am thinking here, for example, of the work of Ellen, Hattie, Siobhan, and Millie. The girls in "Do not try this at home" referenced a wide range of media forms, from the documentary interview to children's TV programs to horror film and to the outtakes from DVD extras. Their aim as expressed to the interviewer was to change and adapt as they went on, to have more "fun" in the accumulation and inclusion of these elements. Their success at the editing stage was more limited, with some elements overrunning and not as coherently or succinctly arranged on the timeline as others, but the process had huge potential in recording aspects of their performed selves in school and this was recognized and invested in by the girls. Only after it was finished did they realize how little came across to an external audience and how much remained private and even disorganized and impenetrable. There are other reasons as this centered on their "play" in the form and this will emerge in discussion in the following section.

In experiencing difficulty in organizing the resources, the girls found themselves struggling to come to terms with decentering their self-representation from their own experiences and conceptualizing their audience's needs in the ways that Raymond and Keiron were able to do. This finding has been noted as an issue elsewhere in youth media production (Buckingham and Harvey 2001) in the analysis of two contrasting outcomes from a shared project. In that project, one of the filmmakers who produced a video based on montage and nonnarrative form, revealed how her conception of the audience and its needs was strictly limited by her wish to please herself. In this research, with much younger children, the girls also revealed that they were absorbed in the making of the piece as a true representation of themselves to the exclusion of other issues. Here, the overarching organizing principle was not that of being audience aware so much as pleasing themselves and hoping that what they made would be understood. By mutual consent, for example, they altered their production substantially when they found that they did not capture their capacity to "have fun" in their original use of the documentary form. This resulted in long sections, which broke into the structure of the piece established in the early interview sections. This was of little concern to them. As they recalled in their interview they simply got bored with the interview format and put in sections with play on the mats and "Sumo wrestling." If the inclusion of these and the other, phantasmagoric episodes and play noted in the analysis, combined with the mats in the hall resulted in audience confusion and disrupted an easy reading, it was, nevertheless, a deliberate choice aimed at a representation that pleased them more.

As a result of their experiences in the project, the same girls discovered that there was a wide gap between successfully organizing traditional written texts, as they had been doing in class up to that point, and organizing media texts. In interview, they went so far as to claim that the status of the production was "unfinished" and they would have enjoyed returning for a second attempt with new thinking about how to organize it. They viewed the process of making meaning in this way as a kind of drafting process, but a much more complex one, engaging with multiple modalities and involving many hours of decision making in front of the editing software of a very different kind from writing. This adds further weight to the lack of a perfect fit of the analogy between writing and media production described earlier. The girls discovered that although all the elements were in place and ostensibly allowed them to be responsive to their compositional intentions and meanings, working with them required more than just inserting different resources into the space on the timeline and hoping they would work. The whole endeavor required knowledge of how media texts actually "speak" to one another. They needed to know more about both grammar and lexis, or to borrow another theoretical frame, which was outlined earlier, they needed to understand how the *centripetal* and *centrifugal* forces of the form (Bakhtin 1981) may work together and be reconciled in successful productions.

Other videos in both schools enjoyed varying degrees of success with organizing resources and in nearly every case, children were pleased with, and proud of, the finished output, even where their audience experienced difficulties with reading the texts. In analysis, almost all the responses across both schools indicated high levels of enjoyment and reasonably positive comments. There was, however, some ambivalence about the ability to quote from other texts and there were frequent admissions of failure and frustration at the editing stage.

This occurred even in productions that included popular and typical elements successful elsewhere. The video from school B, "007 meets Dr X," has some similar cultural touchstones to Raymond and Keiron, as does "Sorry for the disturbance" from the same school. In these productions, we can identify a manipulation of staple media references, from news broadcasts to movie genres, and so on. The difference between their productions and the video by Raymond and Keiron is a lack of coherence across the whole text, a lack of success at both the form and the content, the grammar and the lexis. This neither arises out of a lack of imagination, nor from a failure to gather usable resources or usable self-produced clips, as any scan of the individual elements in the analysis grids will show. The relative lack of success arises from an incomplete grasp of the intertextual possibilities of the medium. Across all productions, the organization of intertextual space emerges as the key determining factor in coherence. At this stage of their development, these children would benefit from privileging editing over other factors. The work at the "multimodal mixing desk" (Burn and Parker 2003) is real work after all, as even adept users such as Raymond and Keiron discovered in their frustration and expressed in interview. One of the longest stretches of conversation in the interview with those boys concerns Raymond's obvious frustration with needing to be accurate and "just right" with the placing of the sound (during the gorilla fight sequence) or concern that the whole segment would not work and would not speak successfully to the other textual elements in the production. This process is more than the simple act of placing things in the right place and joining them together; it is an act of authorship and marshaling of key meaning-making resources into a cohesive whole.

Throughout both projects, editing represented by far the biggest technical challenge to the children. Statements such as the following recurred throughout the interviews:

- "Sometimes it went wrong and we cut out more than we wanted to."
- "We lost a bit of our work."
- "Editing is difficult because of the number of possibilities."
- "Not knowing when it is finished."
- "It was complicated to get the volume up / sound issues."
- "Very frustrating."
- "Working with text—putting it in the right place—is hard."

The "number of possibilities" and "not knowing when it is finished" stand out as key frustrations. They suggest that editing engenders dissatisfaction in the authoring process despite, and perhaps because of, high expectations that it would be straightforward, signal definite pathways and certain endings. It takes place, after all, onscreen with devices that look familiar and on which they experience success in other types of software. The affordances of the software even present them with a partially visually familiar onscreen workshop, as discussed previously (cf. Sefton-Green 2005). The degree of surprise expressed by the children at the difficulty they encountered is high but so too is the overall surprise at the confusing array of opportunities of the process of editing itself.

"Provisionality" is sometimes quoted as an inherently positive feature of Information and Communication Technology (ICT) "tools," which engenders creativity, and represents the potential of technology to confer agency on the part of the user in relation to many possible versions and outcomes, instantly erasable and recreatable again in software (Loveless 2002). The experience of children in this project was that the provisionality inherent in the editing software was certainly engaging and exciting, but was just as equally daunting and frustrating. What was needed was a much closer, more measured integration of skills with knowledge, and of function with ideas about form, which took account of this, alongside time to evaluate the consequences of actions taken and decisions made step-by-step. The children were familiar with the functions of some tools from their use of other software (cf. Sefton-Green 2005) but needed support to realize the greater effect, meaning-making potential, and significance when using them in video editing to weave together multimodal resources, particularly in a high-stakes project involving self-representation.

The placing of editing at the heart of the process links back to thinking about the overall pedagogical design. It is important to allow markers to be placed somewhere in the planning that reflect the eventual possibilities of the editing software and, perhaps, in a future design of these activities to foreground it even more. This may not necessarily take place until some basic familiarity with editing has been established, perhaps through in-camera work initially, as has been suggested before (cf. Burn and Durran 2007, Ch. 4). This would allow part of the process to be reflective and evaluative at an earlier stage and to layer in discussion and development of media literacy skills (this point will be raised and developed later in ch. 7).

Indeed, at the outset, this aspect of the work, of planning and considering form more carefully, could have been signaled even further in the planning paperwork around the two projects. In both of them, the storyboards produced by the children only became significant when they were used as planning spaces that anticipated editing in a multimodal form, rather than as planning tools for shots alone (cf. discussion in Fraser and Oram 2003, pp. 52–57). Others have pointed out that children rarely, if ever, ascribe significant value to storyboards (Buckingham, Grahame, and Sefton-Green 1995).

Raymond and Keiron, however, made use of theirs (pictured earlier in fig. 3.2) as a series of notes to themselves as editors for later use in the process, with spaces for sound design and other notes beneath each of the shots. In their interview, they asserted that if their production had not been planned, it would have been "rubbish." I would argue that it is no coincidence that this most successful production was also one in which the use of the many modes and intertextual possibilities had been signaled most clearly at the outset; perhaps, this is something that could be developed across the ability range represented in the projects. Raymond and Keiron's storyboard showed how the texts would actually be arranged with one another as movable assets arranged in layers and perhaps future pedagogical design should consider carefully how and when to introduce multimodal storyboards into this process; this will be addressed further in proposals for learning and teaching arising from the work. In terms of other project paperwork, certainly the planning sheets themselves were popular in the form of mind mapping the production at the outset and were well used to indicate the direction a production should take.

One aspect of media production that arose out of several videos and that was mentioned in particular in the interviews, was the awareness on the part of the children of the camera as a key "partner" in the process, certainly in terms of its recording of the visual performed mode, even if frequently they were not so sure how to address the recording of sound. I have stated the case for editing to be central in any process above, however, I also believe that consideration needs to be given to the ways in which children act around and with the camera. This is not necessarily to do with the composition of shots or how things were framed in any technical sense, though these would undoubtedly have become a feature of any developmental work. In the projects, on the part of the children, the way of thinking about the camera was frequently *not* to do with looking *through* the camera, or even at the sidebar, so much as looking *at* the camera while it was filming *them*. In these terms, its meaning-making potential in the process was often commented on as though it were personified. Raymond, for example, pondered the fact that the camera gave him ideas, though he couldn't quite explain how ("I don't mean it talks to you"); he addresses it conspiratorially by winking at it throughout the interview. In performance, both James and Poppy in school B quite consciously address the camera in their dance.

In these examples, the camera is a gateway to the audience beyond, one which they realize is a mediating tool influencing their action (Engeström, Miettinen, and Punamäki 1999; Wertsch 1998); but one after which, as they realized later, the action is malleable and mutable through the postproduction process. In some productions, it occurred to the children that the camera was the gateway ultimately to the editing space. By the time Raymond has winked at the camera in the interview, he has already connected it and its presence in the room as something in front of which he alters his behavior and which captures his performed self. He realizes that his action is now also a media asset, which will be collected and may eventually be edited by someone at some stage in the future. I will discuss later how this awareness of making and collecting as part of a continuum in the experience of media production is a marker of a new literacy skill that can be characterized as a form of "curatorship."

Incoherence/Coherence: The Play—Creativity Continuum

In a celebratory mode, it is possible to conclude that the work of Raymond and Keiron provides evidence of an advanced state of readiness by younger children to make successful video productions. The three main achievements of their video seem to have been the way in which the medium was used simultaneously to connect with the wider world of popular media culture, to reflect their lived experiences in school to date, and to address their audience's needs. At the screening to the whole class, it was by far the most popular production. It contains sophisticated shots and tight editing, with an ambitious use of the resource of sound, both diegetic and nondiegetic. Very little instructional adult input was given during its making. Raymond and Keiron were completely reliant on each other and on being left more or less alone to "get on with the show." They are successful with their video on their own terms, in front of an audience with a multilayered piece of work exemplifying forms of media appropriation and intertextuality.

Other productions were successful to a greater or lesser extent, in different ways and for reasons that reveal much about the nature of other shaping forces in the process, some of which are in tension with one another. Some of the videos in which the cues for meaning making were not as immediately accessible or coherently linked revealed themselves as more sophisticated pieces in systematic analysis, ways that give value to certain expressive features of these texts at the same time as acknowledging issues and suggesting ways forward (see further discussion in ch. 7). Furthermore, even at the time or soon afterward, as noted elsewhere, authors such as Katie and Aroti experienced satisfaction with their overall conception; they worked happily and on their own terms, within their own parameters, even if their video was difficult viewing for the target audience. The organizational structures and aims in their production were only revealed after carefully framed viewing, interviews, and conversations outside of the scope of the initial audience. In order to access the meaning-making resources of their production, the viewer required access to the video for longer and a knowledge of the symbolic system employed, and its relation to "habitus" as described in the analysis. This was the case to a greater or lesser extent in nearly every other video across both project schools. There were discontinuities in the organization of shooting, editing, and sound design that impeded a straightforward interpretation. I am thinking here about the way in which the structure of Kyle and Annie's video fractures under the weight of "filming friends" and of the ways in which Ellen and Hattie's production loses focus and direction in the recording of "fun" and anarchic play; similarly in school B, where the narrative drive in "007 meets Dr X" is not sustained beyond the introduction and where in "Morning News" the narrative arc introduced by the news reader is not sustained.

Partly, the explanation for this fracturing lies in the inexperience of the video makers and the pressure of time. Partly, this was due to the relative lack of teaching input in a project designed to research nascent and even innate knowledge of production. Moving away from this deficit model, it is possible that part of the reason for the problematic use of meaning-making resources in some productions lies not in their inability to use the medium in conventional ways but, rather, in their organizational complexity and ambitious scope, which far exceeded the capability of beginner video authors to produce. None of these other productions lacked the ambition of Raymond and Keiron and nearly all of them were felt by their makers to have achieved a measure of success; they agreed that their videos had indeed represented them and their time at school, as per the brief. In other words, something of themselves had at least been partially expressed. Nevertheless, since this account seeks to problematize such texts rather than celebrate every output as successful, there is a message in the lack of coherence and problematic finished output of these videos.

I would argue that there are two ways of thinking about the issue of coherence/incoherence in these videos that arise, first, from recalling the themes of literacy and the wider culture and, second, from conceptualizing play in a Vygotskian sense, as the beginning of an organizing continuum in production.

First, in terms of the issue of dialogism outlined earlier, it seems that the makers of these less coherent pieces were caught in the tension between participation in media language and their own personal dialogic and imaginative response to the task; in other words, they were caught between the centripetal forces and the centrifugal forces of language (Bakhtin 1981), in this case, of media language. As discussed earlier in chapter 3, Bakhtin defines centripetal forces as those that constrain speech acts in their subservience to the unifying organizing forces of the conventions of language systems. These are in continual tension with the centrifugal forces of the wider heteroglossia, the word he used to describe the varied and stratified wider systems in which all utterances take place (ibid.). The two girls, and the others who produced videos that were similarly difficult to understand immediately, immersed themselves in the latter at the expense of the former. By this, I mean that Katie and Aroti, for example, aimed their video squarely at the resources of memory and location without completely fitting either of them into the conventional structures and forms of media language. This is not to say that they were unaware of this as a feature of their work but that they were happy for this video to preserve the relationship of people to place and not to make something that was completely readable in a conventional sense. In terms of their own development and facility with editing, they were operating with the lexis of the system of media language, the actual vocabulary, or units of meaning as disconnected utterance, at the expense of the overall structuring grammar of the form.

A second way to view this issue resides in the notion of "internalisation" drawn from Vygotsky (1978). In the model of child development and language acquisition he proposed, its rules, structures, and forms are internalized and constitutive of understanding in an inner speech. The externalized versions of this speech in which meanings are negotiated in the social world are partial and dependent on the context in which the utterances take place (so there are parallels with Bakhtin's theory above). Where this applies to the productions lies in the partial realization of this process as far as media language and its representative system is concerned. For the members of the groups, the meaning made from the resources can only be apprehended and reapplied on the basis of the dialogue between members of the group, where there exists between them a "zone of proximal development" (ibid.). Mercer (2000), in a similarly useful concept, derives "interthinking" from Vygotsky describing "a process by which *intra*mental (individual) processes can be facilitated and accelerated by *inter*mental (social) activity" (1978, p. 141). In *Words and Minds*, he applies this to teaching and learning to suggest that where learners in a setting are able to sustain an

> "intermental development zone" on the contextual foundations of their common knowledge and aims...if the quality of the zone is successfully maintained...they can become able to operate just beyond their established capabilities. (Ibid.)

Where this has not occurred, it has been so because the potential of the changed nature of the representation, working with multimodal resources has not been fully realized. The group, all of whom are at similar levels of experience in media production has located resources and tried to structure them, but without successfully externalizing them in transformed form. This has implications for pedagogy in the field. As a group engaged in production, knowing where the resources are, thinking through what you would like to say, and being able to express this to each other, is not the same as being able to assemble and externalize that meaning. Neither is *simple*, transmissible instruction enough in this case. If we accept the concept of "interthinking" in this context, the *transformation* occurs in the dialogue around the activity between the users and is dependent for its success on one or more of those participants being able support the others. In the productions where we are seeing less success at conveying meaning beyond the group, we are seeing not so much a finished piece, perhaps, as a version of recorded play (in the Vygotskian sense [1933] of a form of conscious activity, a response to an exploration of what is possible and demanded in a given situation) and its associated internalized references and dissonance. We could take the view that all these productions are in a "halfway house," somewhere on a continuum between internalized play and realizable, communicable, and externalized creative action. The aim for any pedagogical intervention would be to move learners in the direction of creative production, toward an externalized version of the resource in which the meaning-making potential was more fully realized.

Vygotsky in considering the development of creativity in adolescence has another useful to concept to contribute. He proposed that as they grow up, children undergo a gradual "liberation" from concrete thought and "imagistic" features toward a greater integration of "elements of abstract thinking" (1994, p. 274). In some productions this process has not yet taken place, or is only partial, resulting, again, in productions which are not easily understood by an external audience. Such productions have some of the features described above of incoherence and dissonance as a marker, not only due to the lack of transmissibility mentioned in the preceding paragraph but also due to the earlier developmental stage of the children in the process of acquiring abstract thinking.

Bridging Issues: From Forms and Coherence to Self-Representation

Evaluations of media production by children and associated instructional texts have sometimes focused exclusively on teaching formal aspects of narrative and editing concepts, drawn from the tradition of film language (Barrance 2004). While these are important elements to consider in pedagogy around the construction of meaning with the moving image, it is no longer the only way of framing the subject for learners. In an era in which the short-video form is growing rapidly, made and exchanged online, and sits alongside other media assets, readily appropriated and exchanged, we need a way of understanding children's engagement with digital video as a rapidly changing social literacy practice (Marsh 2005; Street 2003; Tyner 1998). In the view of Sefton-Green (2000a) and Buckingham (2003), we further need to align this with a socialized view of creativity that is much more closely connected with group work, situated peer review, and an awareness of group roles in cultural production than connected with individual auteurs and the realization of a personal expressive goal.

The children in these productions would, of course, have benefited from some further instruction at a technical level, about the use of the camera, better ways to record sound, the various rules around the cuts in editing, and so on. However, the practices with which they were engaged in representing themselves no longer depend solely on a foregrounding of these aspects, but, as we have seen, on a range of other overlapping and intersecting factors to do with play, experimentation, appropriation, intertextuality, multimodality, and performance; and all of these operate within a digital literacy context, the exchange of meanings in new media. Even allowing for the fact that a very small proportion of people who use the online video sharing facility YouTube actually produce work for the site (Auchard 2007), the exchange of such short texts is predicated much more on their rapid distribution, mutability, and remixability and, we can probably safely assume this is going to increase over time.

It is possible that, instead, building on viewing and evaluation in the very public spaces of YouTube would allow an eliding of the process of media production with the end product more closely. Writers are already commenting on the ways in which such spaces are changing the nature of the process of composition and consumption of media texts and are becoming a form in themselves, based more on cultural resonance and exchange (Davies and Merchant 2009); this happens frequently, for example, in the presentation of spoof videos on YouTube (Willett 2009). It happened in the social media spaces used in an animation project with younger learners. (Bazalgette 2010)

As the short forms become more common and are perhaps used in social spaces in school contexts in ways suggested by some commentators (Davies and Merchant 2009, pp. 61–63), it should be possible to layer in teaching and learning about structures and the expressive possibilities of media forms over time, alternating analysis and production as suggested by Burn and Durran (2007), adapting them for younger children, and working in self-representational activities, such as those suggested by this study.

The children were making productions at some speed in a medium in which they had previously had little expressive experience as producers, as distinct from their experience as consumers (Buckingham 2003). Their relative levels of success were high on their own terms, and I have shown in the previous section how they employed a variety of forms in pursuit of a video that satisfied the brief of self-representation in a space. They did not all experience the easy levels of success, motivation, or satisfaction that is sometimes claimed for younger users of digital media. Explanations for this have arisen so far in the discussion of both their formal engagement with media literacy, their use of editing software to work intertextually, and their engagement with one another in a process that sees them on a continuum from imaginative play to imaginative fashioning of a resource. However, as is clear from the analysis of the texts, this is only one-half of the issue. The other major starting framework for this work was built on theories of identity, memory, and voice, and I will return to them in the following chapter.

CHAPTER 7

Location and Memory

Storying the Self, Making the Self

Identity was key in these videos; certainly, for the children concerned in both schools this was a high-stakes activity, learning how to make something that represented them in a short space of time and then exhibit it to their peers, family, and the wider community. In school A, leaving and moving to secondary school was an imperative, and so they were making something to record relationships, memories, and spaces. For the children in school B, the focus was again about leaving school (for some) and connecting with a community in which they were marginalized (for those who were staying).

The children in school A certainly had "memories" in mind throughout the project. In addition to the videos, the children were also making personal sculptures, decorating shoeboxes into which they were placing objects of significance to them from their years at school. This was a physical metaphor for their virtual experience (and one that contributed to the eventual theoretical formulation of curatorship as a literacy practice). In school B, the shoeboxes were replaced by the idea of bringing in physical resources from home for filming—media resources (such as songs of significance, etc.)—and contributing to the shaping of the packaging for the resource, their own customized cover designs.

Some of theories of identity provide ways of thinking about the processes, which the children underwent, as well as suggesting ways of looking at the artifacts they made in the schools. To begin with, we have seen throughout the videos that the children used a variety of "symbolic resources for constructing or expressing their own identities" (Buckingham 2008, p. 5) and how in many productions these were layered, to a greater or lesser extent successfully, intertextually in production. The resources included objects from home (Raymond and Keiron's car, Hattie and Siobhan's Chuckie doll, Kyle's fake teeth, and Annie's football), which were used to generate narrative meaning across modes, echoing the storytelling in media found by other researchers who have worked with the use of physical artifacts in this way (Pahl 2003). These kinds of objects ended up in the shoeboxes too (see fig. 7.1), indicating a physical resource, akin to those used with much younger learners to manipulate and construct narrative forms from play artifacts in small worlds in boxes (Bromley 2007).

The organization of content for these boxes was significant in focusing the children on real artifacts, which were of cultural significance as markers of both "anchored" and "transient" aspects of identity (Merchant 2006); the fixed aspects and the transient affiliations that are employed as different markers through time.

In the memory boxes pictured, action figures, Pokémon, and football cards sit alongside rings, trophies, awards, and so on. The intention in the project was to place hard copies of the videos, on disc or tape, alongside these objects in the boxes, for the children literally to leave school with all of these markers of self-representation, with narratives made across all the different modalities. This aspect of construction and performance ran in parallel throughout the second half of that final summer term in school A. Thus, in the boxes, the contemporary memes of the *Matrix*, the England football team, Scooby Doo, and the Hulk sit alongside more personal, anchored objects, and these memetic objects and resources are echoed through the productions in the arrangements of clips from the *Matrix*, from footballing, and from play fighting in, for example, Raymond and Keiron's video.

Some of the theory introduced in chapter 3, notably from Bruner (Bruner 1987), posits the idea that, in their videos, the children were "making the self" at the same time as "storying the self," collecting and assembling visual

Figure 7.1   A selection of memory boxes.

and audio resources that told a specific story. However, identity is not made in isolation. In these projects, the concept of self and "affect" arises from a reimagining of cultural resources in the context of the group and from the transactional nature of the exchange of meaning in relation to the ultimate viewing audience. These transactions are located partly in the cultural markers (the transient) and partly in the lived experience or performed memory (the anchored) (cf. Merchant 2006). The productions sit on a continuum between the two, with, for example, Katie and Aroti's as the most abstracted and reduced form, the most distant from the resources of the wider culture, and Raymond and Keiron's the most related to the markers of time and place. Each contains elements of both aspects, but mixed in different proportions and with different "affective" outcomes for both audience and maker.

Sefton-Green (2000a) has pointed out that school is a setting that, under the right conditions, provides a space, a time, and an audience for the explorations of these kinds of shared cultural and creative productions. This is somewhat at odds with some of the more antithetical positions toward school as an institution that shut down such opportunities for higher order activity with its reductivist stance on activity in the curriculum (Gee 2004a). Certainly, the opportunity to explore the "project" or "trajectory" of the self (Giddens 1991) belongs at least partly in the hugely significant lived experience of school and, clearly, there are ways of creating the halfway house between the two worlds, bridging them with collected and recorded assets from outside and inside the spaces of the formal setting. This may be particularly the case, but not exclusively, in the later years of primary school, looking back. It is this aspect of looking back, within the spaces of school, which the next section goes on to consider.

Locative Memory

All the videos make reference to place and to memory. This is most salient, as seen earlier in Katie and Aroti's production in which the children chose to put themselves into the frame in a variety of locations, talking to camera, quietly and quickly, making an effort to record secret places around the school which were of special significance to them (see fig. 7.2). It did not have many camera or editorial tricks but what it did contain was a measure of performed, embodied identity. Space was marked out around them by gesture and by movement. They existed in the production as a unit of two people in the space, just as they had always remembered and experienced it.

Figure 7.2 Place and memory in Katie and Aroti's video.

Katie and Aroti's video amplified the potential for personal inscription in digital media of a kind that was not self-referential, straightforwardly parodic, or dazzling in its techniques and execution. These techniques of personal inscription in digital form, as noted above, meant a more problematic and less accessible reading for the wider audience in ways in which Raymond and Keiron's video did not. What they achieved, rather than a well-assembled and complex set of quotations from media sources, was to make a collage of quotations from their own lives and experience of living them. And yet, the surface features of the production were much more of an enclosed system, not available fully to the outside world.

For Katie and Aroti, digital video production meant recording embodied action through movement, framing, direction, and selection, which could subsequently become encoded and recorded. In this way, the video itself would be able to take its place in the set of quotable media assets of their own lives in the future, alongside later digital images, web spaces, sound recordings, clips on phones, and so on. In turn, this video would become part of the curating of their life experience—a permanent moving-image recording at a moment in time, shaped and composed by the authors themselves, whose meanings were nonetheless only available by being able to read the different elements and resources in this way, as a system.

Place and memory were, however, key factors in the representation in other ways in other productions. I am thinking here, for example, about the way that Raymond and Keiron moved from interior to exterior shots to record aspects of their play together, as seen in the examples in figure 7.3.

In the still frame on the left, they are standing in front of the shelter they had painted in year 2, playing the music they had performed in year 4 in assembly (see ch. 5). In the middle frame, they have taken ownership of the hall outside their classroom for the long, central "interview" sequence. In the frame on the right, they are out in the playground where they have played football for many years. These shots were composed with specific quotations in mind from the lived experience at the school, layered in alongside the media resources and assets, and their overriding purpose was to

Figure 7.3   Locations in Raymond and Keiron's video.

combine these in ways that made self-representational meaning from them. However, there are echoes in all the locations chosen of Katie and Aroti's need to move around the space and to record embodied play and ways of being at the school (as in the final frame above, breaking a window with a careless shot of a football). They also spoke in interviews about the joys of being able to move around the school as a key element to the work. In this way, they were exploring the freedom of access to the spaces that were sometimes denied to them. This also, of course, had potential for recording their lived experience of the tactics deployed to resist control of their movement therein (cf. de Certeau 1984).

In the study, there are signs of this locative-narrative and embodied experience within other video productions across the two schools. Kyle, Annie, Robin, and Leon introduce themselves in the playground, the hall, and, in the ball pond in the special needs area, enact a scene of mildly transgressive behavior. Ellen, Hattie, Siobhan, and Millie follow a similar path to Katie and Aroti around the school and into some of its more secret locations; for those girls, the purposes are different, connected to the ways in which their production made meaning from play and invention, but they retread many of the familiar paths. In "Morning News," the reporters are in the school hall in front of the apparatus, or taking over the main assembly hall for dancing. In "007 meets Dr X," the school spaces are liberally spread throughout the production, many of them transgressive in nature from the younger children's playground, through to the Audio-visual aid AVA room and the paper shredder, through to the community room where the final dance takes place.

Notwithstanding all of the above, Katie and Aroti's production remains the most intensely realized in terms of recording ways of being in specific spaces (as discussed previously in the context of Bourdieu's concept of "habitus" [1986]). The use of place as a location, and a trigger, for memory is an archetypal response to the task of storying the self in new media. The idea that a video might record and reveal aspects of a child's lived and embodied experience of being in a school at a sophisticated level is a powerful one at a time when the locus of control of the curriculum and its performance is out of the control of most children. Aroti in her interview singles out the "different" nature of the work when she says,

> [Yes, I enjoyed it because]...you get to do something fun in school [lifts right arm up to point back at interviewer, raises eyebrows and then gestures with an upturned hand]...and something new...because we don't normally do projects.

However, there was more taking place in their production than a chance to be off-topic or off-curriculum for a few hours. The elements of the production that are key for successful meaning making for Katie and Aroti are those that enable the recording not only of their friendship and the things they used to do together but also the opportunity to place a high value on a set of ways of being in the world that they can take forward into new experiences. The regular patterning of location and interview creates the cumulative effect of embodied, learned experience. For the viewer of the production, the effect is occasionally frustrating, not particularly technically competent, and at times uncomfortable. Even so, it does have a structure driven by the need to be faithful to representations of space and memory.

Foucault's *Hypomnemata* (1984) was suggested earlier as a further metaphor for the digital inscription in videos made by the children, notably in the one by Katie and Aroti. The choices of framing themselves were significant, repeatedly in two-shots and performing their time together as a way of preserving aspects of their identity and relationship. Some other productions also inscribed names and events into the performance, many with their repeated cycle of interviews (e.g., Ellen, Hattie, Siobhan, and Millie's) and references to events drawn from the past.

The Hypomnemata serves as a useful concept distinct from a diary or journal form, more a record of events and lessons learned and preserved for use in situations in the future. Other videos did not take this on so explicitly and in school B where the purpose was not to make a record prior to leaving, there was less obvious need to sum up and to move on. Nevertheless, even in "007 meets Dr X" and "Morning News" there are recorded ways of being, of dealing with situations and with each other, through role-play and even subversive activity, such as where the wedding is satirized or the school hall is used for the dance.

Where there is apparent assembly without such care to record, we may well view the record more usefully as "palimpsest": a record to be brought together, assembled, wiped, discarded, and begun again. This is not necessarily in tension with the notion of preserved and recorded aspects of the self.

The idea that in new media, one can assemble and reassemble information for different purposes is consistent with the notion of shaping the self and with resisting the structures that attempt to fix and determine our identity through life. The fact that these change over time suggests powerfully that the "curatorship" metaphor may work well in describing these processes: the creation and disassembly of temporary exhibitions. These resources, then, are also memetic but in the exchanges within the world of the class and its relation to the school; for example, in the way of shared patterns of thought about playground activities in the space (Katie, Aroti), transgression in those spaces (Denzil, John, and Lily), and within the school building (Ellen, Hattie, Siobhan, Millie et al.). At the same time, these resources are gathered and presented for these purposes as both a self-reflexive project (Giddens 1991) and a narrative of selfhood (Bruner 1987).

Voice

Many of the videos depend on the organization of particular patterned communication that reflects the children's lived social experiences up to that point; how they have found their voice and exhibited the general, performed self in the spaces of the school. To an extent this is how Annie, Kyle, and the others were organizing their material in this way for themselves and for their audience. They are not simply organizing the scenes in their videos as memes, Lankshear and Knobel's "contagious patterns of thought" (2006), but also as personal communications, which reflect their ways of being in the world as part of a cultural construct (Bourdieu 1986).

Nevertheless, rather than become too celebratory, it is worth noting that some learners find themselves in situations where their preferred mode of learning or mode of expression has little value within current educational assessment systems. In looking for opportunities to reach out to those learners, as outlined in previous sections, media projects are sometimes seen as possible ways of ensuring "authenticity" for the learners and, therefore, engendering participation and even hearing the "learner voice." I discussed earlier how this exaggerates and simplifies the potential of the medium and the process of engagement with learners. Indeed, as we have seen, the situation is far more complex than this in the case of school B; the outcomes are often unexpected, even unwelcome, as in the case of the disruptive and apparently incoherent outcomes. A willingness to engage authentically with learners through media production comes with a price, namely, an ability to work with outcomes that are potentially challenging to authority and a recognition that these may well emerge in the chosen narrative voice.

Figure 7.4 Scenes from "Morning News."

One example, "Morning News" (see fig. 7.4), although criticized by senior managers, was the best received of the productions in school B when it was eventually viewed. Other videos were regarded as being either too subversive or too low in finished quality to be shown to the whole school, running the risk of exposing the makers to ridicule by other children. All the videos were ultimately screened in the community room, a quasi-autonomous space existing—like the videos themselves—somewhere between the informal and the formal worlds of school.

The remaining two productions roamed around the school in similar fashion to "Morning News" but with far less narrative focus. Children in one of these videos explored place with locative narratives as used by Katie and Aroti and the performance of names as used by Kyle, Annie, Leon, and Robin. In the other, there were attempts at improvised play and media quotation as seen in school A by Raymond and Keiron and the larger group of girls.

However, both of these productions fell foul of the school managers because they depicted children talking to each other in "inappropriate" ways (cf. Chan 2008). They also featured trees in the playground that were known to be out-of-bounds. Although they were allowed to be screened in a separate space within the school, to parents and carers, they were deemed anarchic and amateurish, lacking the sheen and literate values of properly finished media productions and therefore unsuitable for a wider audience within the school itself.

This response to an apparently authentic media representation of authorial voice in production was a common reaction to the productions by children in school B. The school managers clearly felt that the adults in the process (including the researcher) could and should have shaped the outcome and exercised more control. However, this would have placed the experience far lower on the previously discussed scale of student voice (Fielding 2004).

Once again, if becoming literate in new media suggests some form of social action, the video makers in both schools, particularly in school B, were more than happy to exploit this potential by testing out school rules, investigating forbidden spaces, and taking part in mildly transgressive behavior in "official spaces," such as the school assembly hall. These playful and transgressive responses are noted in other accounts of media production (Grace and Tobin 1998, 2002). In them, as in the video by the girls in school A, we find versions of recorded play, which Sutton-Smith reminds us is sometimes beyond romanticizing and is frequently challenging (1997). Media representations of these aspects of childhood are often revelatory of transgressive behavior that moves beyond the rules, and we need to know how to account for these and respond to them. I have outlined previously the potential benefits for learning about making media through self-representational video production; these videos suggest that there is nothing simple about this process, that hearing the learner voice in them means accepting their micropolitical (and potentially wider) effects, or risk locking down and suppressing media activity as happens in other settings of youth production with older students (Chan 2008). It has also been noted in looking at the "rhetorics" of creativity that there is a tendency for only pro-social activity to be seen as "creative" and the question has been asked as to whether other sorts of dissident or transgressive activity can be accommodated within a definition of the term (Burn, Banaji, and Buckingham 2006). There will be more to say about he ways in which culture and identity meet the formal activity of the school in video, or not, in activities around new media in the closing chapter. Meanwhile, in the next chapter, I will bring together the twin themes of media literacy and identity and show how the concept of curatorship emerged from the videos.

CHAPTER 8

Theory from Practice

The videos made by the children suggest that digital video production, from initial design through to editing and exhibition is a set of active literacy practices that can be gathered together in the metaphorical conception of "curatorship." This is not curatorship in a sense that suggests the static management of an unchanging set of resources or assets; it is not intended to suggest simply "custodianship" or "guardianship." Instead, I am characterizing it as an active practice and a process involving ways of being active in gathering and assembling the resources needed to represent both the anchored and the transient forms of identity (Merchant 2006) in a variety of spaces for different purposes and audiences.

The acts of self-representation described above could take place in any form in which the user can organize and reengineer combinations of media in an online or offline affinity space. In these projects, the imperative was the making of a self-representational text in the medium of digital video. In both schools, the process was multifaceted, mutable, and malleable, one of continual change and remaking. Even immediately afterward, many of the children were no longer locating themselves as the same people they could see in the productions at the outset; they were aware of themselves as an ongoing project for self-making, for self-representation. In the process, some of the meaning-making resources were no longer applicable, or the ways in which they aligned themselves with them, or affiliated with them, were changed.

The aspects of "curatorship" that suggest themselves as new literacy practices entail the conflation of many skills and attributes into one, all of which involve being literate and functioning in new media. Curating, as a verb, incorporates many subcomponents and actions; it suggests at least the following: *collecting, cataloging, arranging and assembling for exhibition*. Some of these, as we have seen, have been posited as actions taken by young children in assembling their physical collections (e.g., of toys), and refracted through the lens of new media (Mitchell and Reid-Walsh 2002; Pahl 2006).

First, *collecting* resources or media assets: this refers to assets that you create yourself and save, such as video clips, sound files, still images, and more. Equally, it could be assets that you collect from family and friends. These could be in many forms, such as comedy, parody, news, drama, documentary, and tutorial video. You may have found them and gathered them from TV broadcast and mass media, reedited and posted for direct quotation and repurposing. These could take the form of very small clips, barely lasting more than a few seconds or even parts of seconds, or up to much longer sequences. They could take the form of sound from a favorite mp3 file or CD track, recorded from the immediate environment, downloaded, or ripped from a music library. Furthermore, they can, as in the case of many of the videos in this study take the form of reenacted and reimagined media assets. As we have seen in the case of the "Let's get on with the show" video, and in parts of other productions, these reenactments are themselves intertextual references, which are collected, played with, and incorporated.

Second, *cataloging*: As the children discovered, it is much harder to edit in digital video without knowing where your various media assets are, what they are called, and what they contain in the way of meaning-making resource. At the time you come to prepare an edit, you need to be able to locate the files you have made, the files you wish to include, the audio, any still images, and so on. You need to know where these are on your computer or elsewhere. They need to have been organized, cataloged, and tagged for their location in ways that are meaningful to the producers themselves. The software will ask for the location at some point, so that you can import it into the new exhibition. And with social software and online spaces for sharing media assets of course, the cataloging is for others as their tagging and organization is for you, to be shared and incorporated into new exhibitions and spaces. This has already been noted as an area for potential development as both skill set and resource in educational settings, developing learners' capacity for working with user-generated folksonomies as opposed to author-generated taxonomies (see, e.g., Davies and Merchant 2009, esp. Ch. 4, pp. 35–51). It is also a focus for the *Futures of Learning* new media study group in the United States in work directed by Anne Balsamo (2009) as well as for practical application developments in *Steve: The Museum Social Tagging Project* (SteveProject 2009).

Third, *arranging and assembling*: these skills are those of planning for elements to be in dialogue with one another, to suggest specific meanings by their location, and juxtaposition in the timeline of the video, on the screen, in the production when it is complete. This is an active process of working with intertextuality, using the tools in the software to assemble a coherent whole—not necessarily a narrative whole, but a coherent and cohesive whole that stays together for the overarching purpose of the project, of lasting or short duration, and that communicates something of the original intention.

All of these skills map onto those suggested by Jenkins and Gee earlier, and suggest an active authoring practice within lived culture. Curatorship as defined above for new media and identified in these productions incorporates elements of Jenkins's "new skills," such as *play, performance, appropriation, collective intelligence, transmedia navigation,* and *networking* (Jenkins et al. 2006). It further suggests an active engagement with Gee's "affinity spaces" in that it features a version of all of the following at some level:

> "*Common endeavour*" [in which] ... content is *transformed by interactional organisation*... intensive and extensive knowledge are encouraged ... tacit knowledge is encouraged and honoured ... there are many different forms and routes to participation. (2004a, discussed in Ch. 6, pp. 77–89)

In all of the videos something of those processes occurred. Yet, in the study, I have also noted those moments where this process was not as successful or straightforward and working with children in future adapted forms of this self-representational work will entail an engagement with pedagogical design for experiences in digital video.

We saw in the closing sections of chapter 3 how cultural anthropologists were beginning to look at the ways in which new media worked in self-archiving. Miller wrote how, in this respect, digital media create their own "sensual field," which respects "the larger integrity of connections between the media it incorporates" (2008, p. 71). This "integrity of connections" is an important concept because it suggests a set of organizing principles. The particular kind of production in new media dictates these to an extent so that, in the examples of new media in these studies, the short moving-image form has its own conventions, the breaking of which results in incoherence and lack of a viable representational form. Where it works, however, it allows users to control, select, and publish aspects of their performed, recorded self in new media; and we can see here an essential life skill; the management of resources and assets made for, by, and about us in a range of media, as posited in recent work, which focuses specifically on the digitization of personal memories in media assets (Garde-Hansen, Hoskins, and Reading 2009; Williams, Leighton John, and Rowland 2009).

Finally, this kind of curated productive activity extends further, out from the self, to include the creation of cultural resources that record and resonate with wider affiliations, group, and even tribal identities and their associated social and cultural practices. The idea of social relations as a determining factor in the literacy practices within a group was noted in chapter 3, where to be literate was to negotiate cultural and social identity (cf. Buckingham 1993). The socialized version of curatorship as a metaphorical literacy practice in new media is a further marker of its potential role in formal and informal educational spaces and its potential development within literacy pedagogy.

CHAPTER 9

Learning and the New Curatorship

In this chapter, I want to try to map some of this thinking about the new curatorship onto educational practices. Partly this arises from a belief that research and writing should have some impact on the world and on lived culture. As Selwyn has pointed out recently, some research in the field of media, technology and education has tended toward an inherent sloppiness and even technological determinism, pulled that way by, in some cases, large corporate, vested interest. He has identified ten principles for research in the field:

> I would like to make the case for encouraging research and writing that fulfils the following conditions—i.e. research and writing that...
>
> 1. ...has nothing to sell
> 2. ...is certain only of the uncertainty of it all
> 3. ...is close (but not too close) to the digital technologies that are being researched
> 4. ...always asks "what is new here?"
> 5. ...maintains a sense of history
> 6. ...is aware of the global, national and local contexts of education and technology
> 7. ...engages with the politics of education and technology
> 8. ...makes good use of theory when and where it is helpful
> 9. ...is open-minded and curious when it comes to methodology—is rigorous and appropriate when it comes to methods
> 10. ...always considers how education, technology and society can be made fairer. (Selwyn 2012)

This book was designed with a concern for impact in each of the areas outlined above. The specific backdrop is a world in which the gap between home and school cultures is a site of debate in the public sphere and in the popular research literature on educational technology and media. Children and young people are said to be more agentive outside of school and, for some writers, the difference lies in their agency and activity around digital artifacts and media outside of school, to the detriment of their educational experience.

Clearly, the, sometimes, oversimplification of the world outside of school as offering freedom from constraint and a wealth of opportunities for self-expression for those who have access to digital technologies and the ability to be productive with them is a complex issue. At the same time, the formal school world is sometimes regarded as a closed environment in which decisions about teaching and learning are constrained by assessment procedures that also operate against innovative practices. In fact, there is no absolute binary division between these worlds that acts as a solid barrier. Children and young people pass more through a metaphorical semipermeable membrane than a solid barrier when they move between home and school worlds. They leave aspects of their lived experience behind on either side of this when they move between the worlds.

When we explored the differences between home and school in the 7–11 age phase in five primary schools (Selwyn, Potter, and Cranmer 2010), we found some unsurprising conclusions about the low expectations for school technology and media use from children, some of whom were playing games and visiting self-chosen websites. They expected regulation and difficulty with this aspect of their experience of school life, just as they would for other aspects of the daily routine in school that were different from their home life. The hope for the future of technology and media in school was really about building circles of trust, democratic structures that would allow a little of the world outside to inform their experience, permission to be more agentive while acknowledging that school had to be different.

For the research on children's autobiographical filmmaking, in this book, while the work in both schools took place in a formal setting, it was still off the regular timetable in an informally organized space, either because it was at the end of the school year (school A) or the children were not in their normal classes for other reasons (school B). Nevertheless, I wanted to try and discover something of the knowledge of cultural forms and literacy practices that the children had already, and on which teachers could build in the future, not by dragging it wholesale into the curriculum but by examining what practices and approaches could be applied and not swept aside. In taking this line, the study anticipated a time when the organization of the curriculum would be loosened and the debates about changing literacy in schools would perhaps become more focused on moving-image work. However, in the England at least, we have some way to go to move in the direction proposed by the head of Education at the British Film Institute who, as we have seen, has proposed an inclusive "reframing" of "literacy," that involves

> developing children's understanding of how the dominant cultural modes of speech, writing, performance, pictures, and moving pictures with sounds operate; how to choose from a wider range of texts than they might otherwise; how to read, interpret and analyse those texts; how to make them and use their language systems to express themselves. (Reid 2009, p. 22)

In this, Reid was drawing together themes in the work of writers who have linked literacy to popular culture, semiotics, and new media (e.g., Burn and Durran 2007; Burn and Parker 2003; Marsh 2004; Merchant 2005a) into a holistic and inclusive engagement with the reframed version of literacy.

In the preceding chapters, I have outlined the ways in which children took the opportunity in their videos to express themselves in a variety of forms, drawn from their knowledge and experience of popular culture; how they attempted to combine these elements onscreen using editing software, which presented them with options for mixing media assets and different modes together. In carrying out this work, the children in the study produced a very wide range of responses to the task of self-representation. They told personal stories, they made parodic references to other media texts, they composed short sketches, they undertook personal storytelling, they recorded their play and that of others, they improvised, and they sometimes worked from detailed plans. Taken at face value they appeared to suggest an innate understanding of the medium. However, as we have seen, they were not all equally successful in making the elements in their production fit together coherently or accessibly for viewers or, sometimes, for themselves.

So, while the children appeared to have the nascent ability to work with the *lexis* of moving-image forms, on the basis of their previous experience of watching them, when they operated intertextually and mixed assets and sources together, they sometimes struggled with the *grammar* of the medium. What this suggests for schools is some way of working with both in educational settings or in extracurricular clubs that supports children's development in producing moving-image texts but does not risk a lack of engagement.

As a starting point, I would argue, on the basis of this research, that early activities in moving-image production should therefore start with self-representation. This finds a corollary in print literacy where thematic work around the self is often the earliest writing experience. However, as noted above, it was clear in these productions that the activity of moving-image production of itself did not confer a simple, liberating experience of productive creativity on the children. Instead, they found that the ability to edit and successfully organize what they had collected or filmed onscreen was a key determining factor in their production's success or failure. In fact, the children frequently expressed dismay at how the huge potential of the editing tools was hard to use fully in their productions. This suggests that it is time to think seriously about how the affordances of editing tools are introduced to children and to think about how activities may be designed to foreground the organizational aspects of working with the modes of speech, image, gesture, sound, and music in intertextual space much more, much earlier. I would suggest that this notion supports and is supported by thinking about commonalities across software editing interfaces, underlining the approach that Sefton-Green has outlined (2005).

Storyboarding and other paper activities supported some of the children, some of the time, in thinking about content, about media assets, and about some basic shot composition; editing, however, was not supported in quite the same way by this initial work on paper. For many of the children, the use of the editing space or the "multimodal mixing desk" (Burn and Parker 2003) held too much challenge and the paper planning did not support them. They simply could not assemble things in the way they wanted to and, in such a high-stakes activity as self-representation, this became a source of frustration for some of them. The exception to this was Raymond and Keiron's video in school A, which, although they complained about how hard editing was, achieved a high degree of success. It was possible to see the links through from the planning to the final work, including cues on paper, which supported combinations of modes in the editing software. Making this clearer and more obvious in the artifacts used to support the making of the pieces may have helped, although simply producing better planning sheets is unlikely to provide the whole answer. Instead, it makes sense to try to connect with proposals for slightly older children, which appear to result in successful engagement with moving-image work. Burn and Durran (2007), for example, as noted earlier, have suggested analyzing moving-image texts before making them, and layering this alongside significant amounts of simple in-camera work. For primary school children, this could be worked alongside opportunities to make short, simple self-representational texts of the kinds in these projects, with frequent review and evaluation, demonstrating not merely the function of the tools but also how certain juxtapositions and appropriations produce different meanings. In this way, an understanding of the grammar of the moving image, its construction of shots and edits, transitions and cuts can be layered in with critical study of moving-image material in which learners have a real investment. One key aspect that came out of the work was how aware the children were of the camera and of the potential content they could create with it. However, they still needed support to see how the smallest changes in decision at the point of final assembly of their videos, alongside sound, titling, and so on, affected the overall meaning-making process. I believe that this could be achieved in an approach to "learning by doing" that was accompanied by regular reflection and evaluation. This is certainly possible in many of primary classrooms in which large, "interactive" visual displays have been introduced. However, this is certainly *not* the approach that has characterized strategies for print literacy teaching in recent years and that has emphasized teaching of "basics" *before* learners have any wider experience of production and publication. Rather, this is layering in space and time in which to learn in actual production how the many modes may successfully be combined; making media texts, evaluating them, and making more media texts, a progressive model of learning in primary school media work.

As the Cambridge primary review has reported, in recent years in England, the education system has been driven by a "standards" agenda, an unwillingness to undertake activities in which reflection and breadth of experience are the centerpiece, as it stated,

> Primary education is increasingly but needlessly compromised by the "standards" agenda... The most conspicuous casualties are the arts, the humanities and those kinds of learning in all subjects which require time for talking, problem-solving and the extended exploration of ideas... Fuelling these problems has been a policy-led belief that curriculum breadth is incompatible with the pursuit of standards in "the basics," and that if anything gives way it must be breadth. Evidence going back many decades, including reports from HMI and OFSTED, consistently shows this belief to be unfounded. Standards and breadth are interdependent, and high-performing schools achieve both. (Cambridge_Primary_Review 2009, pp. 1–2)

Earlier in the study, I described how recent reconceptualizations of literacy that incorporate new media have been seen to be predicated on problem solving and collaboration, on "tacit knowledge" and "participation" (Gee 2004a; Jenkins et al. 2006), all of which suggest the Cambridge Primary Review's identified "time for talking" and the "extended exploration of ideas." And for the younger learners, described in this study, this productive and inclusive engagement with popular culture, including moving-image forms, which will necessarily frame the redefinition of literacy and pedagogy, also suggests breadth of study and time for critical engagement. In the Cambridge Primary Review, the separation into curriculum subjects for younger children was seen as evolving in primary schools toward "areas of learning." Literacy, as a practice of making and exchanging meaning in culture, was to be the thing that held all of these learning areas together and, since literacy practices reflect lived culture, we could reasonably have expected to see a productive engagement with new media at the heart of learning in the primary school. For the moment in England, this is stalled by yet another review predicated on a change of government and focused back on the narrow picture. Meanwhile, in other educational systems in both the developed and the developing world, literacy is usefully being reframed toward including the moving image.

Progression in a productive engagement with new media in literacy practices in the primary years also suggests an understanding of the developmental aspects of children's lives in preadolescence. The earlier discussion of Vygotsky's notion of creativity in adolescence offered some explanation for the way in which the videos made by the children were positioned on the play-creativity continuum, in parallel to the incoherence-coherence one, with the more successful ones moving away from play or fantasy, and from incoherence to coherence. As seen earlier, Vygotsky proposed that, in adolescence, children undergo a gradual "liberation" from concrete thought and "imagistic" features toward a greater integration of "elements of abstract thinking" (1994, p. 274). For the preadolescents working on these videos, it was possible, in some cases, to see the ways in which this process sometimes overwhelms the authors. In such cases, some audiences, particularly those outside the peer groups in the project schools, could not connect with their videos; they did not find the expected, easily decoded creative forms and instead found themselves witnessing aspects of recorded play, with all of its hidden codes and shared meanings, fully accessible only to the children themselves, and some of their friends. Time and again, they struggled to contain their embodied and performed version of their play within a form that could be understood by an outside viewer. Those who could understand that it belonged to the group and recognized codes, quotations, and affiliations in the responses to the task of representation because they had also enacted and encoded the play. Neither is this a judgmental issue that sets up such productions as somehow failing; nor is it one that celebrates everything as fully formed. Instead, I am positioning these texts on a continuum from incoherence to coherence. Future pedagogical design should therefore be aware of, and responsive to, this issue; in the same way that teaching print literacy involves (or should involve) understanding developmental processes through which children move (Beard 1993, Whitehead 1997). With sensitivity on the part of the teacher, critical awareness of how these forms reach out beyond the world of the children, as well as how this changes over time, could be developed.

Engaging children in a critical response to the work seems to be helpful with regard to the issues raised above; in the interviews, as seen previously, many spoke with real honesty and critical distance about their productions. There was enthusiasm and pride but there was also a degree of self-criticism; even among those who said that they would not change anything, there was an acknowledgment that more could be done another time to make things more communicable to an external viewer.

Many of the children in the study were capable of responding positively to sensitive evaluation. Perhaps, with this in mind, the work suggests that children are ready for taking on some of the metalanguage around media production in order to frame evaluation and reflection. For example, in both schools, some of the children talked about the camera as a key "partner" in the task and, as noted in the previous chapter, it was apparent that they viewed it as a powerful mediating tool that influenced their action (Engeström, Miettinen, and Punamäki 1999; Wertsch 1998). After this initial period of experimentation, they would benefit from reviewing and being introduced to some of the ways of labeling and describing shots that made up their compositions. This would neither be with the purpose of overloading younger learners with unnecessary technical vocabulary, but rather with equipping them with a way to describe some of the processes in production through which they move in creating these short pieces. Nor is it in any way, as with the print literacy strategies, to suggest that the "basics" of shooting should always come first. These principles are wrapped up in making something for meaning, not for undertaking arid and removed technical exercises. The point would be to foster an understanding of moving-image *grammar* as an ally, as a mechanism for making communication in the modes of the moving image clearer and enabling a more successful engagement with the *lexis* of production.

With this in mind, it should be possible to go further still and introduce an age-appropriate metalanguage within the video-editing process, which we have already seen was a key area of development identified by the children themselves. Once the recorded images are loaded on to the computer and are on the shelf or in the bin (depending on the software being used), alongside the other media assets, stills, and sounds, there could follow a similar negotiation with the vocabulary of multimodality at a simple level, enough to enable control over the onscreen organization of intertextual space. Children routinely work within other software at some level of technical vocabulary; in some ways they are already adept at operating with word processors between the "cultural layer" and the "computer layer" (Manovich 2001), choosing *fonts* that are fit for purpose, moving *blocks of text, copying, cutting,* and *pasting* in posters, poems, and stories. Taking this a stage further into video editing is suggested for older children (Burn and Durran 2007) and I pointed out earlier how the affordances of software are convergent, with the representations of controls assuming a common look and feel across editing software of varying kinds (Sefton-Green 2005). It would be worth exploring this notion of control across the modes and developing a vocabulary with children that encompasses the technicalities of controlling the computer layer in an authoring activity that has an outcome in the cultural layer.

In order to map this territory more completely, it would be necessary to take a longer-term view of the work. A study that set out to discover the impact over time of some of the suggestions made in the preceding section on pedagogy would enable a more detailed map to be drawn. In particular, the study would need to focus on areas that have only been hinted at in this and other work in the field. A longitudinal study with aim to map over some years the nature of children's developing metalanguage in regard to moving-image production would help to test some of the assertions made about progressive acquisition of concepts discussed previously. Each of the processes involved would yield findings that could be fed back into teaching and learning in a cyclical, action-research way (Cohen, Manion, and Morrison 2007).

Some of the less explored territory with younger learners is the actual nature of support for different modes in teaching and learning. In the pedagogy section above, I suggested that developing a metalanguage could accompany progressive work with editing and that this could build on the ways it is handled with regard to other kinds of software. Yet, as Burn and Durran (2007) point out in discussing support for older children's experiences of moving-image production, it is not always possible to locate support or expertise for the whole range of modes within a particular setting, particularly one as compartmentalized into subjects as the secondary school. Perhaps, the typical primary school in England, if it returns to one day to the "breadth" suggested by the Cambridge review (Alexander and Flutter 2009), offers greater support for teachers who want to "work with what they have" (Burn and Durran 2007, p. 93) in the way of knowledge of different modes in production.

This study has been focused on learners and the opportunities they have to develop metalanguage, skills, and dispositions in video production. There is potential for research here that takes teachers through similar processes, since they are also present in the setting. I was involved in a project that attempted to do this with regard to teachers in training and their experiences of moving-image production in a cross-curricular context (Potter 2006). In that research, however, there was no direct mapping back onto the areas that have emerged as significant here—namely, the organization of onscreen spaces and the activity of editing as an assembly of multimodal elements with its own specific skills and dispositions, with its own vocabulary. This seems to be another potential site of related research and could be as longitudinal in nature as that suggested by the work with children above.

A further potential area for future research arose from watching the children in both schools, but particularly in school A, work with material artifacts in the context of the video production projects. The memory boxes were a valuable resource and generated much discussion. They were not centrally part of the research but their presence in the project suggested that there was much potential in exploring this relationship further. I would suggest incorporating at an early stage in a future project some space within the work for making an exhibition on the themes of important objects in children's lives to date; this would be particularly important at times of transition. This would have to be handled with sensitivity since there may well be things that children would not wish to reveal and not all experiences may have been happy ones. By locating the autobiographical element in objects of significance, a study that looked more closely at the links between the personal, physical objects and their media representations, in moving-image work, perhaps extending work already done in still images and sharing sites (Merchant 2005b; Pahl 2006; Roberts 2008) would be a significant area of exploration.

In making their videos, assembling cultural resources drawn from their own lives and from wider popular culture, the children took part in a productive engagement with new media in which they were gathering media artifacts and assets together into a new arrangement. I have suggested above that the children thereby took part in a new kind of literacy practice that can be metaphorically characterized as curating. The resources from which they made meaning were collected, cataloged, and arranged for exhibition. These included practices that were previously unseen, acts of memory and habitualized behavior not previously recorded in this way, but that were part of their everyday, lived experience. As some of the projects showed, this revelation was not unproblematic and was not in itself a process without risk or critical issues.

As revealed in the analysis, in the adapted multimodal frames employed in chapter 5, the children's videos were full of references to specific places and memories and their performance in these spaces reveal an embodied and affective response to their "habitus" (Bourdieu 1986). I also described earlier how some of the children used their performance in the spaces of the school to record a version of the "hypomnemata" (Foucault 1984) as both a record and a resource. Others made use of the video form as a kind of "palimpsest," a performed and recorded version of their movement in the space as a kind of strategic resistance to the tactics of control (de Certeau 1984). We have also seen how the concept of anchored and transient versions of identity (Merchant 2006) was a useful one for seeing how the representations moved between aspects of the self that were fixed and those that were demonstrations of affiliation and subject to change over time. Increasingly, participating in lived culture means taking part in a continued project of self-representation in many of these expressive tactical modes, whether in the spaces of social networking, writing the self online in blogs, posting still or moving images, or combinations of all of these. It further involves display of collections of artifacts and texts made by others, shared music, images, or videos that have been found, tagged, and re-presented alongside images that have been created by the person themselves. These may be "anchored or transient" (ibid.) but their selection involves a combined set of skills and practices, which may be gathered into the metaphorical construct of curatorship.

Earlier in the book, I mentioned the *Mark Wallinger curates the Russian Linesman* exhibition in the first half of 2009 at the Hayward Gallery on London's South Bank. The exhibition guide describes *curating* as *making*; it describes the process undertaken by the guest curator, the artist Mark Wallinger as follows:

> An exhibition devised by an artist—especially a multi-disciplinary show such as this—is an *act of creation*, similar in many ways to the *making* of a work of art. Inevitably, as in their own work, the artist's ideas, interests and enthusiasms underpin both the exhibition's *rationale* and the *process* of selection and display. (SouthbankCentre 2009, p. 1, my italics)

The italicized portions of the quotation above show how the language used to describe the process of curating positions it as active, agentive, and evaluative; "creation" and "making" are used alongside "rationale" and "process." Rationale in particular chimes with the earlier discussion of Vygotsky's account of the developing *rational* aspects of creativity (Vygotsky 1994) through adolescence. It also relates strongly to the earlier discussion of *externalization* (Kozulin 2005; Vygotsky 1978), which in this case refers to a process by which assets are curated in such a way as to produce coherence for an audience through their assembly and exhibition.

If we apply the processes of selection, display, and assembly familiar from the language of exhibition creation to video production, we uncover a range of skills and subskills that find corollaries in other media forms and spaces, not least in the associated skills of gathering, cataloging, tagging, and exhibiting in blogs and social networks. Furthermore, the exhibition guide goes on to suggest that the exhibition represents the maker just as much as any individual artifact within the collection. The sum of the parts is the representational act of meaning making about the self at the particular time the collection is made.

This view of production and proposed way of thinking about associated skills and dispositions proposed in chapter 8, namely,*collecting, cataloging, arranging* and *assembling*) represents curatorship as an active but complex literacy practice in new media, multistranded and developing over time. It arises from seeing representational digital video production in its many modes across these projects as a form that makes explicit the processes involved; speech, image, gesture, music, and diegetic sound are all gathered in a collection of self-made assets that have been collected alongside media taken from the existing collection.

An earlier section proposed a developmental model for mapping progression in children's video production. A further proposal for schools, based on curatorship, would be to build on the metaphor and find ways of inviting children to think of themselves as curators across media forms and spaces from an early age. This should not be difficult. Participating in lived culture means making many kinds of digital image and moving image and sometimes all that is required of educators is that they draw attention toward the previously unseen. Children could be encouraged to think of themed exhibitions, self-representation on- and offline, and the use of shared still and moving images to create collections that are stored and archived over time. This implies an active and social engagement with a new literacy practice such as we have seen proposed earlier (Gee 2004a; Jenkins et al. 2006; Lankshear and Knobel 2006; Marsh 2004). It also parallels emergent discussions of "digital memories" concerned with how these are managed through life in the many spaces of new media (Garde-Hansen, Hoskins, and Reading 2009).

Around the time of beginning to write about these films and putting forward curatorship as an active literacy practice, I found myself watching Michael Rosen, the children's writer, performing in front of an audience, a situation I had been in a number of times when I was a teacher. On this occasion, the audience I was among was not children in a primary school; they were student teachers from a partner university in New York. Over the course of an hour and a half, Rosen took them through the process of connecting with the past, with the present, with lived experience and fashioning something from the raw material. In doing so, he presented a way of connecting the elements together; painful experiences lived alongside happier ones, all were performed and embodied with gesture, rhythm, meter, and the tactics of memory. I realized, sitting there, that I had come full circle. With my mind on completion of the study, the principles of literacy as a kind of curatorship activity of selection, organization, and shared cultural markers began to gel as Rosen described a book he is writing, around the methodically recorded and performed notion of his various childhood misdemeanors that his father used to remind him about, and that he now collected and cataloged in a new book, beginning on page one with an incident in which, at the age of two, he threw his mother's ring out of the window. For this talk, for this particular audience, he selected, cataloged, arranged, assembled, and performed from previously created assets, improvisation, and interaction. All the elements were drawn from lived experience and a lifetime of engagement with the act of recombining, realigning, and performing with a particular audience in mind and a particular point in time. The children's video productions also contained those elements; the difference being that the performance drawn from their lived culture and experience was captured and encoded within the meaning-making systems of moving-image production, not that of performance poetry, and took its place within an overall conception of new media as a space in which the various assets could be grouped, shared, viewed, and evaluated.

What we see in these processes of authoring, collecting, and appropriating is a process in which the unperceived accretions of passing time along with the very many processes of growing up and changing relationships with ourselves, and with others, has become the centerpiece of the project of the self. We have also seen how the interdependence between productions and the representations have been of the self within a specific context of others, in the case of the children in school A, for example, their immediate contemporaries and colleagues at a time of profound and accelerated change in their lives.

In the light of the exploration of the children's videos in this study, I would argue that the curatorship metaphor represents a way of expanding our notion of literacy practices in lived, media culture and one that is worthy of future study across a range of modes, media, and settings in years to come.

Afterword: Curatorship and a Media Education Manifesto

In 2010, I was invited to contribute to the manifesto for Media Education Website set up by colleagues at the University of Bournemouth and featuring contributions from around the world. This gave me the opportunity to consider the answer to the question: If there is such a thing as the new curatorship and it connects media literacy and identity what does it mean for teaching and learning in the twenty-first century? I outlined a manifesto for media education for younger learners that incorporated and developed some notions of practice in teaching and learning in the light of the curatorship idea. I called it *Children as Creators, Consumers and Curators: Media Education, Principles and Entitlement for Younger Learners* (Potter 2010), and I presented nine principles, which I would like to adapt for this "Afterword" to the discussions in the book.

1. Context and Entitlement: Let's Widen the Conception of Literacy in Education

Children and young people's experience of lived culture is all consuming and it's no longer tenable to restrict the educational experience to narrow versions of literacy and equally narrow versions of educational technology. We need media education from the earliest years of schooling. We can begin, by "re-framing literacy" (BFI 2008) so that we think about the predominant modes of cultural production and widening our definitions and thinking about what it means to be literate. And if we do that then let's address how children can, for example, learn about time-based texts, how the modes of gesture, image, speech, and music can be made to produce specific meanings in these forms, from the earliest years. In this, as we know from writers in the field (Marsh 2009), we will be building on what they know from their consumption and reappropriation of media from their early years in the play, their talk, and, when they have the opportunity, their own media texts.

2. Building and Maintaining Connections with Learner Lives and Cultures

Another line of argument suggests that we need media education because the skills and dispositions being developed by children and young people outside places of learning threaten to open up a chasm and fracture the relationship between home and school. Some argue the inevitability of this fracturing from a techno-centric perspective because technological advances are seen to be largely unaccounted for in school systems; children and young people use games and social media outside the classroom to do amazing things they could never do in school. These arguments contain elements of undeniable truth, which nevertheless have a tendency to lead their advocates toward a techno-romanticism that stifles any genuine engagement with lived culture and ultimately with curriculum development. They only take you so far and so, in the literature around technology in Education we have thousands of studies that call out for more "curriculum integration" without any notion of how this might happen; they fail the tests that Selwyn (2012) applies to good research in the field. Technological determinism leads us nowhere in the end; however, thinking and learning about the media that gets made and distributed on those devices might. For a further discussion of this issue, see David Buckingham's *Beyond Technology* (2007).

We need to connect with the lives of learners in a curriculum based around the "what" and the "how" of the media that we make, share, consume, interpret, and exhibit in lived culture. In England, a comprehensive review of primary education (Alexander 2010) lists report after report that connects the kind of resulting breadth of curriculum experience with higher achievement. And writers and consultants remind us in presentations about essential connections with skills and dispositions (and lives) of learners now (and in a changing world) (Robinson 2010).

3. Open up a Dialogue with Younger Learners in Shaping Media Education

Ask the learners themselves about school, as myself, Neil Selwyn, and Sue Cranmer recently did in a research project (2010), and you will find that they are quite sanguine about home and school, recognizing that they are, of course, different spaces. At the same time, they call for a freeing up of school structures to take account of their likes, preferences, skills, and dispositions with gaming culture and social media. What we need is a curriculum that understands the agency of children and young people as a factor in their successful learning.

4. Open up a Dialogue between Teachers in Different Disciplines about Existing Media Education Practice Where It Is Happening

In primary schools, I would like to see some building on and recognition of the work of those teachers who ensure that some learning with and around media takes place. Sometimes these are teachers who may have experienced media as part of an educational technology course; sometimes these are colleagues who create media activities with a literacy (re)frame or under the label of the creative arts and humanities. These are starting points for a nascent media education in primary schools, where literacy (in its widest possible sense) and educational technology meet, where the "what" and the "how" are discussed and negotiated. Too often, unfortunately, these activities are seen as peripheral, after the serious curriculum business has happened (e.g., high-stakes league table subjects in the old primary core curriculum in England). Instead, of course, they could be located at the heart of learning activity providing a "digital glue" to hold topics and subjects together with younger learners (Brook 2012). In any case, we need to get some of these people together: Educational technology coordinators, Literacy coordinators, Creativity coordinators, subject area coordinators; and at least start talking to compare, contrast, and plan and to develop what media educators describe as the critical, the cultural, and the creative (see, e.g., OFCOM 2005).

5. Restore Some Balance between Creative and Critical Perspectives

While the creative dimension is sometimes well developed in some activities in digital media and has been written about extensively (Marsh 2010), the critical dimension is underdeveloped. Certainly, as far as moving-image work goes, it is the sense in which the specific properties and possibilities of a time-based text require understanding and experience of a range of forms to develop this critical capacity (see, e.g., Bazalgette 2000). Watching, making, and learning to critique to improve, refine, and understand are important. Once media texts are made, children know that they will be seen and judged. How will they respond and how do they critique others? How do they take account of what viewers say? How do you filter and find the most useful things that are said and written about productions in a critical context? Can you find a genuine community of practice among the diatribes that clog up YouTube comment spaces, for example?

6. Build an Understanding of Culture and Empathy into a New Media Education

Culture—in the sense of seeing how cultures represent and are represented—is of huge importance. When we allow sweeping and unevidenced generalization to dictate patterns of debate and policy, we are in trouble (as we can see at the moment in England). I'm thinking here of arguments made lazily and equally in the press and in various forums that make these announcements: "all children do this," "all children watch that," and "all children play computer games." How about some respect for the complexity of economic and social life as well as cultural difference? I'm sure this could be layered into a new media education. One way would be to talk to learners about these issues.

7. Enough of Media "Projects"; It's Time to Embed Media Education in Regular Recursive Practice across the Curriculum

Many media texts do get produced as a reward, off-timetable activity in schools, or as part of a special "project" that never gets revisited. In an animation research project, which worked differently, Cary Bazalgette, Becky Parry, and I saw evidence of the benefits of repeated experiences across a year; the recursive nature of the practice has benefits for learning about time-based texts and the writing of poetry at the same time (Bazalgette 2010). Each medium retains its distinctive features but supports the other. So, as part of their entitlement, I would expect to see a curriculum structure for younger learners that is broad enough to encompass film, animation, games, and social media on a range of platforms alongside learning from and with older forms of expression. How will we know where to set our expectations of engagement and production? We can look for projects that genuinely connect teaching, learning, and research in the field.

8. Talking about Safety Is Learning about Safety

To some, the location of media activity by younger learners in lived culture is problematic on the grounds of safety. As the social media habits develop earlier, media corporations are having to raise their game to provide safe new online playgrounds for the young protoconsumers. New opportunities for access and expression also carry risk and this is best addressed and brought into the open. Spaces in which children can openly discuss their concerns and learn for themselves how to manage risk will potentially have the greatest effect. Sometimes, as noted above, the learner voice is the last to be heard. So, why not talk about it?

9. Curatorship Is a New Literacy Practice; Think about How We Can Develop Media Education Which Recognizes This

I would like to propose that *Curatorship* is a fourth C alongside those discussed previously, namely *Creative, Cultural,* and *Critical.* Certainly, as discussed throughout this book, in regard to organization and exhibition, children are growing up in a world in which the media they collect and make can be organized, displayed, and re-presented time and again in ways that were not possible before. Some of this will reflect their changing and multiple identities and affiliations as they grow but it is a qualitatively different experience to anything previously possible. It's a new form of cultural production that is pitched partway between making and sharing, creating temporary collections for specific purposes, and then dismantling them again.

I am neither simply talking about archiving, though this is a subset of the skills that go into the new curatorship, nor is this simply about arranging and presenting the texts in a pleasing way. Fundamentally, it is about knowing how the reflexive project of the self with its anchored and transient identities gets made and unmade over time in the various spaces online and how we live with this and function in new media (See Giddens 1991; Merchant 2005b).

Samuel Johnson wrote that the "two offices of memory are collection and distribution" (1759). Video editing, image editing, posting on social media sites, and blogging may well be the current matches for these "offices" of centuries ago. It seems in the age of social media that we can now expand these terms to include "shared" as well as adding "exhibition." If we also imagine that the use of the term "offices" has a vague match with "purpose or function," all of which might be caught by "aspects," we could throw in media education and try this for a working definition in the digital age: "The three aspects of shared memory in new media are collection, distribution, and exhibition." We need a form of educational experience that recognizes curatorship as a cultural and literacy practice whose reach is wide into people's lives and that encompasses many new and emergent skills and dispositions among learners in digital media.

Bibliography

Abbott, Chris. 2001. *ICT: Changing Education*, edited by John Head and Ruth Merttens, *Master Classes in Education*. London: Routledge Falmer.

Alexander, R. J., and J. Flutter. 2009. "Towards a New Primary Curriculum: A Report from the Cambridge Primary Review." Cambridge, UK: University of Cambridge Faculty of Education.

Alexander, Robin. 2010. *Children, Their World, Their Education: Final Report and Recommendations of the Cambridge Primary Review*. London: Routledge.

Auchard, E. 2007. "Participation on Web 2.0 Sites Remains Weak." San Francisco, CA: Reuters.

Bakhtin, Mikail. 1981. *The Dialogic Imagination*. Austin, TX: University of Texas Press.

Balsamo, Anne. 2009. *Virtual Museums: Where to Begin?* 2009 [accessed July 7, 2009]. Available from http://futuresoflearning.org/index.php.

Barrance, Tom. 2004. "Making Movies Make Sense." Cardiff, Wales, UK: Media Education Wales. http://www.mediaedwales.org.uk

Barton, D. 1994. *Literacy: An Introduction to the Ecology of Written Language*. Oxford, UK: Blackwell.

Barton, D., Mary Hamilton, and Ros Ivanic. 2000. *Situated Literacies: Theorising Reading and Writing in Context*. London: Routledge.

Baugh, David, and Dewi Lloyd. 2007. *Digital Video in Education* 2007 [accessed February 1, 2007]. Available from http://www.dvined.org.uk.

Bauman, Zygmunt. 2004. *Identity: Conversations with Benedetto Vecchi*. Cambridge, UK: Polity.

Bazalgette, Cary. 1989. *Primary Media Education: A Curriculum Statement*. London: British Film Institute.

―――. 2000. "A Stitch in Time: Skills for the New Literacy." *English in Education*.Sheffield, UK: Wiley-Blackwell for NATE (National Association for the Teaching of English)

―――. 2010. *Report on the Persistence of Vision Project* 2010 [accessed April 24, 2012]. Available from http://themea.org/pov/volume-3-issue-2/persistence-of-vision /report/.

Beard, Roger. 1993. *Teaching Literacy, Balancing Perspectives.* London: Hodder & Stoughton.

BFI. 2008. "Reframing Literacy." London: British Film Institute.

———. 2010. "Le Cinéma: cent ans de jeunesse." In *BFI / Cinematheque Blog,* edited by Michelle Cannon. London: markreid1895.wordpress.com

Bordwell, David, and Kristin Thompson. 2008. *Film Art,* 8th ed. New York: McGraw Hill.

Bottino, R. 1999. "Activity Theory: A Framework for Design and Reporting on Research Projects Based on ICT." *Education and Information Technologies* 4 (3): 281–295.

Bourdieu, Pierre. 1977. *Outline of a Theory of Practice.* Cambridge, UK: Cambridge University Press.

———. 1986. *Distinction: A Social Critique of the Judgement of Taste.* London: Routledge.

boyd, danah. 2007. "Why Youth Love Social Network Sites: The Role of Networked Publics in Teenage Social Life." In Buckingham, David (ed) *Youth, Identity and Digital Media in The John D. and Catherine T. MacArthur Foundation Series on Digital Media and Learning* (Dec. 2007):119–142. doi:10.1162/dmal.9780262524834.119.

———. 2011. "Social Network Sites as Networked Publics: Affordances, Dynamics and Implications." In *A Networked Self: Identity, Community and Culture on Social Network Sites,* edited by Zizi Papacharissi, 39–59. London: Routledge.

Bragg, S. 2007. "Consulting Young People: A Review of the Literature." London: Creative Partnerships.

Bromley, Helen. 2007. *50 Exciting Ideas for Storyboxes.* Birmingham: Lawrence Educational.

Brook, Tim. 2012. "Digital Glue: A Blog for Media Educators."Norfolk, UK: www .digitalglue.org

Bruner, Jerome 1987. "Life as narrative." *Social Research* 54 (1) :11–17; 21–31.

———. 1990. *Acts of Meaning.* Cambridge, MA: Harvard University Press.

———. 1996. *The Culture of Education.* Cambridge, MA: Harvard University Press.

Buckingham, David. 1993. *Children Talking Television.* London: Falmer Press.

———. 2003. *Media Education: Literacy, Learning and Contemporary Culture.* Cambridge, UK: Polity.

———. 2007. *Beyond Technology: Children's Learning in the Age of Digital Culture.* London: Routledge.

———. 2008. "Introducing Identity." In *The John D. and Catherine T. MacArthur Foundation Series on Digital Media and Learning*:1–24. doi:10.1162 /dmal.9780262524834.001.

———. 2009. "'Creative' Visual Methods in Media Research: Possibilities, Problems and Proposals." *Media, Culture and Society* 31 (4): 633–652.

———. 2011. *The Material Child.* Cambridge, UK: Polity.

Buckingham, David, and Issy Harvey. 2001. "Imagining the Audience: Language, Creativity and Communication in Youth Media Production." *Jounral of Educational Media* 26 (3): 173–184. doi:10.1080/1358165010260303.

Buckingham, David, and Julian Sefton-Green. 1994. *Cultural Studies Goes to School.* London: Taylor and Francis.

Buckingham, David, Jenny Grahame, and Julian Sefton-Green. 1995. *Making Media: Practical Production in Education.* London: The English and Media Centre.

Buckingham, David, Rebekah Willett, and Maria Pini. 2011. *Home Truths? Video Production and Domestic Life.* Ann Arbor, MI: University of Michigan Press.

Burden, Kevin, and Theo Kuechel. 2004. "Evaluation Report of the Teaching and Learning with Digital Video Assets Pilot 2003–2004." Coventry: BECTA.

Burgess, Jean, and Joshua Green. 2009. *YouTube: Online Video and Participatory Culture.* Cambridge, UK: Polity.

Burn, Andrew. 2009. *Making New Media: Creative Production and Digital Literacies (New Literacies and Digital Epistemologies).* New York: Peter Lang.

Burn, Andrew, and James Durran. 2007. *Media Literacy in Schools.* London: Paul Chapman.

Burn, Andrew, and David Parker. 2001. "Making Your Mark: Digital Inscription, Animation and a New Visual Semiotic." *Education, Communication & Information* 1 (2): 155–179.

————. 2003. *Analysing Media Texts,* edited by Richard Andrews, *Continuum Research Methods.* London: Continuum.

Burn, Andrew, Shakuntala Banaji, and D. Buckingham. 2006. "The Rhetorics of Creativity: A Review of the Literature." London: Arts Council England / Creative Partnerships.

Cambridge_Primary_Review. 2009. Briefing paper on "Towards a New Primary Curriculum—A Report from the Cambridge Primary Review." Cambridge, UK: University of Cambridge.

Cannon, Michelle. 2011. "Fashioining and Flow." London: Institute of Education, University of London.

Chan, Chitat. 2008. *Youth, Identities and Media Production in the Digital Age: An Educational Case Study in Hong Kong.* London: PhD, Institute of Education, University of London.

CHICAM. 2004. *CHICAM Website* 2004 [accessed December 10, 2004]. Available from http://www.chicam.net.

Cohen, Louis, Lawrence Manion, and Keith Morrison. 2007. *Research Methods in Education,* 6th ed. London: Routledge.

Connolly, P. 1997. "In Search of Authenticity: Researching Young Children's Perspectives." In *Children and Their Curriculum,* edited by A. Pollard, D. Thiessen, and A. Filer, 162–183. London: Falmer Press.

Cope, Bill, and Mary Kalantzis, eds. 2000. *Multiliteracies: Literacy Learning and the Design of Social Futures.* New York: Routledge.

Craggs, Carol. 1992. *Media Education in the Primary School.* London: Routledge.

Crook, Charles. 2001. "The Social Character of Knowing and Learning: Implications of Cultural Psychology for Educational Technology." *Journal of Information Technology for Teacher Education* 10 (1/2): 19–35.

Csikszentmihalyi, M. 1996. *Creativity: Flow and the Psychology and Discovery of Invention*. New York: Harper Collins.

Cuban, Larry. 2001. *Oversold and Underused—Computers in the Classroom*. Cambridge, MA; London: Harvard University Press.

Cuthell, John. 2002. *Virtual Learning: The Impact of ICT on the Way Young People Work and Learn*. Basingstoke, UK: Ashgate.

Davies, Julia, and Guy Merchant. 2007. "Looking from the Inside Out: Academic Blogging as New Literacy." In *A New Literacies Sampler*, edited by Michele Knobel and Colin Lankshear. New York: Peter Lang.

———. 2009. *Web 2.0 for Schools: Learning and Social Participation*. New York: Peter Lang.

Dawkins, Richard. 1976. *The Selfish Gene*. Oxford, UK: Oxford University Press.

de Block, Liesbeth, and D. Buckingham. 2007. *Global Children, Global Media*. Basingstoke, UK: Palgrave Macmillan.

de Block, Liesbeth, David Buckingham, and Shakuntala Banaji. 2005. "Children in Communication about Migration (CHICAM) Final project report." London: Centre for the Study of Children, Youth and Media, Institute of Education, University of London.

de Block, Liesbeth, and Julian Sefton-Green. 2004. "Refugee Children in a Virtual World." In *Digital Technology, Communities and Education*, edited by Andrew Brown and Niki Davis, 234–248. London: Routledge Falmer.

de Block, Liesbeth, Simon Aeppli, Sezgin Celik, Paul Chivers, Tobi Forsdyke, Steve O'Hear, Julian Sefton-Green, and Fleeta Siegel. 2004. *CHICAM: Children in Communication about Migration*. : Luxembourg: European Commission (Community Research).

de Certeau, Michel. 1984. *The Practice of Everyday Life*. Berkeley, CA: University of California Press.

Deci, Edward, and Richard Ryan. 1985. *Intrinsic Motivation and Self-Determination in Human Behaviour*. New York: Plenum.

DFES. 1998. *National Literacy Strategy*. London: HMSO.

———. 2001. "Special Educational Needs: Code of Practice." London: HMSO.

Engeström, Yrjö, Reijo Miettinen, and Raija-Leena Punamäki. 1999. *Perspectives on Activity Theory (Learning in Doing: Social, Cognitive & Computational Perspectives)*. Cambridge, UK: Cambridge University Press.

Fairclough, Norman. 2000. "Multiliteracies and Language." In *Multiliteracies*, edited by Bill Cope and Mary Kalantzis, 162–182. London: Routledge.

Ferguson, B. 1981. "Practical Work and Pedagogy." *Screen Education* 38:42–55.

Fielding, Michael. 2004. "Transformative Approaches to Student Voice: Theoretical Underpinnings, Recalcitrant Realities." *British Educational Research Journal* 30 (2): 295–311.

Fieser, J., and B. Dowden. 2008. *Merleau-Ponty*. University of Tennessee Martin 2008 [accessed March 18, 2008]. Available from http://www.iep.utm.edu/m /merleau.htm.

Finnegan, Ruth. 1997. "'Storying the Self': Personal Narratives and Identity." In *Consumption and Everyday Life*, edited by Hugh Mackay, 65–111. London: Sage Publications.

Fisher, T. 2004. "Information and Communication Technologies and Teachers' Work." *Canadian Journal of Educational Administration and Policy* 32:1–19.

Foucault, Michel. 1984. *The Foucault Reader,* edited by Paul Rabinow. London: Penguin.

Fraser, Pete, and Barney Oram. 2003. *Teaching Digital Video Production,* edited by Vivienne Clark, *Teaching Film and Media Studies.* London: BFI Education.

Fursteneau, M., and A. Mackenzie. 2009. "The Promise of 'Makeability'—Digital Editing Software and the Structuring of Everyday Cinematic Life." *Visual Communication* 8 (1): 5–22.

Garde-Hansen, J., A. Hoskins, and A. Reading. 2009. *Save as...Digital Memories.* London: Palgrave.

Garfield, Simon. 2006. "Me.com—How the People Took over the Internet." *The Observer,* June 18, 2006, 6–7, 9.

Gee, James Paul. 2004a. *Situated Language and Learning: A Critique of Tradiional Schooling.* New York: Routledge.

———. 2004b. *What Video Games have to Teach Us about Learning and Literacy.* New York: Palgrave Macmillan.

Gibson, J. J. 1977. "The Theory of Affordances." In *Perceiving, Acting, and Knowing: Toward an Ecological Psychology,* edited by R. Shaw and J. Bransford, 67–82. Hillsdale, NJ: Lawrence Erlbaum.

Giddens, Anthony. 1991. *Modernity and Self-Identity: Self and Society in the Late Modern Age.* Cambridge, UK: Polity.

Gilje, Oystein. 2009. "'What Does This Mean?'—Students Negotiating Filters and Special Effects in Digital Editing Practices." Oslo: Institute for pedagogical research, University of Oslo.

Goffman, Erving. 1990. *The Presentation of Self in Everyday Life,* new ed. London: Penguin.

Govt., UK. 1988. *The Education Reform Act.* Office of Public Sector Information 1988 [accessed December 29, 2008].

Grace, Donna, and Joseph Tobin. 1998. "Butt Jokes and Mean Teacher Parodies: Video Production in the Elementary Classroom." In *Teaching Popular Culture: Beyond Radical Pedagogy,* edited by David Buckingham. London: UCL Press.

———. 2002. "Pleasure, Creativity, and the Carnivalesque in Children's Video Production." In *The Arts in Children's Lives,* edited by Liora Bresler and Christine Marme Thompson. Netherlands: Springer.

Gregory, Eve. 1996. *Making Sense of a New World: Learning to Read in a Second Language.* London: Paul Chapman.

Greiner, G. 1955. *Teaching Film: A Guide to Classroom Method.* London: British Film Institute.

Grossberger-Morales, Lucia. 2000. "Sangre Boliviana: Using Multimedia to Tell Personal Stories." In *Digital Desires: Language, Identity and New Media,* edited by Cutting Edge—The Women's Research Group, 184–193. London; New York: I. B. Taliris.

Haas Dyson, Anne. 1997. *Writing Superheroes: Contemporary Childhood, Popular Culture, and Classroom Literacy.* New York: Teachers College Press.

Haas Dyson, Anne. 2006. "Foreword: Why Popular Literacies Matter." In *Popular Literacies, Childhood and Schooling*, edited by Jackie Marsh and Elaine Millard, xvii–xxi. London: Routledge.

HackneyPirates. 2012. *The Hackney Pirates Homepage* 2012 [accessed March 24, 2012]. Available from http://www.hackneypirates.org.

Harvey, Issy, Megan Skinner, and David Parker. 2002. "Being Seen, Being Heard: Young People and Moving Image Production." Leicester: National Youth Agency.

Heath, S. B. 1983. *Ways with Words*. Cambridge, UK: Cambridge University Press.

Hepp, Pedro, J. Enrique Hinostroza, and Ernesto Laval. 2004. "A Systemic Approach to Educational Renewal with New Technologies." In *Digital Technology, Communities and Education*, edited by Andrew Brown and Niki Davis. London: Routledge.

Hills, J. 1950. *Films and Children: The Positive Approach*. London: British Film Institute.

Hoad, T. F. 1992. *The Concise Oxford Dictionary of Etymology*. Oxford, UK: Clarendon Press.

Holloway, S., and G. Valentine. 2002. *Cyberkids—Youth Identities and Commnities in an Online World*. London: RoutledgeFalmer.

Jenkins, Henry. 1992. *Textual Poachers: Television Fans and Participatory Culture*. New York: Routledge.

———. 2006. *Convergence Culture: Where Old and New Media Collide*. New York: New York University Press.

Jenkins, Henry, Katie Clinton, Ravi Purushotma, and Alice J. Robison. 2006. "Confronting the Challenges of Participatory Culture: Media Education for the 21st Century." In *Building the Field of Digital Media and Learning*. Chicago: MacArthur Foundation.

Johnson, Samuel. 1759. "The Use of Memory Considered." *Idler* no. 044 [accessed date April 21, 2012]. Available from http://www.readbookonline.net/readOnLine/29909/.

Jones, Diana Wynne. 2000. *Archer's Goon*. London: Collins.

Kearney, Chris. 2003. *The Monkey's Mask—Identity, Memory, Narrative and Voice*. Stoke on Trent, UK: Trentham Books.

Kenner, Charmian. 2005. "Bilingual Families as Literacy Eco-Systems." *Early Years* 25 (3): 283–298.

Kimbell, Richard, Graham Brown Martin, Will Wharfe, Tony Wheeler, David Perry, Soo Miller, Tristram Shepherd, Phil Hall, and John Potter. 2005. "e-scape Portfolio Assessment: Report of First Pilot Stage." London: TERU (Goldsmiths).

Knobel, Michele, and Colin Lankshear. 2007. *A New Literacies Sampler*. New York: Peter Lang.

Kozulin, Alex. 2005. "The Concept of Activity in Soviet Psychology: Vygotsky, His Disciples and His Critics." In *An Introduction to Vygotsky*, 2nd ed., edited by Harry Daniels. London: Routledge.

Kress, Gunther. 2004. "Learning, a Semiotic View in the Context of Digital Technologies." In *Digital Technology, Communities and Education*, edited by Andrew Brown and Niki Davis. London: Routledge.

Kress, Gunther, and Theo Van Leeuwen. 2001. *Multimodal Discourse: The Modes and Media of Contemporary Communication*. London: Arnold.

———. 2006. *Reading Images: The Grammar of Visual Design*, 2nd ed. London: Routledge.

Kristeva, Julia. 1980. *Desire in Language: A Semiotic Approach to Literature and Art*. New York: Columbia University Press.

Lankshear, Colin. 2003. "The Challenge of Digital Epistemologies." *Education, Communication & Information* 3 (2): 167–186.

Lankshear, Colin, and Michele Knobel. 2006. *New Literacies: Everyday Practices and Classroom Learning*. Maidenhead, Berks, UK: McGraw Hill Education / Open University Press.

Larson, Joanne, and Jackie Marsh. 2005. *Making Literacy Real: Theories and Practices for Learning and Teaching*. London: Sage.

Leander, Kevin, and Amy Frank. 2006. The Aesthetic Production and Distribution of Image/Subjects among Online Youth. *E-Learning*, 3: 185–206.

LeCourt, Donna. 2001. "Technology as Material Culture: A Critical Pedagogy of 'Technical Literacy.'" In *ICT, Pedagogy and the Curriculum*, edited by Avril Loveless and Viv Ellis, 84–103. London: RoutledgeFalmer.

Lievrouw, Leah H., and Sonia Livingstone. 2006. *The Handbook of New Media*, updated student ed. London: Sage.

LKL. 2012. *London Knowledge Lab Homepage* 2012 [accessed April 24, 2012]. Available from http://www.lkl.ac.uk.

Lorac, C., and M. Weiss. 1981. *Communication and Social Skills*. Exeter, UK: Wheaton and Co.

Lord, Pippa, Megan Jones, John Harland, Cary Bazalgette, Mark Reid, John Potter, and Kay Kinder. 2007. *Special Effects: The Distinctiveness of Learning Outcomes in Relation to Moving Image Education Projects*. Slough, UK: Creative Partnerships.

Loveless, Avril. 2002. "Literature Review in Creativity, New Technologies and Learning." In *Nesta Futurelab Reviews*. Bristol, UK: NESTA Futurelab.

Mackay, Hugh. 1991. "Technology as an Educational Issue." In *Understanding Technology in Education*, edited by H. Mackay, M. Mackay, and J. Beynon, 1–12. London: Falmer Press.

———. 1997. *Consumption and Everyday Life*. London: Sage Publications.

Manovich, Lev. 2001. *The Language of New Media*. Cambridge, MA: MIT Press.

Marsh, Jackie. 2004. *Popular Culture, New Media and Digital Literacy in Early Childhood*. London: Routledge.

———. 2009. "Productive Pedagogies: Play, Creativity and Digital Cultures in the Classroom." In *Play, Creativity and Digital Cultures*, edited by Rebekah Willett, Muriel Robinson, and Jackie Marsh. New York: Routledge.

———. 2010. "Childhood, Culture and Creativity: A Literature Review." In *Creativity, Culture and Education Series*. Newcastle: CCE.

Marsh, Jackie, and Elaine Millard. 2000. *Literacy and Popular Culture: Using Children's Culture in the Classroom*. London: Paul Chapman.

Masterman, L. 1980. *Teaching about Television*. London: Macmillan.

McDougall, Julian. 2006. *The Media Teacher's Book*. London: Hodder Arnold.

McNamara, Gerry, and Sean Griffin. 2003. "Vision in the Curriculum: An Evaluation of the FIS Project in Primary Schools in Ireland." Dublin: National Centre for Technology in Education.

Media_Literacy_Task_Force. 2005. "The Media Literacy Charter." The Media Literacy Task Force.

Mercer, N. 2000. *Words and Minds: How We Use Language to Think Together*. Abingdon, Oxon, UK: Routledge.

Merchant, Guy. 2005a. "Digikids: Cool Dudes and the New Writing." *E-Learning* 2 (1): 50–60.

———. 2005b. "Electric Involvement: Identity Performance in Children's Informal Digital Writing." *Discourse: Studies in the Cultural Politics of Education* 26 (3): 301–314.

———. 2006. "Identity, Social Networks and Online Communication." *E-Learning* 3 (2): 235–244. doi:10.2304.

Merleau-Ponty, M. 1962. *Phenomenology of Perception*. London: Routledge and Kegan Paul.

Metz, Christian. 1974. *Film Language*. Chicago: Chicago University Press.

Miller, Daniel. 2008. *The Comfort of Things*. Cambridge, UK: Polity.

Mitchell, Claudia, and Jacqueline Reid-Walsh. 2002. *Researching Children's Popular Culture: The Cultural Spaces of Childhood*. London: Routledge.

Moss, Gemma. 1989. *Un/Popular Fictions*. London: Virago.

MuseumVictoria. 2005 *Ara Irititja (Stories from Long Time Ago) Introduction on Bunjilaka Gallery Page*. MuseumVictoria 2005 [accessed June 4, 2009]. Available from http:// museumvictoria.com.au/bunjilaka/whatson/past-exhibitions/ara-irititja/.

———. 2009. *Indigenous Collections Introduction*. MuseumVictoria 2009 [accessed June 4, 2009]. Available from http://museumvictoria.com.au/collections-research /our-collections/indigenous-cultures/.

New London Group. 1996. "A Pedagogy of Multiliteracies: Designing Social Futures." *Harvard Educational Review* 66 (1): 60–92.

Nixon, Helen, and Barbara Comber. 2005. "Behind the Scenes: Making Movies in Early Years Classrooms." In *Popular Culture, New Media and Digital Literacy in Early Childhood*, edited by Jackie Marsh, 219–236. London: RoutledgeFalmer.

November, Alan. 2001. *Empowering Students with Technology*. Arlington Heights, IL: Skylight.

Noyes, A. 2004. "Video Diary: A Method for Exploring Learning Dispositions." *Cambridge Journal of Education* 34 (2): 194–209. doi:10.1080/0305764041000 1700561.

OFCOM. 2005. *Ofcom's Strategy and Priorities for the Promotion of Media Literacy—A statement*. OFCOM 2005 [accessed May 20, 2005]. Available from http://www .ofcom.org.uk/consult/condocs/strategymedialit/ml_statement/.

Orr Vered, Karen. 2008. *Children and Media Outside the Home: Playing and Learning in After-School Care*. Basingstoke, UK: Palgrave Macmillan.

Pahl, Kate. 2003. "Children's Text-Making at Home: Transforming Meaning across Modes." In *Multimodal Literacy*, edited by Carey Jewitt and Gunther Kress. New York: Peter Lang.

————. 2004. "Narrative spaces and multiple identities: Children's textual explorations of console games in home settings" in Marsh, Jackie (Ed) *Popular Culture, New Media and Digital Literacy in Early Childhood*. London: Routledge.

————. 2006. "An Inventory of Traces: Children's Photographs of Their Toys in Three London Homes." *Visual Communication* 5 (95): 95–114.

Parry, Ross. 2007. *Recoding the Museum: Digital Heritage and the Technologies of Change*. London: Routledge.

Pearson, Matthew. 2005. "Splitting Clips and Telling Tales." *Education and Information Technologies* 10 (3): 189–205.

Perry, Grayson. 2011. *The Tomb of the Unknown Craftsman*. London: The British Museum Press.

Peters, J. 1961. *Teaching about Film, Press, Radio and Television in the World Today*. Lausanne: UNESCO.

Pink, Sarah. 2006. *Doing Visual Ethnography*, 2nd ed. London: Sage.

Porter, Roy. 1994. *London: A Social History*. London: Hamish Hamilton.

Potter, John. 2002. *PGCE Professional Workbook: Primary ICT, PGCE Professional Workbooks*. Exeter, UK: Learning Matters.

————. 2006. "Carnival Visions: Digital Creativity in Teacher Education." *Learning, Media & Technology* 31 (1): 51–66.

————. 2010. *Children as Creators, Consumers and Curators: Media Education, Principles and Entitlement for Younger Learners*. CEMP at the University of Bournemouth 2010 [accessed April 23, 2011]. Available from http://www.manifestoformediaeducation.co.uk/2011/03/john-potter/.

Potter, John, and Harvey Mellar. 2000. "Identifying Teachers' Internet Training Needs." *Journal of Information Technology for Teacher Education* 9 (1): 23–36.

Prensky, Marc. 2005. Listen to the Natives. *Educational Leadership*, 63: 8–13.

Reid, Mark. 2009. "Reframing Literacy: A Film Pitch for the 21st Century." *English Drama Media: The Professional Journal of the National Association for the Teaching of English* (14):19–23.

Reid, Mark, Andrew Burn, and David Parker. 2002. "Evaluation Report of the Becta Digital Video Pilot Project." BECTA/BFI.

Roberts, Lynn. 2008. *Digital Shoeboxes: Online Photosharing in a Cross-Contextual Literacy Project*. London: Masters Dissertation, London Knowledge Lab, Institute of Education, University of London.

Robinson, Ken. 2010. "RSA Animate—Changing Education Paradigms." YouTube.

Robinson, Muriel, and Bernardo Turnbull. 2005. "Veronica: An Asset Model of Becoming Literate." In *Popular Culture. New Media and Digital Literacy in Early Childhood*, edited by Jackie Marsh. London: Routledge.

Rosaldo, Michelle. 1984. "Toward an Anthropology of Self and Feeling." In *Culture Theory: Essays on Mind, Self and Emotion*, edited by Richard A.

Shweder and Robert A. LeVine, 137–157. Cambridge, UK: Cambridge University Press.

Rose, Gillian. 2007. *Visual Methodologies: An Introduction to the Interpretation of Visual Materials.* London: Sage.

Rosen, Michael. 1989. *Did I Hear You Write?* London: Andre Deutsch.

Schuck, Sandy, and Matthew Kearney. 2004a. "Students in the Director's Seat: Full Report." Sydney: University of Technology, Sydney.

———. 2004b. "Students in the Director's Seat: Teaching and Learning across the School Curriculum with Student-Generated Video." Sydney: Faculty of Education, University of Technology, Sydney.

Sefton-Green, Julian. 1998. *"Writing" Media : An Investigation of Practical Production in Media Education by Secondary School Students.* London: PhD, Institute of Education, University of London.

———. 2000a. "From Creativity to Cultural Production." In *Evaluating Creativity,* edited by Julian Sefton-Green and Rebecca Sinker, 216–231. Routledge.

———. 2000b. "Introduction: Evaluating Creativity." In *Evaluating Creativity,* edited by Julian Sefton-Green and Rebecca Sinker, 1–15. Routledge.

———. 2005. "Timelines, Timeframes and Special Effects: Soft and Creative Media Production." *Education, Communication and Information* 5 (1): 99–110.

Sefton-Green, Julian, and David Parker. 2000. *Edit-Play – How Children Use Edutainment Software to Tell Stories.* London: British Film Institute.

Sefton-Green, Julian, and Rebecca Sinker. 2000. *Evaluating Creativity: Making and Learning by Young People.* London: Routledge.

Selwyn, Neil. 2002. *Telling Tales on Technology—Qualitative Studies of Technology and Education.* Aldershot, UK: Ashgate.

———. 2012. "Ten Suggestions for Improving Academic Research in Education and Technology." *Learning, Media and Technology,* 1–7. doi:10.1080/17439884 .2012.680213.

Selwyn, Neil, Daniela Boraschi and S. Özkula. 2009. "Drawing Digital Pictures: An Investigation of Primary Pupils' Representations of ICT and Schools." *British Educational Research Journal.* 35: 909–928.

Selwyn, Neil, John Potter, and Sue Cranmer. 2008. "Learners and Technology," 7–11. End of Project—Full Report. Coventry: BECTA.

———. 2010. *Primary ICT: Learning from Learner Perspectives.* London: Continuum.

Sharp, Jane, John Potter, Avril Loveless, and Jonathan Allen. 2002. *Primary ICT: Knowledge, Understanding & Practice,* 2nd ed. Exeter, UK: Learning Matters.

Silverstone, R., and E. Hirsch. 1992. *Consuming Technologies: Media and Information in Domestic Spaces.* London: Routledge.

Sinker, Rebecca. 2000. "Making Multimedia: Evaluating Young People's Multimedia Production." In *Evaluating Creativity,* edited by Julian Sefton-Green and Rebecca Sinker, 187–215. London: Routledge.

Sneddon, Raymonde. 2000. "Language and Literacy: Children's Experiences in Multilingual Environments." *International Journal of Bilingual Education and Bilingualism* 3 (4): 265–282.

Somekh, B., and D. Mavers. 2003. "Mappping Learning Potential: Students' Conceptions of ICT in Their World." *Assessment in Education-Principles, Policy & Practice* 10 (3): 409–420.

SouthbankCentre. 2009. *Exhibition Guide: Mark Wallinger Curates the Russian Linesman.* London: Hayward Gallery, South Bank Centre

SteveProject. 2009. *Steve: The Museum Social Tagging Project* 2009 [accessed July 7, 2009]. Available from http://www.steve.museum/.

Street, Brian. 1985. *Literacy in Theory and Practice.* Cambridge, UK: Cambridge University Press.

———. 1995. *Social Literacies: Critical Approaches to Literacy in Development, Ethnography and Education.* London: Longman.

———. 2003. "What's 'New' in New Literacy Studies? Critical Approaches to Literacy in Theory and Practice." *Current Issues in Comparative Education* 5 (2): 77–91.

Sutton-Smith, Brian. 1997. *The Ambiguity of Play.* Cambridge, MA: Harvard University Press.

Sykes, J. B. 1979. *Concise Oxford English Dictionary,* 6th ed. Oxford, UK: Clarendon Press.

Thomas, Michael. 2011. *Deconstructing Digital Natives.* London: Routledge.

Twining, Peter. 2002. *Enhancing the Impact of Investments in "Educational" ICT.* Milton Keynes, UK: Open University.

———. 2005. *dICTatEd—Discussing ICT, Aspirations and Targets for Education* 2005 [accessed November 2, 2005]. Available from http://www.med8.info /dictated/.

Tyner, Kathleen. 1998. *Literacy in a Digital World.* Mawhah, NJ: Lawrence Erlbaum Associates.

Unsworth, Len. 2008. "Explicating Inter-modal Meaning-Making in Media and Literacy Texts." In *Media Teaching,* edited by Andrew Burn and Cal Durrant. Kent Town, South Australia: Wakefield Press.

Van der Velden, Maja. 2006 *A License to Know: Regulatory Tactics of a Global Network* 2006 [accessed May 27, 2009]. Available from http://www.globaagenda.org.

Van Leeuwen, Theo, and Carey Jewitt. 2001. *Handbook of Visual Analysis.* London: Sage.

Vygotsky, Lev. S. 1933. *Play and Its Role in the Mental Development of the Child.* Psychology and Marxism Internet Archive (marxists.org) 2002 1933 [accessed April 14, 2009]. Available from http://www.marxists.org/archive/vygotsky /works/1933/play.htm.

———. 1978. *Mind and Society: The Development of Higher Psychological Processes.* Cambridge, MA: Harvard University Press.

———. 1994. "Imagination and Creativity of the Adolescent." In *The Vygotsky Reader,* edited by Rene Van der veer and Jaan Valsiner, 266–288. Oxford, UK: Blackwell. Original edition, *Paedology of the Adolescent* (1931).

Wertsch, J. V. 1998. *Mind as Action.* New York: Oxford University Press.

Whitehead, Marian. 1997. *Language and Literacy in the Early Years,* 2nd ed. London: Paul Chapman.

Willett, Rebekah. 2009. "Parodic Practices: Amateur Spoofs on Video Sharing Sites." In *Camcorder Cultures: Media Technology and Everyday Creativity*, edited by D. Buckingham and R. Willett. New York: Palgrave Macmillan.

Williams, P., J. Leighton John, and I. Rowland. 2009. "The Personal Curation of Digital Objects: A Lifecycle Approach." *Aslib Proceedings: New Information Perspectives* 61 (4): 340–363.

Williams, Raymond. 1961. *The Long Revolution*. London: Chatto and Windus.

Yancey, Kathleen Blake. 2004. "Postmodernism, Palimpsest, and Portfolios: Theoretical Issues in the Representation of Student Work." *College Composition and Communication* 55 (4): 738–761.

Index

GPSR Compliance
The European Union's (EU) General Product Safety Regulation (GPSR) is a set
of rules that requires consumer products to be safe and our obligations to
ensure this.

If you have any concerns about our products, you can contact us on

ProductSafety@springernature.com

In case Publisher is established outside the EU, the EU authorized
representative is:

Springer Nature Customer Service Center GmbH
Europaplatz 3
69115 Heidelberg, Germany